PRAISE FOR ECOCOMMERCE 101

The concept of *EcoCommerce 101* and the frame that Tim Gieseke applies is, I believe, the start of something big...I suspect it will gather steam slowly and be real and long term rather than a fast fad... really good thinking and base presentation...a. tremendous job - very well done!

> *Robert O'Donnell*
> *General Manager, AquaNexus*
> *www.aquanexus.com*
> *New York*

"*EcoCommerce 101* is a seminal body of work. Tim Gieseke has thoughtfully and thoroughly pulled together a grand concept and a mechanism to make it work...an excellent study about combining the economic and ecological systems into a unified program that promotes and encourages appropriate use of Natural Capital. Students, faculty, policy makers and the general public will be enlightened and enriched by absorbing the compelling case presented by Tim Gieseke in *EcoCommerce 101*".

> *Eric Jackson*
> *Senior Carbon Expert*
> *Environmental Change Institute*
> *University of Illinois*

"*EcoCommerce 101* offers a concrete vision and pragmatic approach to understanding the emergence of markets for payments for ecosystem services (PES). EcoCommerce principles applied to urban ecosystems and other business activities, such as retailing or water services, could mean the emergence of a truly-green global economy; one which would be based on investing in ecosystem management and restoration."

> *Joël Houdet PhD*
> *AgroParisTech*
> *President of Synergiz*
> *Vincennes, France*

"Finally - finally someone with dirt (or worse) in the treads of their boots has produced an approachable explanation about how the academic and theoretical potential of environmental market forces might actually look in the real world. Tim's experience working with the land and with landowners makes the day-to-day decision-making of real people less of a mystery. I don't know if ecoservice markets are going to stay just over the horizon for *another* decade, but I do know when they do rise they will follow the principles Tim lays out in his book."

Steve Woods
Agricultural Engineer and State Conservation Agency Manager
St. Paul, Minnesota

EcoCommerce 101 is an inspiring book that allows the reader to think through all the issues as it relates to the new emerging bio-economy. The readers will know Tim Gieseke writes from a practical point of view, thus recognizing that it's not all about the final end game, but how as a country we will get there. His experience as an ecologist and farmer gives him the perspective to create a logical pathway that naturally corresponds with economical goals and targets proper planning while we protect our resources.

Steve Flick
Board Chair, Show Me Energy Cooperative
Centerview, Missouri

EcoCommerce 101 provides a wonderful entry point for those interested in where our economy is right now and where it should go. With an amazing level of research, this book takes you by the hand and shows that the old system need not be broken in order to bring more sense into it. This book should be in many libraries and I would definitely recommend it and I will put it on the shelf where I keep my useful books.

Ronny Daniel
M.Sc. Strategic Leadership Towards Sustainability
Blekinge Institute of Technology - Sweden

EcoCommerce 101

Adding an ecological dimension to the economy

Tim Gieseke

BASCOM HILL
PUBLISHING GROUP

Bascom Hill Publishing Group

212 3rd Avenue North, Suite 290

Minneapolis, MN 55401

612.455.2293

www.bascomhillpublishing.com

ISBN - 978-1-935098-42-3

LCCN - 2010911457

Graphic Art by Rayanna Eckhardt

Cover Design and Typeset by Wendy Arakawa

Printed in the United States of America

List of Figures, Tables and Boxes

Figures

Tables

Boxes

LIST OF ACRONYMS

USDA	United States Department of Agriculture
WWTP	Waste Water Treatment Plant

ACKNOWLEDGEMENTS

I would like to acknowledge that the concept of this book would not have coalesced without the insight and feedback from hundreds of interested individuals and professionals with whom I have discussed this evolving topic over the last five years. More specifically, I would like to thank Steve Woods for his offer and effort in providing comments and to Mark Lindquist, Minnesota Department of Natural Resources, for his ecological and economic perspectives. I would like to thank David Changhoon Kim, a partner attorney for Gislason and Hunter LLP, for his legal counsel, guidance, encouragement, and support from the beginning of this effort. I also want to extend my appreciation to Rayanna Eckhardt for her graphic art assistance. And finally, I would like thank my wife, Jenny, and my family for their encouragement and patience as the ideas of the book were explored.

FOREWORD

For the past 20 years, I have spent considerable time evaluating the impact that agriculture production has on environmental quality. Our view of this research and the outcomes was to evaluate how different management systems would impact different environmental endpoints. As the laboratory director of the USDA-Agricultural Research Services National Laboratory for Agriculture and the Environment, I have had not only the responsibility for developing research teams to address these problems but also the personal satisfaction of conducting research on agricultural systems and environmental quality that has fostered a foundation for the ecosystem management.

At the beginning of this century, a whole new series of questions began to emerge when we were asked to quantify not only how much each of the different management practices affected a particular environmental endpoint but also the potential value of these endpoints on the environment. The value assessment has broadened from the concentration of a particular chemical in soil, water, or air, to the monetary value of these constituents. This was the beginning of a whole new series of requests in which the value of environmental components was to be considered as part of the evaluation process. The emergence of the consideration of the ecosystem as part of the agricultural systems was not something that had been part of the vocabulary within the research community. The development of a terminology that describes ecosystem services has created a completely new view of how we merge the ecosystem. We now freely talk about water quality trading, carbon credits, cap and trade, wildlife habitat, ecotourism, and social aspects of landscapes although there is not a common structure of how we view the values of these components. *EcoCommerce 101* provides such a framework, not only for how we value these ecosystem services but for the process through which we quantify this value. This effort can be summarized in the following statement from the beginning of this book. "EcoCommerce is more significant than a compilation or organization of ecoservice markets as it provides the framework to build an ecological intelligence system that allows the public arena of commerce to define sustainability." This is a unique feature because what has been lacking in the discussions of ecosystems or their monetary value has been a framework from which the value could be evaluated.

More and more we are examining the links among the monetary value of ecosystems. This book focuses on agricultural systems and their value, bringing the concepts into play in an area in which ecosystem services need to be understood from an economic perspective. There should be a series of questions in everyone's mind: What is the value of soil? What is the value of ton of carbon? What is the value of clean water? We frame these questions but lack a rigorous framework from which to develop a measure of the values. An interesting aspect of this book is the illustration of the role of conservation practices and their monetary value through the history of the Soil Conservation Service extending into the current Natural Resource Conservation Service. Working through this example provides insights into the foundation of EcoCommerce. Producers and landowners have received payments for various conservation practices, and, with the development of a broader set of ecosystem services, there will continue to be questions about the value of these services. This book will be a valuable asset to anyone who wants to understand how this economy will emerge and to anyone who wants to ask the critical questions about the process used to derive the value. There will continue to be expanded discussions on the economic value of ecosystem services, and this book will have value for undergraduates and graduate students to understand how economic services will be generated from components of the ecosystem. However, the greatest value for this book is for those policymakers and traders who will be the driving force in the development of policies and practices associated with ecosystem services. This group will benefit from understanding the complexity of this process because, through this understanding, there will be a more consistent development of the processes used to value ecosystems.

We are moving into a whole new ecosystem structure in which there are both physical and economic values to ecosystem components. What is the value of clean water and the practices that will have to be implemented to garner this value as parts of a viable EcoCommerce? What will be the interaction between soil management practices that sequester carbon or reduce greenhouse gas emissions and the role of these practices as part of the economic structure to value carbon? These are only a couple of the questions that are emerging and ones that we are going to have to answer to develop a strong ecological-based economy. We are all going to have to become conversant in a whole new set of terms in which ecosystem services have monetary value and will enter into the trading picture. For us who have spent a lot of energy investigating the physical, chemical, and biological basis for environmental impacts of different practices, there is a new set of parameters, which will include the economic value of these environmental impacts. If we are to continue to serve the world by which we are entrusted to be good stewards, then we will have to understand all of the dimensions of sustainable systems, which can only come through understanding the economic value. Those who understand these dynamics will emerge as the leaders in sustainable ecosystems. The challenge will be there, and we need to be ready to evaluate these programs and be able to offer our insights into these dynamics. The question that you can answer from this book is: How will EcoCommerce be developed and how will it function?

Jerry L. Hatfield
Laboratory Director
National Laboratory for Agriculture and the Environment
Ames, Iowa

PREFACE

As someone who has the opportunity to farm in America's Upper Midwest and to raise the fifth generation of our family on our farm, I feel fortunate to have had the experience to explore the depth and breadth of EcoCommerce. EcoCommerce has the potential to value the management strategies that improve the natural-resource base of our farm and nation, while allowing us to apply innovations to continually expand the production capacity and productivity of our farm. As importantly, EcoCommerce provides a process to allow corporate and individual consumers of natural and production resources to value the management strategies that improve the resource base of our farm and nation. There are unique challenges for those whose occupation is directly related to the production capacity of the natural resource. One must keep abreast of emerging technologies and keep learning the ancient secrets of the biological aspects of soil, the primary natural capital of our farm and our world. The value and risks associated with such resources are reflected in the extent of government policies that manage those attributes. As many farmers do, I participate in the commodity and conservation titles of the USDA Farm Bill – the far-reaching policy that significantly influences many of the production decisions through the use of various price supports, safety nets, insurances, and compliance provisions.

Along with my 15-year career in farming, I have also viewed agriculture through an academic lens studying biology, chemistry, having earned a M.S. in environmental sciences. As a local government staffer, I viewed agriculture from another on-the-ground perspective by providing technical support to implement conservation practices. As a non-profit policy specialist, I participated in the policy processes of the 2002 and 2008 federal Farm Bills and was introduced to the many perspectives that are held in the various political camps. As a business owner assessing production and natural resources for farmers, my intentions are to provide farmers with an assurance document that provides communication and a valuation platform on how their farms are being managed.

From these personal and professional viewpoints, I saw that the production-resource management and natural-resource management source pollution from the landscape is immeasurable as it relates to source and quantity. Non-point-source pollution consists of such things as sediment, nutrients, and chemicals that are washed off the landscape and into water bodies via countless pathways. A type of positive externalities is called ecosystem services or ecoservices. Ecoservices are benefits derived from the landscape management such as fertile soils, clean water, and habitat. Ecoservices could be considered the immeasurable opposite of non-point-source pollution. Both are derived from the landscape and are greatly influenced by how the land is being managed and the particular weather conditions before and during the weather episode.

In addition to the inability to directly measure these externalities, no public institutions have uniformly identified reasonable processes and standards that are needed for the market economy or the government agencies to be confident of the values associated with these externalities. It is the lack of the interconnection among our markets, institutions, and policy that sets up a significant hurdle for these externalities to interact within a market system.

No Free Lunches

As Milton Friedman, a renowned market economist, stated, "There is no such thing as a free lunch." In other words, all resources have an economic value in relation to their scarcity; they are limited, while the human desire for goods and services is virtually unlimited (Gwarty 2005). This free-lunch scenario is only true for any particular transaction if no externalities occur. In that case, all positive and negative results are figured in the cost of the good or service. If pollution or ecoservices are generated and no costs or benefits are applied, those costs and benefits are still borne by someone. Friedman's statement is correct if that assumes that lunch will always be paid by someone, regardless if that payment is made by someone else either in the past, present, or future. As this pertains to natural capital, it was as if the economists considered natural resources and the regenerative capacity of natural capital to be infinite in supply and, therefore, free (Dasgupta 2004). Ironically, the economists who attempt to educate the non-economists about this cyclic nature of currency and how no one step in the process is given a free pass, may have been the greatest violators of this economic law. By not recognizing that natural capital is limited and that its productive capacity can be diminished through its use to generate financial capital, economists omitted the cost for this item on the capital "menu." A common rationale for this omission is that the capacity of natural capital cannot be measured, and, if it could be measured, it has characteristics of a public good and its value cannot be legally owned. That rationale may be true to some extent, but it does not relieve the economic participants of paying for this lunch eventually.

The Bio-Economy

The term "Bio-Economy" has been used to describe different sectors of the economy in recent years, such as the bio-technology and the bio-energy sectors, both of which are components of a bio-economy. In this book, bio-economy is defined broadly to include the goods and services that are produced by the world's fisheries, forests, and breadbaskets, the world's economic natural capital.

Natural Capital

Natural capital is the stock of natural ecosystems that yields a flow of valuable ecosystem goods or services, also called ecoservices. The rationale in defining natural capital is the extension of the economic definition of capital that refers to "factors of production" that are used to create goods and services, but are not themselves directly consumed. Natural capital can be compared to physical capital in that a factory has the capacity to produce goods that the public can purchase. If that factory is left in ill repair or if it is destroyed, it no longer contains the capacity to produce goods. Financial capital must be reinvested into that factory for it to regain its productive ability. Natural capital exists in both renewable and nonrenewable forms and may or may not be revived with financial investment. Investing and divesting wealth among the differing capitals does occur, and the industrial age has been ear marked by the harvesting of natural and social capital to produce physical and financial capital (Senge 2008, 353). Theoretically, an economy could, through consumption, convert the vast proportion of natural capital into financial capital and end up with an economy flush with cash, but lacking in robust fisheries, forests, and breadbaskets. Each capital subset is needed to create wealth, and an imbalance of any one of the capitals will reduce the overall capacity to create wealth.

This fact can be illustrated by a fishery (natural capital) whose reproductive stock is completely harvested and can no longer produce fish. Due to the reduced capacity of the natural capital, it can no longer support the fishing boats and processing plants (physical capital), the fishermen and community (social capital), and the repayments on the operational costs (financial capital). The same parallel can be stated that if all the fishing boats sank (physical capital), then the natural capital, other physical capital, social capital, and financial capital could not be utilized or serviced. Of course, physical capital can be rebuilt at a cost, whereas natural capital is prohibitively costly to rebuild, or it may take long periods of time to regenerate, if possible at all.

Corporate Bio-Economic Supply Chain

The impact that corporations have on natural capital may be considered immense and derogatory. Hawken (1993) stated that business contains our blessing. It must because no other institution in the modern world is powerful enough to foster the necessary changes. The Millennium Ecosystem Assessment report states that it is in business's self-interest to take a leadership role in reducing poverty, improving human well-being, and protecting the environment. Doing so will help secure stable and safe societies, preserve open and free markets, ensure access to critical resources, provide new product and business opportunities, avoid abrupt social and environmental changes, and, for the most astute and agile, carve out competitive advantage (MEA 2005).

Businesses depend on ecosystem services directly for inputs to their operations, including water, timber, fiber, fuel, genetic materials, and food. The consumption of ecosystem services, which is already unsustainable in many cases, will continue to grow even while population growth is expected to level off mid-century. For example, during the next 50 years, demand for food is projected to grow by 70–80 percent as calculated by several scenarios run by the MEA. As the pressure on ecosystem services grows, businesses may find either access to these inputs impaired or the costs of securing them increased. Whether or not a business directly uses natural resources, these trends could affect supply chains, access to markets, competitive dynamics, and corporate reputation. Some specific implications for businesses of these trends include increased regulatory constraints as governments seek to protect degraded services; risk to reputation and brand image for businesses most directly tied to threatened ecosystems and services; substantial increase in costs of important inputs (such as water or agricultural products); increased vulnerability of assets to floods or other natural disasters; and conflict and corruption that may arise in areas plagued by scarcity of ecosystem services (MEA 2005).

Corporations are beginning to recognize that their product and profit are directly related to the regenerative capacity of the landscape to produce food, feed, biomass, clean water, or wildlife. They are beginning to understand that they will no longer be able to make profits if their resource "holdings" can no longer yield profit. These holdings could be defined as the natural capital of the world: the oceans' fisheries, the continental forests, and the breadbaskets that produce renewable economic goods. These corporations are beginning to sense an ownership of access, not of the actual lands, but of the regenerative productive capacity of those lands. Corporations are recognizing the limits of supply in relation to the relatively unlimited demand on ecological systems. With this recognition comes the realization of the finite, and perhaps, diminishing capacity of the natural capital.

The other bio economical fundamental is simply the primary production of the earth's vegetation and its relationship to the land and other organisms. It is estimated that of net primary production on the earth's land, 40 percent of this flows into human-based consumption, which leaves 60 percent for all other species and maintenance of the natural capital. For corporations to maintain their income stream, they must also maintain the regeneration capacity of natural capital (Vitousek 1986). With world population and effluence growing, it could be estimated conservatively that more than half of the net primary production of the land would be needed to support humans in the next 20 years. Allocating half of the world's net primary productivity on one species could presumably cause an increased risk associated with fragility and imbalance of both the economy and ecology.

It was perhaps these types of scenarios that led World Economic Forum CEO, Leo Apotheker to state, "We believe we have the potential to create new business models that build lasting prosperity for the many and not for the few; that make wise use of natural resources; that internalize social and environmental capital; and that focus on innovation to thrive in a low-carbon, dematerialized economy driving smarter consumption" (WEF 2010).

Consumer Demands

But despite the sheer dominance that corporations have acquired in the economic sector, they, by themselves, cannot consume the world's resources. As author and farmer Wendell Berry stated, "There are not enough rich and powerful to consume the whole world; for that, the rich and powerful need the help of countless ordinary people (Hawken 1993, 15)

In *Our Ecological Footprint,* Wackernagel (1995) calculates the ratio between the land resources available and population. Due to the increase in population and the increase in per capita consumption, that ratio has fallen from five hectares per person at the beginning of the 20th century to one-and-a-half hectares per person in 1995. At the same time, the average North American's land-base demand has grown to four hectares. If everyone on the planet today lived the same life style of North Americans, it would take the production capacity of two additional planets to meet these needs.

Chamber of Commerce, but as an extension and influence. Due to its stance on climate change legislation, businesses such as Apple, Exelon, Levi Strauss, and Pacific Gas and Electric Co. have quit the U.S. Chamber of Commerce, the nation's leading business organization. Nike resigned from the Chamber's board but maintained its membership, and companies like Duke Energy, General Electric, Alcoa, and Johnson & Johnson have disavowed the Chamber's positions on global warming (Williams, D. 2009). Members of an organization such as the Chamber of EcoCommerce would have a similar mission statement as the current Chamber's, "To advance human progress through an economic, political, and social system based on individual freedom, incentive, initiative, opportunity, and responsibility." But the Chamber of EcoCommerce mission statement would presumably include "ecological systems to support the regenerative capacity of many business," to include the perspective of natural capital.

In addition to the ability to exchange value for ecoservices, EcoCommerce will generate information that describes how the land resources are being managed. This "landscape intelligence" will be valued by entities that desire to know how particular geographical areas are being managed relative to an economic activity. Biomass processors' demands, including those that use food, feed, and cellulosic materials, have a direct impact on how the landscapes are being managed. Watersheds, river basins, and wildlife zones are directly affected by resource management activities. How these ecological and economical activities can be integrated and valued is a foundation component of EcoCommerce. This intelligence can generate ecological indices that can interface with the economical indices at the scale desired. In this manner, EcoCommerce is more significant than a compilation or organization of ecoservice markets as it provides the framework to build an ecological intelligence system that allows the public arena of commerce to define sustainability. If the public market is provided succinct and transparent information, and a functioning ecology has value, then EcoCommerce should flourish. With this structure, EcoCommerce should function, if for the only reason that maintaining and improving the capacity of natural capital creates wealth and when it is degraded, it creates less wealth. Aldo Leopold, one of the great conservationists of the 20th century, understood the value of natural capital. He also understood the challenges of motivating landowners to maintain this natural capital value. In his 1934 essay "Conservation Economics," he stated that successful conservation will likely entail rewarding the landowners who conserve the public interest (Leopold 1934). EcoCommerce is a system that recognizes these opportunities and challenges and supports those with the intentions of advancing "Conservation Economics."

SECTION 1
ECOSERVICE MARKET BEGINNINGS

CHAPTER 1

Oikos Commerce

Our "Houses"

Oikos, derived from the Greek word meaning *house*, is the root word for both "ecology" and "economy." Ecology, from Greek *oikos* and *logy* (the study of), is defined as the scientific study of the distribution and abundance of resources and the interaction between organisms and their natural world. Economy, from Greek *oikos* and *nomos*, is defined as the study of how humans use, supply, and distribute the resources that are available to them (Harper 2008). Ecological and economical systems have functional similarities and are linked in ways that humanity must understand. It is for this reason that ecologists and economists have much incentive for interaction (Levin 2006). Both systems operate by the consumption of energy and the transfer and transformation of nutrients (in the natural economy) and currency (in the man-made economy). The realm of our economic house today does not include the values associated with our ecological house. Simply put, today's economy does not apply a price to ecological services even though they have economic value. Expanding our economic house to include our ecological house is the essence of EcoCommerce. To state in a more far-reaching fashion, one could quote Ray

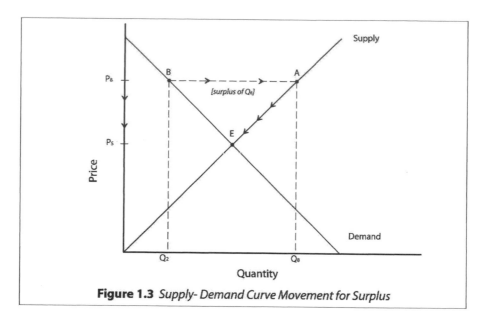

Figure 1.3 *Supply- Demand Curve Movement for Surplus*

Seeking Long-term Equilibrium

For markets to seek equilibrium in the long-term, adjustments are made by *shifts* of the slope to the left or right. These shifts in supply-and/or-demand curves occur because of overall market restructuring, and the shifts are made independently from price changes. They may represent an increase in demand (Figure 1 .4) due to an over-arching condition such as a growth in population that would lead to a permanent higher demand of food as represented by line D$_2$. A shift of the supply curve to the left (reduced supply) in Figure 1 .5 may represent the loss of agriculture production due to soil degradation or the loss of arable land. In that case, the supply was reduced in response to factors other than prices. A result of these shifts may be higher or lower prices, but prices are not the cause of the shift. In economic reality, these shifts may exhibit more complex behaviors, such as a change in slope steepness, a slope that maintains its course through its origin or other patterns.

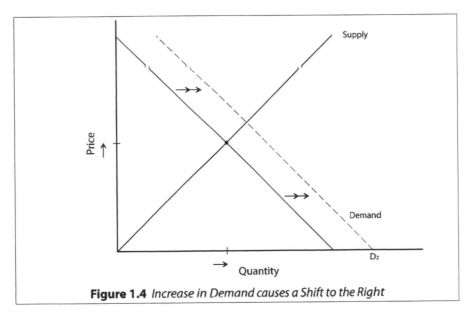

Figure 1.4 *Increase in Demand causes a Shift to the Right*

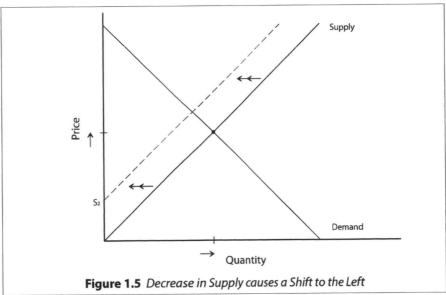

Figure 1.5 *Decrease in Supply causes a Shift to the Left*

Ecosystem Supply Curve

All rivers have a certain capacity to process and assimilate pollution. In supply-and-demand terms, a river has the capacity to supply clean water through its biological and physical functions. The rippling water adds oxygen, the currents mix, and the biota break down wastes. If the river experiences changes, which over time reduce its capacity to process and assimilate pollution, then its capacity-to-supply (water-cleansing function) would be reduced. This would be represented by a shift of the supply curve to the left. Viewing the river as natural capital that has a capacity to supply "water-cleansing functions" is analogous to viewing automobile factories as physical capital that has a capacity to supply cars. In either case, a degradation of the physical or natural capital reduces the capacity-to-supply.

Market Changing Scenarios
      There are four possible market changes, with each market change causing a uniquely identifiable change in the price and quantity combination as the market seeks equilibrium:

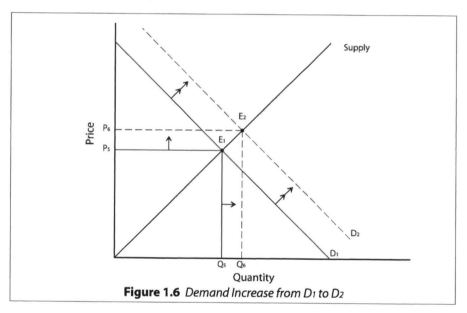

Figure 1.6 *Demand Increase from D₁ to D₂*

Figure 1.6: Demand Increase from D_1 to D_2: New equilibrium causes price increases and quantity increases. To seek new equilibrium (E_1 to E_2) the price moves from P_5 to P_6 and the quantity produced moves from Q_5 to Q_6.

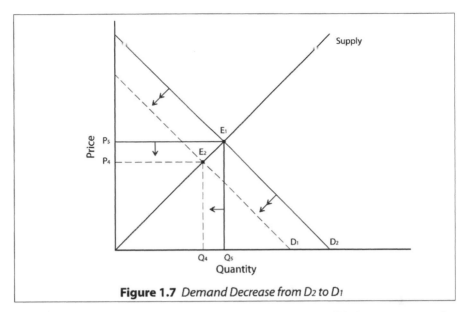

Figure 1.7 *Demand Decrease from D2 to D1*

Figure 1.7: Demand Decrease from D_2 to D_1: New equilibrium causes price decreases and quantity decreases. To seek new equilibrium (E_1 to E_2) the price moves from P_5 to P_4 and the quantity produced moves from Q_5 to Q4.

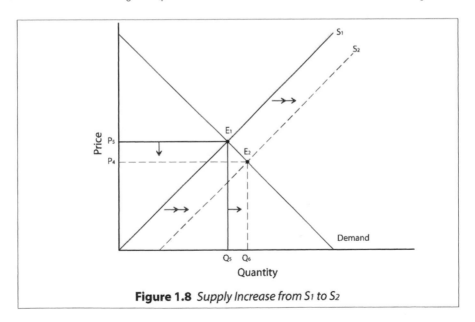

Figure 1.8 *Supply Increase from S1 to S2*

Figure 1.8: Supply Increase from S_1 to S_2: New equilibrium causes price decreases and quantity increases. To seek new equilibrium (E_1 to E_2) the price moves from P_5 to P_4 and the quantity produced moves from Q_5 to Q6.

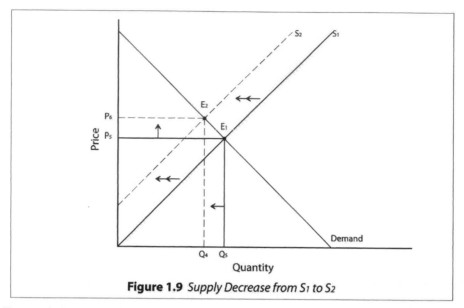

Figure 1.9 *Supply Decrease from S₁ to S₂*

Figure 1.9: Supply Decrease from S_1 to S_2: New equilibrium causes price increases and quantity decreases. To seek new equilibrium the price moves from P_5 to P_6 and the quantity produced moves from Q_5 to Q_4.

These shifts and the corresponding market adjustments in price and quantity can be determined due to the market's ability to assimilate the market information that allows market participants to make decisions related to their self-interests. This is often taken for granted in today's efficient market systems, but a market must be highly evolved for that to occur.

Changing Scenarios in Ecosystems and Ecoservice Markets

Participants in ecoservice markets do not have the luxury of identifying market conditions that cause a uniquely identifiable change in the price and quantity combination as the market seeks equilibrium. This is due to the lack of market information, but also due to the unique nature of ecological-economical supply function. Unlike a man-made economy that responds to an increasing shift in demand by increasing price and quantity, the natural economy (ecology) is not connected and cannot be directly connected to this system. This disconnect can be represented by an economic graph having a vertical supply slope if there is nothing people can do to increase the quantity in relation to price. In other words, regardless of price, the same quantity is produced. Likewise, an increase shift in the demand on a river's capacity-to-supply a "water purification function" obviously will not motivate the river to increase its purification capacity. Conversely, the river does not stop its water-purification functions if there is no economic value placed on it. As long as some level of that capacity remains, the natural capital will contain the "will-to-supply" ecoservices such as clean water, wildlife, carbon sequestration regardless of whether an economic value is applied toward it. Due to this innate "will-to-supply," the shifts in the natural capital supply-and-demand functions do not cause the uniquely identifiable market changes as illustrated in Figures 1.6-1.9. The shift is real, as it represents a corresponding change of the capacity of the natural capital. But unlike manmade capital whose production capacity is utilized based on conscious decisions, natural capital will produce goods and services in direct relation to its capacity. A successful ecoservice market would incentivize land-management activities that increase the capacity of the natural capital as this directly corresponds to an increase in the production of ecoservices.

Production Possibility Frontier

The Production Possibility Frontier (PPF) represents the point at which an economy is most efficiently producing its goods and services and, therefore, allocating its resources in the best way possible. The arc in Figure 1.10 represents the maximum amount of total production that can occur given the resources available. This PPF graph illustrates the production choices of grain and wildlife. Point A represents the grain and wildlife outcomes in a field that is managed for wheat production, and Point B represents the outcomes in that field enrolled in the Conservation Reserve Program (CRP), a USDA program that pays farmers to convert fields used for crop production to perennial vegetation that supports wildlife. The wheat-production system (Point A) produces a Q_9 quantity of wheat and a Q_4 quantity of wildlife. The CRP system (Point B) produces Q_0 of wheat and Q_{10} of wildlife. The reason for these outcomes is that a crop field does provide some wildlife benefits and unharvested perennial vegetation provides no crop production. Point x on the graph represents a production outcome that is less than the capacity of the available resource and Point y represents a production outcome that is not attainable (or identified) considering the resources available.

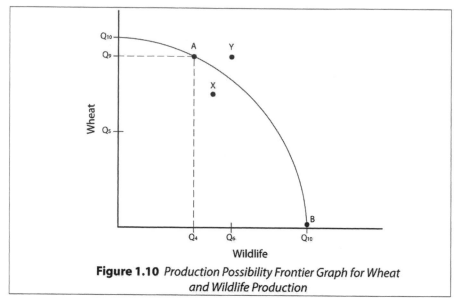

Figure 1.10 *Production Possibility Frontier Graph for Wheat and Wildlife Production*

To expand the economy that is, in this case, to produce more wheat and more wildlife, a higher level of resource efficiency could expand the PPF arc, representing an increase in production possibilities.

Figure 1.11 illustrates this concept by expanding the arc outward resulting in a wheat production level of Q_9 and a wildlife production level of Q_6 (Point C). This production-possibility expansion occurred due to a strategy to maintain the wheat-production level and increase the wildlife production within the same production system.

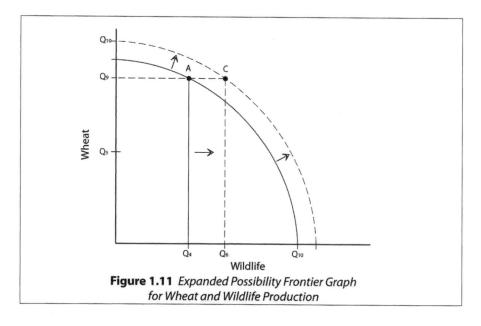

Figure 1.11 *Expanded Possibility Frontier Graph for Wheat and Wildlife Production*

EcoCommerce and PPF

The intention of EcoCommerce is to also account for economic costs and benefits associated with natural capital and ecoservices. If ecoservices provide economic values and they are not being accounted for, then the current PPF arc does not represent that sector of economic activity and the area under the arc is set artificially less than the total economic value.

Opportunity Costs

Opportunity cost is the value that is foregone to obtain one good or service in order to obtain another. In relation to the PPF example in Figure 1.10, value can either be applied toward wheat or wildlife. The result is less of one good or service and a greater amount of the other. The USDA CRP example illustrates how the decision to enroll in that program gives up the opportunity to grow grain. Opportunity cost is different for each individual, business, or nation.

Demand Elasticity

Demand elasticity refers to how flexible people's choices are in obtaining goods and services. Food demand would be considered very inelastic because, regardless of the cost, people cannot be flexible in whether they are going to buy it or not. On the other hand, demand for eating food at a restaurant would be considered elastic; as relative costs of eating out go up, people will generally make their food at home. How elastic demand for a good or service is depends on the availability of a substitute. Ecoservices such as clean water and productive soils would be considered inelastic, as few or no substitutes exist.

Summary of Economic and EcoCommerce Principles

Of course, the depth and breadth of the study of economic principles is far greater than discussed in this chapter. But due to relative newness of ecoservice markets, these basic economic principles and illustrated tools will serve the process of developing EcoCommerce principles, concepts, and related graphs. The basis for EcoCommerce is the acceptance that natural capital exists, that natural capital is finite, that the capacity of natural capital to produce ecoservices can be influenced by human activities and that human behavior change will occur relative to the economic values applied to those activities. Accepting that these parallel EcoCommerce principles exist alongside economic principles allows for the incorporation of these principles within an economic system. As principles, they exist regardless of the economic system being employed, but their influences on the market vary by what economic system is most prevalent.

Economic Systems

Economist Milton Friedman described the two types of arrangements for organizing economic activity commonly designated as "command economy" (centrally planned) and "market economy" (Friedman 1981).

Centrally Planned Economy

The ideal type of centrally planned economy is one in which individuals act not as principals for themselves, but as agents for someone else. They are carrying out an order, doing what they are told (Friedman 1981). This is an economic system in which the central government makes all [most] decisions on the production and consumption of goods and services. Its most extensive form is referred to as a centrally planned economy in that it controls all major sectors of the economy and formulates all decisions about their use and about the distribution of income. The planners decide what should be produced and direct enterprises to produce those goods. Less extensive forms of planned economies include those on which the state employs influence, subsidies, grants, and taxes, but does not compel. This latter is sometimes referred to as a *planned market economy*.

Components of the U .S economy have varying degrees of a planned market economy. The Commodity, Conservation, and Energy titles of the 2008 Farm Bill contain significant subsidies, insurance assistance, reduced loan rates, and other incentives to influence the types and quantity of crops grown, and encourage management of both production and natural resources (characteristics of a planned economic system) while the crops and biomass are sold within a market economy.

Market Economy

The ideal type of market economy is one in which individuals act as principals in pursuit of their own interests. If any individual serves as an agent for someone else, he does so in a voluntary, mutually agreed-upon basis (Friedman 1981). A market economy or that of capitalistic economy typically refers to an economic system in which trade, industry, and the means of production (also known as capital) are privately controlled and operated for a profit. In a capitalist system, investments, distribution, income, production, pricing and supply of goods, commodities, and services are determined by private decisions, usually within the context of markets. In a capitalist state, private property rights are protected by the rule of law of a government through a limited regulatory framework. The most commonly held notion about capitalism is that it is a free-market economy; however, this interprets capitalism so narrowly as to make it almost non-existent. In a free-market capitalist state, legislative action is confined to defining and enforcing the basic rules of the market, although the government may provide some public goods and infrastructure (Case 2004).

Mixed Economy

In society, there are no pure centrally planned or market economies, either as ideals or in practice. Every system is something of a mixed system that, on the one hand, includes command elements and, on the other, relies predominately on voluntary cooperation. Friedman states that the problem is one of proportion, of keeping command elements to a minimum and, where they are introduced, doing so in a way that interferes as little as possible with the operation of the market while achieving the objectives other than productivity efficiency that are being sought (Friedman 1981). This struggle can also be described as allowing the *invisible hand* of the economy to go unfettered, or to allow the *visible hand* of the government to control the economy.

The Invisible Hand

The *invisible hand* is a concept described by Adam Smith (1952), and is broadly accepted by today's economists as a means to explain the forces of a free market. In Smith's words, "every individual necessarily labors to render the annual revenue of the society as great as he can. He generally, indeed, neither intends to promote the public interest, nor knows how much he is promoting it. By preferring the support of domestic to that of foreign industry, he intends only his own security; and by directing that industry in such a manner as its produce may be of the greatest value, he intends only his own gain, and he is in this, as in many other cases, led by an invisible hand to promote an end which was no part of his intention. By pursuing his own interest he frequently promotes that of the society more effectually than when he really intends to promote it." Smith also provides a more direct scenario. "It is not from the benevolence of the butcher, the brewer or the baker, that we expect our dinner, but from their regard to their own self interest. We address ourselves, not to their humanity but to their self-love, and never talk to them of our own necessities but of their advantages."

According to the invisible-hand theory, each of us, acting in our own self-interests, generates a demand for goods and services that compels others to deliver those goods and services in the most efficient manner so that they may be able to receive compensation from others and make a profit in doing so. In this process, resources are allocated in the most efficient manner, in contrast to a process that relies on a centrally planned system.

It should be noted that Smith's book contains many other descriptions of how economies function, and the often-quoted invisible hand can be misleading. The invisible hand concept as used in *EcoCommerce 101* refers to the profit motivation of individuals that drive an economy and not the overarching application that Smith's invisible hand is a recommendation that all economies should function unfettered by taxes, regulations, and incentives. As that, apparently, was not the intention of Smith.

The extent of the value of the invisible hand goes beyond the transaction between two individuals, as the information generated by each transaction is absorbed by the economic participants to guide the division of labor to most efficiently allocate resources. This information and division of labor is described by Leonard Read in his 1958 essay written in the first-person from the perspective of a pencil. "I, Pencil, the creation of a pencil is a complex combinations of miracles: a tree, zinc, copper, graphite and so on. But to these miracles which manifest themselves in Nature an even more extraordinary miracle has been added: the configuration of creative human energies – millions of tiny know-hows configuring naturally and spontaneously in response to human necessity and desire, all in the absence of any human masterminding! Since only God can make a tree, I insist that only God could make me. Man can no more direct these millions of know-hows to bring me into being than he can put molecules together to create a tree" (Read 1953).

Read identifies not only the allocation of resources, but the coordination of all the information and decisions that it takes to create the "simple" pencil as miraculous. It takes the flow of information throughout the production system to create a pencil in the most efficient and cost-effective means. Read continued, "The lesson I have to teach is this: Leave all creative energies uninhibited. Merely organize society to act in harmony with this lesson. Let society's legal apparatus remove all obstacles the best that it can. Permit these creative know-hows freely to flow. Have faith that free men will respond to the Invisible Hand. This faith will be confirmed. I, Pencil, seemingly simple though I am, offer the miracle of my creation as testimony that this is a practical faith, as practical as the sun, the rain, a cedar tree, the good earth."

Friedrich Hayek, a modern economist, called the market system a "marvel" because just one indicator, the market price of a commodity, spontaneously carries so much information that it guides buyers and sellers to make decisions that help both obtain what they want. The market price of a product reflects thousands, even millions, of decisions made around the world by people who don't know that the others are doing (Gwarty 2005).

The extent of the influence of the concept of the invisible hand can be realized in a speech Chairman Ben S. Bernanke gave at the New York University Law School, New York, New York, on April 11, 2007, entitled

"Financial Regulation and the Invisible Hand" (Federal Reserve Bank 2007).

"Market forces determine most outcomes in our economy, a fact that helps to explain much of our nation's success in creating wealth. Markets aggregate diffuse information more effectively and set prices more efficiently than any central planner possibly could. The result is powerful competitive incentives for businesses to produce, at the least cost, the goods and services that our citizens value most." Bernanke's focus of the speech was on financial regulation, but he did use an example of market forces to address environmental protection.

"In recent decades, public policy has been increasingly influenced by the insight that the market itself can often be used to achieve regulatory objectives. For example, in the area of environmental protection, the trading of emissions permits has been widely embraced as a cost-effective means of controlling pollution. That market-based approach is regulation by the invisible hand, as opposed to the very visible hand of direct government regulation and enforcement. The invisible-hand approach to regulation aims to align the incentives of market participants with the objectives of the regulator, thereby harnessing the same powerful forces that allow markets to work so efficiently."

The extent of the influence of the invisible hand, as described by leading economists in the last 200 years, is significant as it pertains to exchanging goods and services. And while the concept is valid, in that the invisible hand does have a tremendous force on the economy and that it does efficiently allow individuals to better their lives through a free market, it is equally apparent that market failures – the result of a market not being able to efficiently allocate resources for their best use – do routinely occur.

To continue with Bernanke's speech, he added how hedge funds provide a second illustration of how the invisible hand can be used to support regulatory objectives.

"Their rapid growth is one of the most important developments in U.S. financial markets in the past decade or so. Regulatory oversight of hedge funds is relatively light. Since hedge funds deal with highly sophisticated counterparties and investors, and because they have no claims on the federal safety net, the light regulatory touch seems largely justified. However, the growing market share of hedge funds has raised concerns about possible systemic risk. The complexity and rapid change inherent in the strategies of many funds make them relatively opaque to outsiders, and so the concern arises that the collapse of a hedge fund might come with little warning. Congress could impose a much more intrusive regulatory regime on private pools of capital. However, doing so would be costly and technically difficult, would have increased moral hazard by relieving investors and counterparties of the responsibility for monitoring the funds, and likely would have reduced the social benefits of hedge funds by hampering the ability of their managers to respond quickly and flexibly to changing market conditions. I have argued today that, in many situations, regulation that relies on the invisible hand of market-based incentives can complement direct government regulation. For market-based regulation to work, the incentives of investors and other private actors must align with the objectives of the government regulator. In particular, private investors must be sophisticated enough to understand and monitor the financial condition of the firm and be persuaded that they will experience significant losses in the event of a failure. When these conditions are met, market discipline is a powerful and proven tool for constraining excessive risk-taking."

As with most concepts, philosophical or otherwise, a long line forms of those who agree or disagree with the invisible hand. But what is generally agreed on is that the invisible hand is a ubiquitous and powerful force that influences and is influenced by individuals interacting within the economy. The other agreement is that the invisible hand does create market failures, in that resources are not always efficiently allocated.

Not the Infallible Hand

Regardless of the invisible hand's ubiquitous force, it is not infallible or incapable of failure or error. A market can only function "perfectly" if all economic participants are perfectly rational, that information is perfect, and that market exchange has no costs associated with the transaction. These are not the cases in which the economy operates, but it operates with "bounded rationality." In other words, people make the best decisions they can, given what they know and their capacity to analyze the information (Landell-Mills 2002, 12). In ecoservice markets, there is much less information available.

Societal Failures

As it pertains to the decline in natural resources, three major societal failures are occurring that prevent ecoservice markets to function (Cork 2002):

1. Failure is caused by individuals and communities that do not have the basic knowledge of how their management activities relate to the natural world.

2. Market failure is caused by economic transactions that do not

cause the supply and demand of resources to be in balance.

3. Institutional failure is caused by inadequate policies, programs, and rules that do not adequately recognize ecological values.

Economic Failures

These societal failures are expressed in four generally recognized classes of economic failures (Ribaudo 2008):

1. Externalities, such as water pollution, arise when buyers or sellers are neither charged nor compensated for the economic impacts of their choices on others.

2. Public goods, such as national defense [or ecoservices], do not lend themselves to market allocation because it is difficult to exclude individuals from enjoying the good or service once it is produced and because it costs nothing for an additional individual to use.

3. Insufficient information about the characteristics of a good or service may prevent markets from forming even though, with more complete information, consumers would be willing to buy and manufacturers would be willing to sell.

4. Market power, where a few buyers or sellers are able to exert significant power over prices, can dampen production and exclude some otherwise willing market participants.

If allocating or rationing scarce resources is an attribute and responsibility of the invisible hand, then the combined intelligence of the consumer and producer population must be complete for it to function at its most efficient level. Bernanke (Federal Reserve Bank 2007) stated, "Markets aggregate diffuse information more effectively and set prices more efficiently than any central planner possibly could. The result is powerful competitive incentives for businesses to produce, at the least cost, the goods and services that our citizens value most."

If the combined intelligence of the consumers and producers is nowhere near complete, and the invisible hand is omnipresent, then the invisible hand will fail in one or a combination of aspects. In other words, giving the invisible hand the power, but not the intelligence, will create a market that is destined to fail. This difference between market success and failure is the result of the quantity and quality of the information that gets fed into the economic system to allow the invisible hand to guide each of us in a manner that allows production, consumption, and rationing of our economic (and ecological) resources. The success of the market then depends on the information that is available and the ability to incorporate that information into the invisible hand.

Externalities

As in the case of externalities, it is well known that pollution degrades water quality and erosion reduces productivity of the land and contributes to water degradation, but that information is still not able to become incorporated into the invisible hand in a market-based fashion. Since neither the consumer nor the producer can, in any practical manner, consider these externalities, the invisible hand cannot "know" about these ecoservices, and, therefore, cannot provide guidance on the proper price needed to produce, consume, or ration them to achieve market equilibrium. The negative externality graph (Figure 1.12) represents the price and costs of unit PC and the ecological costs (line EC). At price P_5 and quantity Q_5, the market equilibrium is at Point E_1. Unknown to the economic participants is line PC+EC, the combined production and ecological costs. If they were included in the transaction, then a cost of P_6 would result in a decrease in the production to Q_4 and market equilibrium would occur at E_2. This additional cost is often obtained from applying a tax, or imposing regulation costs.

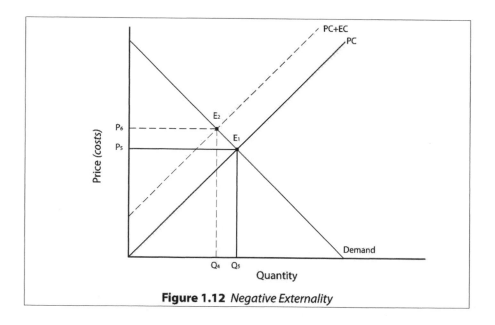

Figure 1.12 *Negative Externality*

Positive externalities are beneficial impacts imposed on parties not participating in that particular transaction. The intention of EcoCommerce is to include positive externalities into the economic system to allow a shift in the demand for ecoservices. Figure 1.13 represents the demand for goods and services including the ecological benefits. At price P_5 a quantity of Q_5 is produced on line D_1 and market equilibrium is produced at Point E_1. By including a demand for ecological value (EV) within the production system, the price increases to P_6 and the quantity generated increases to Q_6 as it shifts to equilibrium point E_2 on line D+EV.

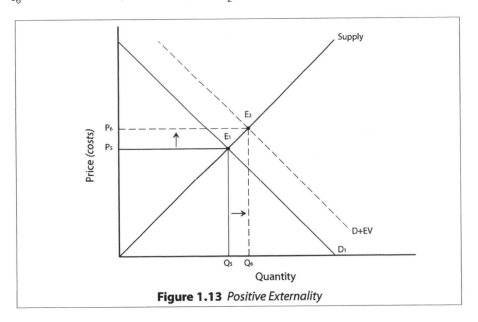

Figure 1.13 *Positive Externality*

For example, fertile soil does produce abundant crops and that productivity is a function of the ecological resources of soil type, topography, and rainfall along with human inputs that can increase the production. Due to these known parameters and the resulting economic feedback and signals, the invisible hand of the economy provides guidance on the price of the land, the type of crops to be grown, the price and amount of human-based inputs, and the price these commodities can bear. Management activities to improve the soil condition produce ecoservices such as long-term productivity capacity, cleaner water, reduced erosion and sedimentation, nutrient assimilation and sequestration, microbial, insect and annelid habitat, all of which are significant components of a functioning ecosystem. Combining man-made capital with the natural capital of an agro-ecosystem has produced significant bounty. The challenges for the invisible hand are to recognize the economic symbiosis of that relationship and increase the incentive to apply economic value toward the natural capital functions. If those incentives are employed, the natural capital will receive its due value, and economic participants will be compelled to work toward the market equilibrium point at E_2 in Figure 1.13.

Failure to recognize the economic value of natural capital and its management will have economic consequences. In the case of the fertile field, the topsoil may be at a depth of 18 inches. In an economic sense, each inch of that soil has value, but the invisible hand may not begin to recognize that value until that topsoil has been reduced to about 10 inches.

It is about at that point that the reduced production capacity begins to be more apparent (Cruse 2009). If nutrient inputs are relatively inexpensive and grain prices are relatively high, the invisible hand could continue to promote intensive cultivation of the topsoil. The resulting tillage, as well as water and wind-induced erosion will reduce the soil's nutrient cycling and other beneficial capacities. Since topsoil and the multiple ecoservices are not renewable, the temporary loss becomes a near-permanent loss. When the cost of nutrient inputs becomes high enough and the invisible hand guides the farmer to again manage the soil to gain back some of its natural capacity, this natural capital of soil may be too degraded to reverse this trend in any appreciable time frame. The invisible hand will then compel the price of foodstuffs to rise to encourage more production and less economically productive lands may be brought into the economy. These marginal lands may be more beneficial to society from an ecological perspective than to the farmer from an EcoCommerce perspective, but the invisible hand will be silent to those values. Reducing the capacity of the natural capital to provide wealth generated by man-made capital, whether that is fisheries or topsoil, does not create long-term wealth regardless of new technologies and efficiencies. Losing the capacity of natural capital is akin to a factory or industry becoming dilapidated and no longer able produce widgets, except that the widget maker can be restored and possibly even made more efficient. Ecosystems are quite efficient at producing outcomes, and agro-ecosystems are quite productive as well. To refer back to the topsoil example, the economic value of the eight inches of topsoil lost will be recognized after it has been reduced to a marginal productive state.

Natural Capital-Financial Capital Comparison

The financial market failure that occurred shortly after Bernanke's speech demonstrates that pending economic failure can be unforeseen. While there were several economists predicting the impending collapse, the economic leaders and participants were not compelled to listen as their self-interests were apparently being addressed. To make a statement today that an ecological failure in some fashion will occur or that a downward trend has begun would generate about as much interest of the media, leaders, and direct participants in the natural capital-based economy as the interest that was generated in the financial capital-based economy on the day of this particular Bernanke speech in 2007.

This is expected, as the self-interests of the leaders and the direct participants in the natural capital-based economy are being met. Participants who are directly involved, but are more passive (such as individual mutual fund investors in the financial markets and consumers of food and fuel in the agricultural markets) do have a responsibility to correct the market's failure. But due to the lack of transparency and understanding in both markets, these direct, but distant, participants do not have avenues to express themselves in a practical or efficient economic manner. Determining risks in the hedge fund market and the agro-ecological market would generate significant costs to them, either in time or money.

If Bernanke's speech was about our nation's natural capital and the impending increase in demands from an expanding population or a biofuels market, rather than about our nation's financial capital and its hedge funds, it could have read like this (with financial capital terms replaced with natural capital terms in [brackets]):

"The rapid growth of [biofuels] is one of the most important developments in U.S. [agricultural & forest] markets in the past decade or so. Regulatory oversight of [natural capital] is relatively light. Because [agriculture & forestry] deal[s] with [USDA policies], and because [farms and forests] have no claims on the federal safety net, the light regulatory touch seems largely justified. However, the growing market share of [biofuels] has raised concerns about possible systemic risk. The complexity and rapid change inherent in the strategies of [production and processing] make them relatively opaque to outsiders, and so the concern arises that the collapse of an [ecosystem] might come with little warning.

"Congress could impose a much more intrusive regulatory regime on private pools of [natural] capital. However, doing so would be costly and technically difficult, would have increased moral hazard by relieving [farmers & foresters] of the responsibility for monitoring the [lands], and likely would have reduced the social benefits of [food & fiber production] by hampering the ability of the [farmers & foresters] to respond quickly and flexibly to changing market conditions.

"I have argued today that, in many situations, regulation that relies on the invisible hand of market-based incentives can complement direct government regulation. For market-based regulation to work, the incentives of [farmers & foresters] and other private actors must align with the objectives of the government regulator. In particular, [consumers] must be sophisticated enough to understand and monitor the [ecological] condition of the [farms & forests] and be persuaded that they will experience significant losses in the event of a failure. When these conditions are met, market discipline is a powerful and proven tool for constraining excessive risk-taking."

In response to the financial market collapse, significant changes are taking place that many are describing as "socialism." In essence, they are saying that the nation's planned market economy is incorporating more centrally planned aspects in it, rather than more market-based aspects.

As Bernanke described, "The invisible-hand approach to regulation aims to align the incentives of market participants with the objectives of the regulator, thereby harnessing the same powerful forces that allow markets to work so efficiently."

Of course, market failures will occur, but it is not to say that harnessing the powerful forces of the invisible hand is not applicable to meeting government and societal goals. In fact, attempting to achieve outcomes by ignoring or opposing the forces of the invisible hand seems futile.

Incorporating the invisible hand into natural capital management for the purpose of generating ecoservices will allow for two important aspects of natural capital management:

- The exchange of monetary and non-monetary values for ecoservices and presumably a functioning ecosystem

- Creation of ecoservice and ecosystem intelligence – the information that allows resource management stakeholders to understand the state of an ecosystem and to develop pricing, policy, and programs to further motivate those who have self-interest in providing ecoservices

Hybrid Economy

An ideal hybridized economy would reduce the undesirable traits such as the externalities generated by a market economy and the inefficiencies of a centrally planned economy. Such an economic system would contain Hayek's "marvel," the price that spontaneously carries so much information that guides millions of decisions. And that price could not have been generated with disregard to positive and negative externalities. First, the function of price is to enable commerce to be coordinated by transmitting information about resource availability and the demands placed on them.

Second, it provides incentives for people to adopt the least costly methods of production and to use available resources for their most highly valued uses. And third, prices determine how much income is distributed and to whom (Friedman 1981, 8).

A hybridized EcoCommerce economy, as all economies, would use price for the same three reasons, of course, but EcoCommerce incorporates a structure to include resource values that are not directly included within the transaction. In EcoCommerce, a bushel of corn grown within a cropping system that is prone to erosion and consumes a significant amount of energy in the process is worth less to the economy than corn that is produced under a cropping system that increases the soil tilth and generates a higher return on the energy investment. Most people can recognize those values, but without an economic system to present these values, they cannot be expressed. EcoCommerce can then emerge as not just a mixed economy but a hybrid economy that aligns the incentives of market participants to achieve government and societal goals. If there is, indeed, economic value associated with the natural capital, then EcoCommerce will have the result of expanding the economic base and value, rather than being a tax-like burden on the bio-economy. EcoCommerce will be validated as an economic system if it allows the three functions of price to occur for the commodity within the context of the additional values that are generated in the process of producing the commodity.

EcoCommerce as a hybrid economy can be further explained by applying it to the description posed by Ernest Sternberg (1993). Sternberg sees government and business – once antithetical pillars of the economy – combining to funnel their operations through hybrid "partnerships." Decisions will be made through a variety of forums that are neither public nor private. These entities, conceived in the decades after World War II, consist of university-industry collaboration, military-industrial cooperation, and industrial consortia in which public authority is implicitly transferred to non-government groupings and other non-classifiable arrangements. He states that these partnerships that are shaping a new overall hybrid economy have proliferated to a significant degree and represent a substantial historical tendency.

The ideological attraction to EcoCommerce, as a hybrid economy, is for new partnerships to arise that are often considered being at odds, such as environmentalists, farmers, government, conservationists, and economists. They could arise from the desire to privatize activities, such as the USDA's conservation delivery system that is predominantly public. Also non-profit organizations could increase public intervention into the economy such as incorporating externalities [pollution] and these costs within the economy. In the best of situations, EcoCommerce would draw on the strengths of each major stakeholder and components while also minimizing their inherent weaknesses.

For example, EcoCommerce would tap into the innovation and creativity of the agricultural sector but would apply the resource management assessment tools and standards developed by government agencies, universities, and institutions. In this manner, the invisible hand is allowed to pursue the most efficient means to address the national and global resource concerns, but the processes become standardized so that a variety of stakeholders, private, non-profit, government, and industry could participate. The decisions on how the natural and production resources are managed remain with the resource managers—farmers, ranchers, and foresters—while the valuation of those decisions can reside within any sector of the economy, including the government. EcoCommerce would allow the farmer to become the primary-resource-management supplier to the federal government, rather than their current niche as a resource-management customer of the federal government.

As a hybrid economic system, EcoCommerce measurements and standards are rooted in government, university, and institutional assessment tools. These unified standards allow for open trade among producers of ecoservices, (private landowners), and buyers (governments, industry, retail markets, and landowners). Verification of producing the ecoservices is conducted in a joint process between government and the private sector. As an emerging hybrid economy, EcoCommerce has the ability to respond to transformation forces as retail institutions, such as Walmart Stores, Inc ., become interested in marketing products and produce using a "sustainability index" and government entities seek other avenues to address natural resource issues other than regulation and practice-based incentive payments.

Contrary to the financial markets moving in the direction of a more centrally planned economy from a market-based economy, EcoCommerce gravitates the opposite way. Under EcoCommerce, the existing centrally planned conservation-delivery system of the USDA and its state and local partners moves significantly toward a market-based allocation process. The centrally planned components of the conservation-delivery system will not be dismantled under an EcoCommerce system, but they will evolve into supporting systems of EcoCommerce rather than the transaction system for ecoservices. The hybrid economic structure also parallels recommendations that emerged from the Millennium Ecosystem Assessment in 2005.

The MEA stated that even though existing institutions may have a mandate to address degradation of ecosystem services, they cannot always enable cooperation across sectors. Therefore, changes of institutions or new institutions may be necessary.

Their recommendations and mentions of promising instruments include five elements (MEA 2005):

• Integrate ecosystem management with other sectors. The most important decisions affecting ecosystems are often made by parties who are not involved with ecosystem protection.

• Increase coordination among multilateral (environmental) agreements and institutions.

• Involve the stakeholders in decision-making to create institutions and instruments that are more likely to be effective.

• Ecosystem management problems have been exacerbated by both overly centralized and overly decentralized decision-making. This can be prevented by development of institutions that carry out decision-making based on effective coordination across scales and management needs.

• Strong institutions must be developed that regulate interaction between markets and ecosystems.

Institutional frameworks should develop that promote a shift from highly sectoral resource management to integrated approaches. Since in most countries separate [agencies] are in charge of different aspects of ecosystems, there is seldom political will to develop effective ecosystem-management strategies.

EcoCommerce will compel the development of institutions described and could include an EcoCommerce Registry that identifies standards, measurements, and outcomes as well as licenses professionals. An EcoCommerce Exchange and Clearinghouse should be developed that exists on local, regional, and national bases depending on how the ecoservices are generated and marketed. These institutions will be, in part, anchored in the federal governments with delegated authorities to the states with the price and transactions that motivate individuals and entities remaining within the public arena.

System of National Accounts

For any economic value to be recognized at the national and global scale, it must be measured within the accounting system of the nation. The System of National Accounts is a conceptual framework that sets the international statistical standard for the measurement of the market economy. It is published jointly by the United Nations, the Commission of the European Communities, the International Monetary Fund, the Organization for Economic Co-operation and Development, and the World Bank. The System of National Accounts consists of an integrated set of macroeconomic accounts, balance sheets, and tables based on internationally agreed concepts, definitions, classifications, and accounting rules. Together, these principles provide a comprehensive accounting framework within which economic data can be compiled and presented in a format that is designed for purposes of economic analysis, decision-taking, and policy-making (UNSD 2010).

Conventional measures of economic activity include Gross Domestic Product (GDP) and Net Domestic Product (NDP). National accounting dates back to 1758 when Francois Quesney attempted to capture the workings of the French economy in a matrix. However the real incentive to understand the flows of money in a national economy came during the Depression, with the notion that understanding the relationship between macroeconomic variables was the key to controlling economic events (Wright 1990).

Conventionally, GDP is constructed as a measure of the output of the market sector, yet in its interpretation as nation's income, it is often presented as a measure of standards of living, and thus a proxy for social welfare. In this manner, GDP has serious deficiencies in regard to natural resource stocks, whose use contributes to current income flows (Harris 2002). Although the "environment" is not completely invisible in national accounting, its treatment produces some curious results. Wright states that it is often better, economically speaking, to cause environmental damage and then repair it than to avoid causing the damage in the first place; this is hardly an efficient form of economic growth. A commonly cited example of the inappropriateness of the GDP to measure the progress of society is the Exxon Valdez oil spill of 24 March, 1989., where 10 .8 million U.S. gallons of crude oil were spilled into the sea, covering 28,000 km^2 of ocean. Thousands of animals died immediately, including an estimated 500,000 seabirds, 1,000 sea otters, 300 harbor seals, 250 bald eagles, and 22 orcas, as well as the destruction of billions of salmon and herring eggs. Oil can still be found on the beaches of Prince William Sound today. Economically speaking, the accident generated an estimated $5 billion U.S. in more economic activity, much more than the straight delivery of the cargo would have produced (ANEW 2010). In a more general statement, the shortfalls of GDP were clearly articulated by Repetto (1988) who stated that, "a country could exhaust its mineral resources, cut down its forests, erode its soils, pollute its aquifers, and hunt its wildlife to extinction, but measured income would rise steadily as these assets disappeared."

The shortfall of the conventionally measured GDP can also be illustrated by the drop in GDP when investments are made in the production of ecoservices. In this case, the GDP will fall when private firms invest in conservation activities because some of the resources of landholders are diverted from producing commodities and into ecoservice production. The example used by Stoneham (2008) supposes a landowner excludes livestock from part of the farm to allow habitat to regenerate. In this case, GDP will fall because the reduction in livestock production will be accounted for, but not the production of ecoservices and or the increase in the capacity of natural capital.

By no means is there universal agreement that the GDP is an inappropriate measurement tool. Wright states that the fundamental issue is whether SNA statistics should be improved as measures of economic welfare or left as measures of a subset of economic activity. It is not generally known that most economists recognize GDP as performing only the latter task. Economists frequently express concern about the misinterpretation of the SNA. Wright quotes Anne Harrison: "At first it may seem counterintuitive that the degradation of permanent resources leads to an increase in GDP. This reflects the common lack of awareness that the 'gross' in GDP means 'before allowance has been made for consumption of capital" (Wright 1990).

This perspective gives a sense that the GDP is not a perverse system as it relates to natural capital. But the challenge still remains to have a system that can generate an economic allowance when the consumption, degradation, or improvement in the capacity of natural capital occurs.

CHAPTER 2

Natural Capital

Natural Capital

As listed in the Introduction, natural capital is one of the five generally accepted economic capitals identified along with financial, physical, human, and social. The definition of natural capital is based on an extension of the economic definition of capital, which refers to "factors of production" that are used to create goods and services, but are not themselves directly consumed. Natural capital, the stock of natural ecosystems, yields a flow of valuable ecosystem goods or services, also called ecoservices. Ecoservices consist of a multitude of resources and processes that are provided by nature, such as soil, pollination, clean water, wildlife, and oxygen. Ecoservices are generated in quantities directly related to the capacity of the natural capital and how the ecosystems are managed. Boyd and Banzhaf (2006) define ecoservices as "the benefits of nature to households, communities, and economies." If ecosystems and their components are viewed as natural capital, and this natural capital acts as "factories" to produce ecoservices, then people can apply their labor (and other capitals) toward this natural capital to produce a valuable economic component, or commodity.

The concept of natural capital, that is, the notion that nature's functions can even be described as "capital," is not universally accepted by economists. This is, in part, due to the difficulties related to appropriately modeling and pricing both market and non-market environmental resources, the lack of willingness to pay, a lack of knowledge about minimum levels or time spans required for resources to replenish or renew, a lack of knowledge regarding the interaction and dependences between resources and their true value, usefulness, or necessity.

But even in the 18th century there was an understanding of the varying potential of natural capital. In defining various forms of capital, Adam Smith (1952) made a comparison of man-made capital to that of natural capital of a farm. "An improved farm may very justly be regarded in the same light as those useful machines which facilitate and abridge labour. An improved farm is equally advantageous and more durable than any of those machines, frequently requiring no other repairs than the most profitable application of the farmer's capital employed in circulation." In speaking of the productivity of farming, Smith (1952, 157) states that after all their labor, a great part of work always remains to be done by her [nature].

Repetto (1988) makes a similar, albeit more modern analogy, by stating that as man-made assets (buildings and equipment) age, they become worthless and money is set-aside for their replacement in order that the income flowing from their use is sustainable. Gross domestic product is adjusted for such depreciation to give net domestic product. But the value of natural assets also falls if the assets are depleted. Thus, in the same sense that a machine depreciates, soils depreciate as their fertility is diminished, since they can only produce at higher costs or lower yields. Repetto and his colleagues treat natural resource depreciation as asset depreciation in order to put man-made capital and [natural] capital on the same footing. Thus, in this methodology, GDP remains unchanged, but NDP is changed [reduced] (Wright 1990).

Smith (1952) recognized, as most others who work in or study agriculture have, that there is an inherent natural capacity unique to each tract of land on the quantity of crops it can produce. How the soil resource is managed has a direct influence on the short- and long-term productivity and capacity. Natural capital may also provide services like groundwater recharge, carbon sequestration, and erosion control. In the United States, nearly 87 percent of all of the country's fresh water supply originates from forests and agricultural lands, and more than 200 million people rely on their drinking water from public and private forests and grasslands (USDA 2009). Since the flow of services from ecosystems requires that they function as whole systems, the structure and diversity of the system are important components of natural capital.

Awareness of Natural Capital Limits

The United States has had significant events in the last 100 years providing evidence that humans can reduce the capacity of its natural capital.

The Dust Bowl was a period of severe dust storms causing major ecological and agricultural damage to American prairie lands in the 1930s. The phenomenon was caused by severe drought coupled with poor soil and vegetative management that led to extreme rates of erosion. This awareness led to the creation of the USDA Soil Conservation Service.

The Cleveland, Ohio, Cuyahoga River fire in 1969—though not the first or last river fire—provided an obvious example how point-source or factory-generated pollution can limit the production and assimilation capacity of a river system. Since point-source pollution is definable and measurable, it can be quite efficient to pass a regulation that requires a limit on the amount of pollution, either by concentration or by total amount over a given time. This led to the Clean Water Act in 1972.

But following the reduction of point-source pollution, it became apparent that another significant source of water pollution was from non-point sources. According to the U.S. Environmental Protection Agency (EPA), non-point-source pollution is the leading cause of water pollution in the United States today originating with polluted runoff from agriculture along with urban runoff of items like oil, fertilizers, and lawn chemicals. As rainfall or snowmelt moves over and through the ground, it picks up and carries away natural and human-made pollutants. These pollutants are eventually deposited into bodies of water, such as lakes, rivers, wetlands, coastal waters, and underground sources of drinking water. Such pollution led to the development of Clean Water Act's Total Maximum Daily Load policy in which a designated amount of both point-source and NPS pollution can enter a water body. But because NPS pollution is diffuse and impossible to measure in relation to its source, a process to adequately reduce NPS pollution and increase ecoservices has not been created.

Value of Natural Capital

Valuing natural capital is difficult. The economic value of maintaining topsoil can vary greatly, or knowing the genomic value of a plant or animal that is not even known to exist, is of course not possible. Numerous insects could go extinct without a known economic effect and then the loss of

become obvious. An accounting framework for recording numerical information (whether in dollars or not) has enormous strengths (Wright 1990).

To reach this natural-resource accounting framework, Wright (1990) lists six preconditions that Lone (1988) concluded, within his report on the Norwegian experience of natural-resource accounting, which would provide greater success. Wright states that these would certainly apply to an environmental-statistical-system design influenced by the concepts of resource accounting:

1. Identify important resource and environment problems and the major decision-making institutions as users of natural-resource accounting and budgets.

2. Concentrate on a few of the most important of these problems, where it is possible to reach some results in the relatively near future, and where managers are able to use natural-resource accounts and budgets in their planning and management.

3. Involve managers/users and political institutions as early and as closely as possible.

4. Develop the necessary integrated economic/ecologic expertise. Exploit to the utmost existing data-collection routines, management concepts, and management tools.

5. Avoid ambitious theoretical system-building and resist the temptation to engage in large, indiscriminate data collection that very easily may emerge as an end in itself.

Economic indicators such as real GDP, price indices, terms of trade, and numbers of unemployed are published regularly. They cannot be weighted together into a grand economic index, but together build up a picture, albeit a different picture in different minds. Similarly, the interpretation of a set of indicators of sustainability [to represent resource accounts] will not be straightforward. The indicators themselves will, like the economic indicators, be flawed and always in need of improvement (Wright 1990).

Origins of Natural Capital

Natural capital and its subsequent ecoservices, originate with a "natural economic" structure consisting of biomes and ecosystems. Economically speaking, one could refer to the major biomes as the fisheries, forests, and breadbaskets of the world.

Biomes

Biomes are defined as "the world's major communities, classified according to the predominant vegetation and characterized by adaptations of organisms to that particular environment" (Campbell 1996). A biome, or "major life zone," is a large geographic region of the earth's surface with distinctive plant and animal communities. There are both terrestrial, or land-based biomes, and aquatic-based biomes. A biome may be spread over a wide geographic area, or as a grouping of many ecosystems that share similar environmental features and plant and animal communities. Biomes represent a superficial and somewhat arbitrary classification of ecosystems. These are not distinct geographical features such as a mountain range and therefore, biologists are not unanimous in how they classify biomes or in the number of biomes.

Commonly recognized biomes include:

Land-based biomes

- Tundra (permafrost regions)
- Taiga (high-latitude forested regions)
- Temperate deciduous forest
- Grasslands
- Deserts
- Tropical rain forests

Water-based biomes
- Marine
- Estuary
- Fresh water

The grassland biomes are considered the world's breadbaskets, but temperate deciduous forest biomes have been converted into productive agricultural areas. Within biomes are ecosystems. Ecosystems are defined by the physical and biological interactions that occur within them.

Ecosystems

Ecosystems are the interactions between the living things and the nonliving things in a place. In an ecosystem, plants, animals, and other organisms rely on each other and on the physical environment – the soil, water, and nutrients. The first modern textbook developed on the ecosystem concept was by Eugene Odum in 1953 (MEA 2003). Thus the ecosystem concept, central to understanding the nature of life on earth and how it can be interrelated with an economic system, is relatively new and still being developed.

The components of an ecosystem can be categorized by "abiotic" (non-living) and "biotic" (living .) Abiotic components are sunlight, temperature, precipitation, water, and soil. Biotic components consist of plants, herbivores, carnivores, omnivores, and detritivores (generally those smaller organisms that consume decaying plants). Using this definition, the entire biosphere of Earth is an ecosystem since all these elements interact. But for analysis and assessment, it is important to adapt a pragmatic view of ecosystem boundaries.

The Millennium Ecosystem Assessment (2003) developed 10 reporting categories that it felt shared a suite of biological, climatic, and social factors so that the system categories would provide a useful framework for analyzing the consequences of ecosystem change for human well-being. The first three categories encompass this book's focus on EcoCommerce with *Cultivated Lands* being the reporting category that is the primary focus of this book:

1. Cultivated – lands dominated by domestic plant species, used for and substantially changed by crop, agroforestry, or aquaculture production

2. Dryland – land where plant production is limited by water availability and the dominant uses are large herbivores, including livestock grazing and cultivation

3. Forest – lands dominated by trees that are often used for timber, fuel wood, and non-timber forest products

4. Marine – ocean with fishing typically a major driver of change

5. Coastal – the interface between ocean and land and to extend into the land to include all areas strongly influenced by proximity to the ocean

6. Inland Water – permanent water bodies inland from the coastal zone, and areas whose ecology and use are dominated by the permanent or seasonal occurrence of flooded conditions

7. Island – lands isolated by water with a high proportion of coast to inland

8. Mountain – steep and high lands

9. Polar – high-latitude systems frozen for most of the year

10. Urban – built environments with a high human density

Defining the boundaries or identifying categories of ecosystems is not an exact science as those definitions are influenced by what the intentions of the delineation are. The MEA categories do not have definite boundaries and often overlap. The MEA (2003) uses overlapping categories because this better reflects real-world biological, geophysical, social, and economic interactions, particularly at these relatively large scales.

Ecosystems Dissected

There is a broader acceptance that to prevent degradation of an ecosystem, or to preserve the capacity of the natural capital, its components must be both understood and economically valued. To advance EcoCommerce or any ecoservice markets, it is necessary to further dissect ecosystems and identify how ecosystems produce human-related values and how these values can be expressed in economic terms. Ecosystems have processes, functions, and structures that become the base for a level of production capacity of the natural capital. This natural capital eventually dictates the quantity of end-products, whether that is clean water, fertile soil, abundant crops, or all, and many more. In theory, one could value the ecosystem components: the processes, functions, the structure, or end-products individually or in a combination of two or more. One of the challenges and debates in constructing an ecoservice market is deciding where to apply value and how to account for it to generate the desired results.

Ecosystem Processes

Within all ecosystems, certain processes occur to sequester, transform, and move energy and materials through the ecosystem. Ecosystem processes include the following (Ruhl 2007):
- photosynthesis
- plant nutrient uptake
- microbial respiration
- nitrification and denitrification
- plant transpiration
- root activity
- mineral weathering
- vegetative succession
- predator-prey interaction
- decomposition

These processes operate within biological and physical characteristics and constraints. Energy movements are essentially one-way flows that prevent the reuse or recycling of energy. Nutrients, on the other hand, can circulate through different components of an ecosystem and create nutrient cycles and pools. The study of ecology, at its most fundamental level, is quantifying the factors that regulate energy transformation and nutrient cycling within the particular ecosystem defined. Measuring photosynthesis can occur at the level of an individual leaf or within the canopy of a forest. Therefore, defining ecosystem processes must also entail defining the scale at which the process is going to be measured. It should be noted that these processes exist in all ecosystems whether that is a cornfield in Iowa or the rainforest of Brazil. An analogy would be to consider the processes of man-made capital such as a factory using electricity, switches, conveyor belts, chains, hydraulics, and other processes that many other manufacturing plants use to create products.

Ecosystem Functions

As noted, the same biological and chemical processes occur in all ecosystems, but different conditions (such as location, soil parent material, climate, etc.) yield different functions. The processes in the Iowa cornfield and the rainforest are the same, but the functions are quite different. The corn field has the basic function to produce corn, but can also produce clean water, pheasants, and sequestered carbon. The rainforest has the basic function to create a tree canopy habitat and all the interrelations that make it a rainforest. To make a more comparable scenario: a corn field in Iowa that is adjacent to a prairie field has the same processes, location, soil parent material, weather, and climate but they each result in a different function. The ecosystem function is how the processes interact. An analogy would be to consider the functions of man-made capital such as a manufacturing plant that is capable of producing cars or appliances. Both factories use the same processes (conveyor belts, welding, and hydraulics), but since they are organized differently they have different functions.

Ecosystem functions do not occur independently from one another, and the interplay of material cycles and energy flows in large ecosystems generate a self-correcting homeostasis with no outside control or set-point required. Control mechanisms operating at the ecosystem level include those that regulate the storage and release of nutrients and the production and decomposition of organic substances. These mechanisms can influence populations that are regulated by density that provides feedback by way of behavioral changes to reduce or increase the reproductive rate within set limits (Odum 1971).

Ecosystems are information-rich economies that adjust the production and consumption of energy and nutrients via a "natural" invisible hand. Both economic systems, natural and manmade, are most efficient when participants are guided by information-dense feedback that signals production and consumption needs and eliminates or reduces externalities. New ecosystems [or new economic systems] tend to oscillate more violently and are less able to resist outside perturbation as compared with mature systems in which the components have had a chance to make mutual adjustments to each other (Odum 1971).

Ecosystem Structure is Natural Capital

Unique to natural systems, the ecosystem functions contribute to the building of the ecosystem's biophysical structure, which in turn supports the functions themselves (Christensen 1996). A crop-management system can create the biophysical characteristics that are advantageous for crop yields. Perhaps more apparent in the rainforest, the structure of the vegetation supports the functions of the rainforest. It is this structure that supports the processes and functions of the ecosystem and creates value for humans and their economy that is called "natural capital." This natural capital supports the creation and flow of goods and services to humans (Clark 1995). Since ecosystems have self-generative and regenerative characteristics and man-made capital does not, there is no man-made capital comparative. Ecosystems' processes lead to functions that build the "factory" to support it holistically. Economic systems are able to value the outputs of these natural factories (food, fiber, fuel) but have been inefficient or unable to place value on the processes, functions, and structure.

Finite Factories

Ecosystems are finite resources in the sense that their output can be diminished or eliminated or made extinct. They have finite production capacities that can be affected by the management of their components. In an example of the fishing industry, an extensive investment into man-made capital to harvest and process fish could exceed the natural capital capacity to produce fish. Perhaps of all the natural capital components needed to have a robust capacity to produce fish remained (such as adequate shoals, nutrient-rich currents, adequate water temperature, and oxygen supply) except for the reproductive stock. In this case, the production capacity of the fishing industry is dependent on a proper balance and integration of both man-made capital and natural capital. In other words, economically speaking, if the natural capital is the scarcer resource of the two capital sources, the economic value of the man-made capital is relative to the productivity of the natural capital.

Adam Smith's (1952) view of capital and the principles he advanced

run-off water, and attempting to value certain types of wildlife by specific totals.

Direct and Indirect Ecoservice Benefits

Ecoservices have both direct and indirect benefits to human welfare. These benefits can be derived from ecosystem processes, functions, and structure. Most people can appreciate the ecosystem structure—that is the forested mountain—for beauty, for hiking, and for timber. The ecoservices that make this structure possible are the ecosystem processes and functions that humans don't directly interact with, such as the genetic stock of the plants and animals, the food web, and other biochemical interactions. In this case, processes and functions provide an indirect benefit by making the structures (forested mountain ecosystem) possible.

If one stands on or near the forested mountain, he directly consumes oxygen generated by the trees, is immersed in the microclimatic conditions of the ecosystem, and directly experiences or consumes other conditions that are the direct result of that forested mountain ecosystem. All of this is directly dependent on the supporting services of soil formation, nutrient cycling, seed dispersal, and other long-term benefits of this ecosystem. Humans directly and indirectly consume these ecoservices.

To bring this discussion to an agro-ecosystem, humans generate wealth through the production of grain that is directly dependent on the long-term supporting ecoservices and the shorter-term regulating services. To sustain the economic productivity of the farm and to improve the condition of the agro-ecosystem, economic value must be targeted or be eventually allocated toward indirect regulating services such as erosion control, biodiversity, soil fertility, and micro- and macro-climatic stability. In the same way, a factory needs to perform maintenance on their equipment.

These regulating ecoservices, both direct and indirect, are generally excluded from the economic transactions. For indirectly used ecoservices, the link between an ecoservice and its contribution to the ecosystem structure must be made to be valued. Ironically, for directly used ecoservices it is as difficult to make a human-ecosystem connection. Directly used ecoservices, such as pollination, are the result of the ecosystem structure and are dependent on indirect processes and functions. Economically, the value resides in the number of pollen grains that are successfully delivered. But since this is impossible to account for, an indirect measurement is then necessary.

To maintain the theme of comparing natural capital to physical capital, the following direct and indirect comparison is made.

In the man-made economy, identifying direct and indirect benefits is not necessary. The purchase of a car includes within it the price of the steel, labor, interest rates, the cost of the factory, computers, the engineering, and the numerous inputs that are needed to construct a car. The prooooooo and the functions of the factory and the costs associated with them are imbedded in the cost of the car. Physical capital is well-defined economically. To get more cars, people have to demand them (with adequate payment) and in delivering those cars, the processes, functions, and structure of the factory are developed and built. The person who bought the car is also buying the processes and functions so that the structure of the manufacturing plant has the capacity to produce cars. The person who wants a car is dependent, indirectly, on those processes and functions of that physical capital structure. If, in some odd world or culture, cars could not be purchased but were considered public goods, then no one would make cars unless some other component of the car manufacturing plant was valued. If the processes and functions of the manufacturing plant were valued adequately and there was an efficient method to account for and exchange value, then the capacity of that manufacturing plant would be developed at the level needed to construct cars.

Ecoservice Valuation Strategies

It is apparent that valuing ecoservices is not as straightforward as applying value to all the processes and functions needed to manufacture a car and determine its costs. There are numerous strategies to define ecoservices and to place value on them.

A practice-based strategy is a commonly used method and is similar to the USDA conservation programs, in that specific conservation practices and activities that have been identified have incentives allocated to their use and installation. This method is used in the successful markets in the New York City Regional Watershed program and the Nestlé-Vittel effort explained in Chapter 5. Many water-quality-trading markets rely on this framework, and the Chicago Climate Exchange, a voluntary carbon market, uses a practice-based process as well.

Boyd and Banzhaf's (2006) strategy is to restrict the definition of ecoservices to the measurement of the outcomes of processes. This strategy could include pollination populations, soil quality, and water availability as ecoservices for agricultural systems. In their valuation of property damage avoidance as it pertains to flooding, they consider wetlands, forests, and natural land cover as the ecoservices. For climate change and the potential for rising sea waters, they state that the economics will be captured by the damaged beaches and the resulting loss of recreation. They state that although carbon sequestration is important, the climate-related effects of sea level rising is the outcome, and therefore, that becomes the valuation strategy rather than the carbon sequestration that occurs to possibly mitigate the climate change. Although the outcome approach is more conducive to a market-based economy, this strategy does not seem much different than the economic system that is in existence today, meaning that the destruction of the beach by rising sea levels is the same economic signal that we have today to motivate carbon sequestration, and no functioning ecoservice or carbon market exists to address it. Or maybe, more tangibly, degraded waters are the economic signal that excess pollution is entering the water body, but that, too, does not compel an ecoservice transaction to compensate for that. While these are economic outcomes, economic participants are not able to value or respond to them in a manner that is conducive to human behavioral changes, the essence of microeconomics. Beyond this perceived flaw, Boyd and Banzhaf propose two important aspects of ecoservices: (1) that proxies are needed in place of direct measurement in many cases, and (2) that ecoservices are spatially explicit. In their example they state that pollination populations are an ecoservice for an agricultural setting. Rather than count all the pollinators, a practical proxy would be habitats that support a robust bee population. The rationale for ecoservices being spatially explicit arises from the site-specific nature of the ecosystem processes and functions and how ecology interacts spatially. They state that this property is important to measurement, as ecoservice scarcity, substitutes, and complements are spatially differentiated. Unlike cars, which can be transported by buyers and sellers, ecoservices cannot be readily relocated.

A much broader and perhaps more common strategy is Daily's (1997) list of ecoservices that includes processes and functions such as water purification, dispersal of seeds, nutrient cycling, pollination of crops, and similar biophysical and biochemical outcomes. These were also included in the ecoservice categories provided by the Millennium Ecosystem Assessment (2003). These lists provide awareness to the extent that we rely on natural capital for economic and personnel well-being, but applying economic value to each of these ecoservices appears beyond our capacity and beyond the reach of the economy. For example, dispersal of seeds and soil formation are valuable ecoservices, but neither the economy nor economic participants could have much influence on either.

Regulating Ecoservices as EcoCommerce Foundation

The EcoCommerce valuation scheme uses two general criteria: (1) that value only needs to be applied to ecoservices that are not currently valued and (2) that value is only applied to ecoservices that human activities have impacts upon.

If we begin with the MEA list, not all ecoservices are unvalued. Provisional ecoservices such as food, fiber, fuel wood, and other bio-economic products have been priced within a market from the very beginning of trade. The value of these items may not represent the ecological costs and benefits of producing them, and therefore, that is the rationale of developing EcoCommerce. Not all ecoservices can be affected by human activities and, therefore, cannot practically have an economic valued applied to them. Supporting ecoservices, such as soil formation from parent material, primary production, oxygen generation, and the global cycles, are beyond human reach and beyond economic capacity. And while cultural ecoservices are valuable, they represent an ecoservice that resides outside the realm of EcoCommerce and ecoservice markets that have a foundation in the physical, biological, and chemical processes, functions, and outcomes. This leaves regulating ecoservices as the foundation for EcoCommerce. Table 2.1 describes a classification system designed by Longva (1981) that will be used, in part, to define regulating ecoservices.

Table 2.1	Classification of Natural Resources	
Economic Classification	Physical Classification	Physical Properties
Material Resources	Mineral Resources - minerals - hydrocarbons - stone, gravel, sand	Non-renewable
	Biological Resources - in the air - in the water - on the land - in the soil	Conditionally Renewable
	Inflowing Resources - solar radiation - hydrological cycle - wind - ocean currents and waves	Renewable
Environmental Resources	Status Resources - air - water - soil - space	Conditionally Renewable
Source: Longva, 1981		

Applying the MEA list to Longva's classification system, one could conclude that regulating ecoservices are found within the Material Resources - Biological Resource classification that are listed as having a conditionally renewable physical property. The Environmental Resources – Status resources are affected by both the renewable Inflowing Resources and the

and cut down every tree in North America and bury them. In the lump sum scenario, it could be assumed that the permanently sequestered needs would be accounted for many decades or centuries. But in reality, the rate of carbon sequestration would plummet and the emissions would continue at the same rate. Actively sequestering carbon at a rate greater than what is being emitted is the solution to reducing carbon dioxide from the atmosphere, rather than crediting sequestered carbon. Preventing the harvested sequestered carbon from being reemitted into the atmosphere is part of the solution, but not a regenerative solution.

On the other hand, accounting for the rate of carbon being sequestered in a standing forest is relatively straightforward as long as growth rates are agreed upon. Since information related to the growth rates of timber currently has economic value, stakeholders are well aware of the existing capacity of forests to add growth and carbon. It may be stated that the consequences of a rate system will promote the removal of older stands of trees that are in a lower sequestration rate to be replaced by younger timber stands that have a higher sequestration rate. And that would be the case if we advance ecoservice markets one ecoservice parameter at a time, or develop them independently from each other. A mature forest has significant timber value and a reduced carbon sequestration rate relative to a maturing forest. But it also has a more complex ecosystem with higher biodiversity and stable soils. This provides water storage and water purification for the watershed and downstream users. Wildlife species that thrive in older forests generally do not thrive in younger forests. Older forests provide a livelihood for wildlife while the younger forests are aging. Wildlife without a place to survive can't wait for the younger forests to age. Advancing individual ecoservice markets one ecological parameter, such as the current focus on just a carbon market, will create perverse policy, programs, outcomes, and unintended consequences. An EcoCommerce framework that provides a valuation process for numerous regulating ecoservices is consciously structured to reduce or prevent ecoservice imbalances from occurring.

Crops as a Permanently Supplied Ecoservice

Crops fall under the provisional ecoservice category and are already included in the economy, and, therefore, new ecoservice markets do not need to be created. But crops are fairly dependable ecoservices, and how they are valued can provide a model on how to value regulating ecoservices. Crops are the result of how the agro-ecological system is managed, and farmers are, in essence, paid to manage their lands in a manner that produces bushels of grain. The world's economy wants a "permanent" supply of grain, as any disruption in this permanent supply would be catastrophic. But the agro-ecosystems only have the ability to provide a rate of crops that meets the economy's needs. This rate fluctuates both temporally and spatially as crops are grown in the northern hemisphere during the carbon sequestration seasons and in the southern hemisphere during their growing season. Crops are produced for a market-driven economy whose production is supported by centrally planned economic policies involving numerous governments and trade agreements. The point of drawing a parallel with these provisional ecoservices and regulating ecoservices is that both will be provided in a permanent, fluctuating rate that is influenced by the seasons, market forces, and centrally planned economies. Both types of ecoservices will be generated simultaneously within the same management unit. How these two types of markets interact or become hybridized is a function of market, government, and institutional forces.

To generate crops, the market does not pay the farmer directly for how the land is managed because there are readily available methods to measure the result in a succinct and transparent fashion: bushels of grain. It is the outcome that the market desires and the value that is placed on the outcome provides motivation to farmers to manage their land to achieve those outcomes. It is this framework that EcoCommerce will rely on to create a demand and to motivate a farmer to bring an ecoservice commodity to the market. And regardless of the type of ecoservice, a relative rate of production rather than a permanent supply is much more efficient to integrate with other ecoservice markets and therefore, more accountable.

Non-point-Source Pollution

Non-point-source (NPS) pollution is the other side of same coin as ecoservices. NPS pollution is generated by the management activities imposed on natural capital. In contrast to ecoservices, NPS pollution is a negative economic externality. Unlike point-source pollution, which is generated by a factory or wastewater treatment plant that discharges pollution via a pipe, non-point-source pollution is generated in a diffuse manner and cannot be satisfactorily or economically measured due to the landscape scale and the variable nature of weather. According to the EPA (1994), NPS pollution, unlike pollution from industrial and sewage treatment plants, comes from many diffuse sources. NPS pollution is caused by rainfall or snowmelt moving over and through the ground. As the runoff moves, it picks up and carries away natural and human-made pollutants, finally depositing them into lakes, rivers, wetlands, coastal waters, and even our underground sources of drinking water. These pollutants include many elements:

• Fertilizers, herbicides, and insecticides from agricultural lands and residential areas

• Oil, grease, and toxic chemicals from urban runoff and energy production

• Sediment from improperly managed construction sites, crop and forest lands, and eroding stream banks

• Salt from irrigation practices and acid drainage from abandoned mines

• Bacteria and nutrients from livestock, pet wastes, and faulty septic systems

• Atmospheric deposition

States report that NPS pollution is the leading remaining cause of water quality problems. The effects of NPS pollutants on specific waters vary and may not always be fully assessed. However, these pollutants have harmful effects on drinking water supplies, recreation, fisheries, and wildlife.

Myth of Measurement

The inability to directly measure NPS pollution and ecological benefits has been a primary reason that these components are not included within microeconomic transactions. Since it is impossible to accurately measure these externalities, government agencies have limited ability to regulate non-point-source pollution or to pay directly for ecoservices. Some indirect attempts to reduce NPS pollution include banning phosphorus fertilizers or requiring the capture and treatment of the run-off in storage ponds and created wetlands. The inability to measure NPS pollution as it pertains to its source and quantity is difficult for legislators to accept. For example, in three separate testimonials at the Minnesota State Capital, legislators suggested that funds that are being spent for NPS reduction must include a direct measurement component. A December 10, 2008, session with the Legislative and Citizens Commission on Minnesota Resources, and two other senate hearings related to environmental legislation all included statements toward the need to directly measure the water quality improvements related to conservation practice being applied. The funds were not being requested for research to determine the efficacy of conservation practices; funds were being requested for the application of conservation practices that are included in the *USDA NRCS*

Field Office Technical Guide, the official federal government document for proper application of conservation practices. The explanation that the cost of directly measuring water quality improvement related to the implementation of conservation practices often costs several times the cost of the conservation practice was not accepted as justification to use other measurement methods. In discussing this situation with Minnesota state conservation agency professionals, the experts stated that these direct measurement demands from the legislators that are being directed to their agency and other stakeholders involved with addressing NPS could be considered irrational.

Basic Limitations

With continual demands being placed on institutions and government agencies to directly measure the effects of conservation practices have on NPS, it becomes difficult for government agencies and universities to acknowledge that NPS pollution and ecoservices cannot be directly measured. Since funding is often based on agreeing to accomplish the demands of the legislators, it is in the self-interest of the conservation agency professionals to conduct this irrational behavior. This measurement myth is not just embraced by many legislators, but it is prominent in environmental, conservation, and agricultural communities. This is probably considered a rational thought, due to the many technological wonders that exist in our world today: automated samplers, geographical positioning systems, satellite controlled devices, wireless communication, and laboratory analytic techniques that can measure impurities from several perspectives and levels of detail. With knowledge of these technologies, legislators and others expect that an agricultural operation could set up an automatic sampler in the stream as it enters the farm and in the stream where it leaves the farm. The samples retrieved from each sampler can be compared to determine if the farm caused the water quality to decline, improve, or remain constant. At face value, this appears rational, but what is not considered is that NPS pollution and ecoservices are generated in the out-of-doors and are subject to ecological forces that are inconsistent, constant, and dynamic.

Even this relatively simple sampling strategy to identify NPS pollution sources or ecoservices related to water quality for the purpose of understanding what is occurring on the farm operation is flawed from several perspectives:

1. Geographical limitations. None or very few farms are situated geographically so that the management activities that are used on the farm will be represented within the water quality of the stream corridor, if such a stream corridor even existed on the farm operation.

2. Geological limitations. If such a stream corridor and farm operation existed, the geological characteristics of water percolation, soil capacity, surface irregularities, and modified subsurface flows would prevent a reasonable, representative measurement to occur.

3. Financial limitations. If the geological limitations were overlooked and a stream corridor existed, the costs to install and manage the sampling equipment and analyze the water samples would be prohibited. Considering that three samplers would be needed for every two farms, as the adjoining farms could use the same sampler, and that operation of those samplers would need to continue for at least three years, but preferably between five-10 years to get a representative sampling year, the costs could easily exceed $50,000 for the shorter duration period. There are approximately 80,000 agricultural operations in Minnesota and two million in the nation.

4. Control limitations. Even with sampling equipment on each end of this stream corridor, the sampling environment is outdoors and the samples are subject to influences beyond the management of the farm operation. Stream corridors attract and house a variety of mammals, fowl, fish, and amphibians that conduct activities that cause water impairments related to sedimentation and bacteria. Samples collected at one end of the farm and compared to the other end of the farm would not be conclusive to a high enough degree as to what actually caused impairment.

Limitations Realized
These limitations have been stated in numerous research and educational documents from various perspectives and the following examples represent a small percentage of documented attempts to measure NPS pollution.

In the *Journal of the American Water Resources Association*, Horan and Ribaubo (1999) state "that [lack of information] stems mainly from the fact that NPS pollution from agriculture is impossible to measure with existing technology."

As it pertains to geological conditions, the Kentucky Non-Point-Source Pollution Control Program states that groundwater and surface water are often difficult, and sometimes impossible, to separate (KDEP 2008).

In Arizona, the EPA-funded Chino Winds Project plans to develop a surrogate system to measure water quality impacts because the flow of surface water on Arizona rangelands is intermittent and changes in water quality are difficult to determine. Therefore, measurable improvements from best management practices (BMPs) may be impossible to document. This project correlates coverage vegetation to sediment discharges and extrapolates water quality information by measuring the amount and biodiversity of the vegetation (EPA 2010).

A Cooperative Extension document by the University of California acknowledges that agriculture is one of several industries that have been identified as contributing to non-point-source pollution. It states that while it is impossible to locate the source of the pollutants, it is known that certain growing practices will contribute more to non-point-source pollution, while other practices can minimize water quality problems (Robb 1998).

In the Vittel watershed in France, the nitrate rates were still below the maximum level authorized by law, and a legal action could not be justified. Even if such an action had been intended, it would have been impossible to prove the responsibility of individual farmers – making a lawsuit an unlikely, and costly, solution (Perrot-Maitre 2006).

Both NPS pollution and ecoservices cannot be directly measured in relation to their source and is one of the primary reasons that these externalities have not been included within the market economy or even the centrally planned economy of the government conservation delivery system with sufficient success. This is not to say that research to directly measure the effects of land-management practices on pollution and ecoservices is not possible or necessary. In fact, this direct research and monitoring is vital to provide a greater understanding on how conservation practices impact resources for specific or controlled sites. But we must begin to view these measurement limitations not as obstacles to overcome, but as realities that we need to accept and can safely say we will never be able to directly measure.

Home Energy Efficiency Analogy

An example of a directly immeasurable objective is to determine how well a home retains its heat in the cold months. Comparing the process of conducting home-energy assessment to non-point-source pollution and ecoservices generated on a farm reveals that immeasurable conditions can be "measured" in a manner that is efficient and effective at locating solutions.

A home loses heat through many pathways that are relatively understood from a generic perspective. Homes lose heat through windows, outlets, walls, ceilings, crawl spaces, attic roofs, and the list continues. A farm also transports non-point-source pollution and generates ecoservices through many pathways, and they, too, are relatively understood from a generic perspective. Water and any pollutants from a farm leave through countless surface and soil channels, tile lines, and ditches and recharge groundwater or pools in a wetland. And because these pathways are generically understood, a list of numerous practices and activities can be generated that describes what a home owner or farm operator could do to improve their heat loss or non-point-source pollution reduction.

The challenge comes when an individual farm is considered or an individual house is considered. Over the life of the farm and house, many management decisions are implemented since no one implementation plan will fit very many farms or homes. Home owners could caulk all their windows or replace them all; they could insulate the walls, floors, or attic with a certain R-value product; they could install solar, geothermal, or upgrade their furnace and the list goes on. Farmers could install grassed buffers, adjust their tillage, change their crop rotation, plant trees, install terraces, and that list goes on as well.

If the home owner and the farmer began installing practices and changing activities, they both would most likely reduce their heat loss and non-point-source pollution, but they would not know to what extent or when they met a practical limit of reduction. And since heat loss cannot be measured directly, just like non-point-source pollution cannot be measured directly, methods to assess these systems have been created. In homes, energy audit questionnaires provide a home-specific assessment of what are the most cost-effective and energy effective measures to take. While caulking is relatively cheap compared to replacing windows, it may or may not be the best management practice to use. Farmers face a similar situation, and the use of management indices provides a "measurement" to the immeasurable. Applying practices to the home without an assessment may be saving "heat" resources but may be misusing other resources or not using them wisely. The same applies to farms, but at a larger and more expensive scale.

If legislators demand that all investments into reducing a home's heat loss and a farm's non-point-source pollution must be accompanied by directly measuring both pre- and post- conditions of the area receiving the conservation practice, it would become cost-prohibitive and inefficient. The demand placed on the home improvements would seem ridiculous to most observers as many are acquainted with how homes function in relation to heat loss. Since this same level of awareness does not exist with farms and non-point-source pollution or ecoservices, the requests to directly measure non-point-source pollution and ecoservices seem reasonable.

CEAP Search

One of the most comprehensive efforts to measure the effects of land-management practices undertaken by the USDA is its Conservation

Effects Assessment Project whose goals were to establish the scientific understanding of the effects of conservation practices at the watershed scale and to estimate conservation impacts and benefits for reporting at the national and regional levels (Duriancik 2008).

CEAP focused on developing approaches, methodologies, and databases to produce scientifically credible estimates of environmental benefits of conservation. Initially, the project studied water quality, soil quality, and water conservation on cropland and CRP land. Eventually, CEAP will assess benefits to water quality, soil quality, water conservation, and wildlife habitat on cropland, grazing land, and wetlands. Work is underway to develop suitable and affordable analytical approaches for these other land uses and natural-resource concerns (USDA NRCS 2009).

In its first five years, this effort established 38 research sites to quantify the measurable effects of conservation practices on the quality and quantity of water and soils. In the synthesis of its preliminary findings, it determined that certain types of conservation practices had positive effects in certain regions of the country, and also that certain conservation practices had positive effects for specific resource concerns. The report concluded that the accomplishments demonstrated that CEAP has been effective in identifying and quantifying the effects of conservation practices, though much work remains to be done to provide more definite answers on the effectiveness of conservation practices and their value to the U.S. environment, economy, and general public (Duriancik 2008, 603).

A new direction for the CEAP was recommended, and the focus of CEAP in the future will include the following goals (Duriancik 2008, 199):

1. To research and assess conservation effects on croplands, wetlands, wildlife, and grazing lands

2. To research how to best manage agricultural landscapes for environmental quality

3. To establish a framework for determining and reporting the ecosystem services provided by conservation

4. To broaden assessment capabilities to address priorities for future program design and implementation

5. To reduce uncertainty in model estimates of conservation benefits

Since the CEAP is focused on a relatively few watersheds (38) and had sufficient funding, it was able to overcome some of the geographical, geological, financial, and technical limitations that cannot be overcome by a non-point-source pollution and ecoservice measurement program for all farms. But even with a focused effort, the evasive pinpoint effects of conservation practices and activities cannot be captured. Even within an intensively managed ecosystem, such as agriculture, too many uncontrolled variables and too few controllable variables are involved with the potential outcomes. Barring significant abuse or extreme natural events, soil type and topography remain constant. Beyond that, the farmer can decide what type of vegetation will be planted and, to a degree, what management practices will be applied. All other conditions related to the impact that the cropping system has on the resources are greatly influenced by the variables of the planting date, germination rate, weed and pest types and populations, soil moisture, precipitation rate, timing, intensity, temperature, weather extremes, and the management decisions made within the window of opportunity that is available. The variables are present in varying degrees within any agricultural land use such as annual, perennial, herbaceous, or woody. In general, estimating the complete range of ecoservices [or NPS] from any particular ecosystem [or watershed] is beyond scientific ability (NCR 2005).

By examining 38 watersheds across the country, the CEAP participants can get a sense of what types of conservation practices and activities will have a positive or negative effect within the context of the mentioned variables and across a timeframe of five or 10 years or longer. This data will be of great value in developing conservation recommendations, fine tuning assessment techniques, calibrating measurement tools, and even in beginning the process to value the environmental outcomes and the ecoservices provided by different management systems applied with agro-ecosystems.

But neither the CEAP nor any other attempt to diagnose the precise cause and effect will be able to provide the units of sediment saved, tons of carbon sequestered, gallons of water infiltrated or shed, number and type of wildlife inhabitants, tons of soil created, or any of the resource impacts associated with non-point-source pollution and ecoservices. The CEAP can be used to develop and utilize index-type measurement tools and use the knowledge gained over the next five, 10, 20, 50 and 100 years to fine tune these measurement tools.

EPA Office of Policy, Economics and Innovation program analyst Manale's (2008) viewpoint states that the science of environmental management is never good enough. The models are never complete, the scientific linkages uncertain, the data too few or at the wrong spatial or temporal scale. Then there are institutional barriers to successful conservation whereby the effectiveness of one intervention depends on or requires knowledge of what has happened or is being tried elsewhere. Manale sees that an adaptive- management approach, one that establishes a method for acquiring feedback in changing or unanticipated circumstances, will allow us to set on a course toward achieving the resource-management objectives. A successful application of adaptive management will require a platform— whether it is CEAP or another vehicle—for applying it to strategic resource management as change occurs, as new or unanticipated problems arise and opportunities present themselves.

The adaptive-management approach is aligned with how farmers achieve their production objectives. From the moment a farmer decides what to plant and where to plant, he is engaged in an adaptive-management approach to account for the variables previously mentioned. The current system of the USDA's centrally planned, program-driven conservation delivery system does not mesh with the adaptive-management process that includes a resource-driven, outcome-based production system employed by farm managers. Since farmers do not have the option to convert to a practice-based production decision process, the USDA conversion to an adaptive-management process appears inevitable.

purifying his wastes before releasing them. Since this is true for everyone, we are locked into a system of "fouling our own nest," as long as we behave only as independent, rational, free-enterprisers within the context of the economic structure.

The "tragedy," as Hardin explains, is the degradation and eventual failure of the natural capital. And since this natural capital had the capacity to produce wealth, it is also an economic "tragedy." This loss of economic capacity is due to the inability of the invisible hand to account for both positive and negative externalities. The inability of the invisible hand to recognize positive externalities is as great a failure as its inability to recognize negative externalities. Ecoservices are being generated on farms and ranches with grasslands, croplands, and forested lands, but the relative extent of these ecoservices is unknown on an individual farm basis, and it is this scale at which land management activities begin to generate the ecoservices for all landscape scales.

To compensate for this tragedy, government institutions create policies that encourage economic participants to seek uncompensated changes. These attempts to influence the allocation of natural resources rely on taxation, regulation, public investment, and ownership and management of those resources. All of these methods present one interest group or another with at least the hope of getting something for nothing, while others often feel threatened with uncompensated injury. An institutional process to bring compensation, rather than injury, often brings those into a genuine consensus for change.

This institutional change may reside in the finding of Ostrom (2009) that under conditions that enable harvesters and local leaders to self-organize, effective rules to manage a resource will occur. Conditions are often based on size. Large land-related resources such as forests are unlikely to be self-organized due to the costs of defining boundaries, monitoring land use, and gaining ecological knowledge. Very small areas do not generate enough ecoservices of value to warrant coordination. Thus, moderately sized territories are most conducive to self-organizational structures. This is true with fishers who consistently harvest from moderately sized coastal zones in comparison to fishers who travel the ocean. Other variables include productivity of the system, mobility of resources, number of users, leadership skills, and social norms. Understanding how self-organization is most likely occurring will provide insights on potentially successful policies (Ostrom 2009).

EcoCommerce Supply/Demand Curves

The conundrum then, is how can the economy value the act of maintaining the capacity of the natural capital (which is impossible to directly measure), and how can the economy place market incentives or government regulation on non-point-source pollution, which is also impossible to directly measure. In addition to this market valuation, a greater conundrum of the ecoservice market is to identify what values must be applied to generate more ecoservices. To address this conundrum, EcoCommerce graphs were created to illustrate a relationship among ecological and economical functions. The supply line in these EcoCommerce graphs represents the ecological capacity-to-supply, rather than the economic capacity and its participants' willingness-to-supply. The demand line is the man-made economy's willingness-to-consume. The EcoCommerce graph illustrates the relationship the manmade and natural economic systems may have relative to their capacities. The exercise of creating these graphs illustrates that some level of ecological capacity is needed in relation to some level of economic consumption that is desired. Developing a system to allow both these information-dense economic systems to interface is the intent of this book.

Locating Sustainability

Unlike the traditional supply-and-demand curve (Figure 1.1) that represents the economic supply-and-demand relationship and contains a zero point on the graph representing a willingness-to-supply value of zero, the EcoCommerce supply-and-demand curve (Figure 3.1) represents the ecology's capacity-to-supply (line S_1) and the economy's capacity-to-consume (line D_1). The supply curve on the EcoCommerce graph lies at some value greater than zero to represent some level of ecological function (line S_1) that is provided regardless. The quantity between $Q_0 - Q_1$ could be considered the economic "free lunch," perhaps the exception that proves that economic rule. If the current minimum ecological supply capacity (or so-called sustainability level) lies above this Q_1 level, then sustainability can either be achieved by shifting the ecological supply curve to the right or by shifting the demand curve to the left. On this EcoCommerce graph (Figure 3.1), three theoretical points of sustainable equilibrium include SE_1, SE_2, and SE_3. In relation to SE_1, SE_2 assumes that we will need to increase the supply capacity of natural capital, and SE_3 assumes that we will have to reduce our demand. And it is highly unlikely that the demand curve will shift to the left, as the increases in world population and standard of living are well-established trends.

biofuels, regional food systems and supply chains, and forest restoration and private land conservation (Vilsack 2010). All five areas either support an EcoCommerce system or are supported by an EcoCommerce system.

Despite this trend toward ecosystem markets and highly visible legislative and administrative efforts, farmers and ranchers still receive the clearest market signals and the vast majority of their income from the more tangible and traditional production resources that are grown on the farm operation, such as crops and livestock. That said, a continual increase in incentives or regulations on the management of land as it pertains to ecoservices and non-point-source pollution will carry more influence on how the farm is managed to produce those more tangible production resources. The question becomes: How will land managers receive the ecoservice signals, and will the signals emerge from the market or the government?

As previously discussed, the invisible hand generates and seeks out market signals that eventually create the market marvel of efficient commerce. The absence of a market signal is also valuable as it also communicates the market's lack of desire and prevents or reduces the production of a particular product or service that the economic participants no longer want at a particular price. Of course, a weak or lacking market signal for goods and services that are desired is not ideal and it is considered a type of market failure. This lack of signal for ecoservices, in part, creates the tragedy of the commons described by Hardin. In the case of a drinking water supply, a municipality may have a great desire to have access to clean surface water and land managers in the watershed may have the ability to manage the land in a manner that sheds clean water, but if the market does not provide a signal, then a reliable supply of clean water from the watershed is highly unlikely.

To illustrate the range and depth of these land management signals, a table and several paragraphs in this chapter's section, *Today's Agriculture Management Signals,* will describe how market and government signals are received on a fictional, but realistic farm operation.

Kimball Farm Operation and Situation

The fictional farm is owned and managed by Mr. Kimball, and he receives management assistance from his son and daughter. He also hires several agricultural professionals, including a veterinarian and an agronomist. Mr. Kimball farms 500 acres, 400 of which he owns and 100 of which he rents. Most of land soil type is a clay loam, and his farm operation includes about a dozen soil type variations. Twelve percent of his farm is considered highly erodable by USDA definition, and he has a 12-acre wetland that is located in a wooded area on his farm. He milks 100 dairy cows and sells his milk to Butter Land Company. The manure is collected in a manure-containment system and applied to his fields to increase his soil fertility. In addition to producing milk, he grows the food and feed resources of corn, alfalfa, wheat, soybeans, and timber. Of the 400 acres of land that he owns, 50 acres are wooded. Kimball owns a share in Etank Ethanol and provides corn to them. He also sells corn, wheat, and soybeans on the open market. He has five acres of land enrolled in a USDA program that pays Kimball to plant a buffer strip along a creek.

Kimball's farm is located in the Valley River watershed, and the Little Fork Creek flows along the farm's east border before it flows into the Valley River. The Valley River watershed drains 250,000 acres and is the drinking water supply for several cities on the river. In one incident a decade ago, the runoff from a heavy spring rain caused a fish kill in Valley River. The investigation could not determine the exact cause, but many farmers were questioned about their manure application, and there was talk about significant fines associated with whatever caused the fish kill. Kimball, like most farmers in the area, did not carry environmental liability insurance, but he has been considering buying such a policy. Kimball does farm in as environmentally conscious manner as possible, but he knows that the challenging weather conditions may cause results not intended. Subsequently, in recent years water-quality monitoring has been conducted in the river, and the Environmental Protection Agency (EPA) 303D list states that the Valley River water quality is impaired because of low oxygen levels and excess sediment and nutrients. Since the river is put on the 303D list, it requires the state's EPA to develop a Total Maximum Daily Load Plan to describe how the water quality will be improved. Downstream from Kimball's farm, the town of Valley Creek has a waste water treatment plant (WWTP) that does not meet its effluent limitation set by the EPA and is considering forgoing a $5 million upgrade to pursue the option of paying for water quality credits generated by upstream farmers.

On Kimball's farm, there are two species of birds listed as "species of concern" in their area, the bobolink and the red-headed woodpecker. Kimball occasionally sees bobolinks on his farm and in the area, but has not seen a red-headed woodpecker on the farm for a decade. Kimball has also been hearing a lot about the honey bees "colony collapse disorder" and the role that pollinators play in the agro-economy. The farm is also 3/4 of a mile from Duck Lake, one of the largest freshwater marshes in the state. The organization Game Bird Habitat Unlimited has been promoting duck-nesting habitat on farms near Duck Lake, and Kimball received a mailing that offered some technical assistance to farmers who want to improve their duck-nesting habitat.

The Kimball farm is also located in the Valley River Watershed District. This district is one of the local units of government that has developed a watershed plan with stated objectives and goals related to cleaner water in the Valley River. The district mapped out the entire watershed and provided all the landowners within the watershed a map with the steepest areas next to the stream noted. The letter that came with the map stated that these areas are prone to erosion and their proximity to a stream makes them likely to cause excess sediment to enter the stream. The district's letter also stated that they would like the farmer to provide them with a management plan to explain how he would address these erosion-prone areas.

In response to these ecological issues, Kimball's landlord recently decided that all the land that he rents out, and not just the lands considered very prone to erosion by the federal government, should be monitored for erosion. The landlord wanted assurance that Kimball and his other renters were farming the land in manner that was not detrimental to long-term soil productivity and water quality.

Kimball recognizes that natural-resources issues are gaining prominence in the community, media, nation, and the legislation. He considers the management of his farm operation does not excessively pollute the waters and preserves the natural resources. Despite the high standards Kimball places on his farm operation, he still feels somewhat overwhelmed and confused by what the expectations are of him. Mr. Kimball feels he is in a conundrum. He understands the competitive nature of agriculture and the demands that consumers and the market place on production and his operation responds to those signals. He also is well aware of the pressure that social organizations, consumers, and the government place on natural-resource management but does not know how to respond to those signals.

Today's Agriculture Management Signals

In both a conscious and subconscious manner, each of us gets up in the morning and understands who values the productive efforts that we engage in by the economic signals we receive. It is in our self-interests to be acutely aware of these signals and demands. When these demands are diminished, or absent, our behavior often changes toward other productive efforts that are valued. Mr. Kimball is no different. Over decades, his farm operation has responded to signals from both government and the market, and today his operation receives the signals from the following business, industries and government. These commodity and ecoservice market signals are listed on Table 3.1.

Butter Land Company

Butter Land Company is a processor that procures milk from about 1,000 dairy producers and processes it into dairy products and fluid milk for Walmart Stores, Inc. It strives to offer dairy producers a competitive price for their milk. Its market signal is $15.00 per hundred weight. It also encourages dairy producers to produce their milk in an environmentally friendly manner and presents a dairy producer with an environmental award each year.

Etank Ethanol

Etank Ethanol is a farmer-owned bio-refinery that processes corn into ethanol. Each share owner is required to deliver at least 5,000 bushels of corn to the facility. It pays the farmers the market price for corn, and profits from the ethanol plant are paid to shareholders. One of its major costs is fueling the natural gas-fired boiler, which share owners plan to convert to a synthetic gas boiler. To do so, they will buy cellulosic material such as corn stover and woody materials and will offer $45.00 per ton dry material.

Round Wood Company

The Round Wood Company, a log processor, has purchased furniture-grade lumber from the Valley Creek area for more than two decades. It also provides forest management service to its suppliers and encourages them to provide wildlife habitat. The company pays an average price of $0.05 per board foot.

Electric GenCo

Electric GenCo is a local electrical utility plant that primarily burns coal in the process of generating electricity. It has recently added a biomass-fuel boiler and is purchasing corn stover, woody materials, and other cellulosic materials that can be burned and is offering $50.00 per ton dry material. Electric GenCo has applied to the federal government to be listed on their approved list of biomass converters to become eligible to participate in the USDA Biomass Crop Assistance Program. It is planning on converting 100,000 tons of biomass into heat energy in the production of electricity.

Commodity Exchanges

To facilitate trades of commodities, the Chicago Board of Trade manages several dozen commodities including traditional grains such as corn, soybeans, wheat, oats, etc. Prices are offered and trades are made between buyers and sellers. The Chicago Climate Exchange is a nationally based exchange that facilitates trades between carbon emitters and carbon sequesters. It is a voluntary market with the anticipation that restrictions put in place by Congress or the Environmental Protection Agency on the amount of greenhouse gases (GHG) that can be emitted. Prices for commodities fluctuate regularly and are dependent on supply-and-demand forces. Commodity prices used in the Kimball scenario include corn at $4.50, wheat at $6.50, and soybeans at $10.00 per bushel. GHG are traded on a per-ton basis of carbon dioxide equivalents (CO_2e) with a market price of $0.15 per ton.

USDA Farm Service Agency Farm Bill Provisions

The USDA FSA administers the commodity title provisions of the federal farm policy, called the Farm Bill. For farmers to be eligible for various commodity supports, the farmer agrees to farm highly erodable land in a manner that reduces erosion and restricts farmers from draining wetlands. This is referred to as meeting "conservation compliance." This is a very strong signal, as violating these requirement may cause ineligibility for Farm Bill payments. Management on all lands other than these steep slopes and wetland basins is not subject to restrictions.

USDA Farm Service Agency Biomass Crop-Assistance Program

The USDA FSA administers the Biomass Crop Assistance Program that is designed to create financial incentives to produce and process biomass. This incentive is a payment of $45.00/ton for every ton delivered to an approved conversion facility. One of the eligibility requirements is for the farmer to meet the conservation compliance provisions of the Farm Bill.

USDA Farm Service Agency Conservation Reserve Program

The USDA FSA administers the CRP program that was created in the 1985 Farm Bill. It is designed to provide multiple resource benefits related to soil, water, and habitat. It provides a signal through a rental payment based on an Environmental Benefits Index that includes land type, rental rate, and land-management plans. There are about 32 million acres enrolled in the CRP, and farmers engage in somewhat of a silent auction process to enroll.

USDA NRCS Conservation Stewardship Program

The USDA Natural Resource Conservation Service administers the Conservation Stewardship Program that provides monetary payments to producers who meet certain resource-management thresholds. It is a new program concept in that it attempts to pay for outcomes of resource-management activities rather than paying for the cost of the conservation practices. While the CSP provides a market signal toward management goals of soil, water, air, habitat, and energy resources, the signal is relatively weak in that units are not transparent and prices are not posted. Eligibility is determined through a type of winnowing process that does not allow market interaction.

Additional Signals

In addition to the signals provided by the three processors, other entities have regulations and standards that require farm operations to be managed in a certain manner. Regulatory signals may include building site set-backs, limits on animal units, and types of facilities. Incentive programs include conservation practice cost-share programs that provide a percentage of the cost of installing conservation practices on a farm operation. Commodity support programs include maintaining price floors, subsidized crop insurance, and revenue insurance. These are important signals for farmers to adhere to, but to keep Kimball's scenario manageable they will not be addressed. It should be noted, though, that dozens of signals exist for each farm operation depending on numerous scenarios.

Market Signal Summary

It is beyond the capacity of any individual or entity other than the farm operator and their advisors to be keenly aware of all the opportunities. One of the greatest challenges posed to any centrally planned economy is to invest the resources to understand the dynamic signals that are available to each and every land manager. It is at this point in the process that the efficiencies of land management diverge when comparing market-driven and centrally planned economies. Table 3.1 below represents the major government and market signals that Kimball receives. The strong market signals (bold font) are for the commodities corn, milk, wheat, soybeans, and lumber. Kimball perceives the biomass signals to be medium, but with the additional BCAP subsidy, he feels that it may be a strong enough signal for him to respond to. The GHG signal is very weak at only 15 cents a ton. Of the signals he receives for the ecoservices, he considers the FSA Conservation Compliance signal to be very strong, and the CRP offer medium-weak. The CSP signal he considers to be very weak for the reasons that a unit and price are not defined in manner that Kimball can interpret.

photo that shows how the land use is patterned across the farm. This photo interpretation would vary by season as annual vegetation patterns change. This photo could be enhanced by overlaying various land data such as streams, topography, and wetlands. The farmer could complement the aerial photo with a list of best management practices (BMPs) that were installed on the farm, but a list of BMPs does not provide a quantification of resource management. Finally, Kimball could offer a tour of the farm operation and show firsthand how the conservation practices are installed or used on the land. If it were raining, the observers or inspectors could see how the various BMPs protect the soil and other resources. Obviously, some of these are cumbersome processes and all are somewhat inefficient to communicate how the management of the farm operation is providing ecoservices or is reducing non-point-source pollution. In all these cases, these are snapshots of a particular moment within a cropping season and do not or cannot represent the resource-management outcomes as they pertain to how ecosystems function in seasonal, yearly, and multi-year cycles. Kimball feels the most straightforward method he has to communicate his resource-management outcomes is the Environmental Benefits Index used by the USDA in the Conservation Reserve Program. The EBI uses the land-management activities that Kimball proposes to apply on a specific parcel of land with its own unique characteristics. But the EBI has only been applied on five of the 500 acres of land that he manages, or just 1 percent. He is not aware of any other organizations using the EBI or other management indices to determine outcomes.

River Friendly Farmer

To establish his operation as an environmentally friendly farm, Kimball enrolled into the Valley River Friendly Farmer Program, a program based on the Minnesota River Friendly Farmer Program that interviews and grades farmers on how they address the farm-resource issues (Wagar 2000). Farmers who satisfy criteria related to residue cover, soil loss, fertilizer-application rates, use of BMPs, permitted feedlots, an integrated-pest-control plan, and an overall goal that the farm is profitable and productive as compared to surrounding farms in the region. Kimball was recognized as a River Friendly Farmer. Unfortunately, none of the natural-resource stakeholders or government units that are demanding ecoservices would accept the River Friendly Farm certification as a valid assurance document. It lacked common or universal units of exchange.

Environmental Quality Assurance Program

Kimball was also aware of the Livestock Environmental Quality Assurance (LEQA) Program, a program initiated by the Minnesota Milk

Producers Association (MMPA) in 2001 and adopted by the Livestock Environmental Assurance Consortium (LEAC) in 2007. The LEAC is a 20-member consortium consisting of farm groups, non-profits, and government agencies that have vested interests in both production and natural resource issues in agriculture. The program addresses five key areas of water quality, air and odor, soil and nutrients, habitat and diversity, and community image. Kimball understood that by achieving the LEQA 5-Star Certification, he may receive a higher ranking for state grants associated with both production and natural-resource objectives on his farm.

Kimball had his farm assessed and implemented some of the practices that allowed him to achieve the 5-Star Certification. Kimball soon realized that while the LEQA program provided him with several values, it was not widely recognized either.

Natural Resource Conservation Service Conservation Plan

Kimball has engaged in NRCS Conservation Planning process for guidance on resource-management issues, but it did not provide a resource-assurance document that could be used by any of the mentioned entities.

In Need of a Singular Resource Assurance Process

Kimball remained in the natural-resource-management conundrum. It was obvious that a universally accepted resource-assurance document was needed to communicate his resource-management outcomes and to provide assurance for those stakeholders who value ecoservices. Kimball's priority is to farm long-term and possibly allow a son or daughter to continue the farm operation. He is well aware of the environmental issues that have emerged in the last couple of decades, and he plans on addressing the soil, water, air plants, animals, and energy resource issues. He has worked with the local conservation agency, but they no longer have the capacity to conduct resource assessments, and they do not provide a resource-assurance service. In today's farming, Mr. Kimball realizes that the agricultural community is going to be ultimately responsible for resource assessments and assurances. In the near future, he thinks farmers will be provided monetary and non-monetary incentives for how they manage their farm operations, in relation to ecoservices. He also realizes that if ecoservices have value for society and the economy, these values must be expressed in a succinct, transparent, and comprehensive manner that allows buyers and sellers to interact. Kimball needs a singular process that provides resource-management assurance to all or most of the public and private stakeholders.

The Economic Conundrum

Despite Kimball's intentions and actions, he is not able to communicate the resource-management outcomes to the organizations concerned with soil, water quality, and habitat. Of his net income of $64,550, a sum of $750 came from natural-resource incentives or about 1 percent. Kimball realizes that only 1 percent of his land was assessed for natural- resource outcomes. It occurs to him that if the remaining 495 acres of his farm operation are not being measured for natural-resource outcomes, it is probably reasonable to expect that ecoservice value cannot be applied toward those 495 acres. He figures the conundrum is caused by the lack of information that is not being generated during the process of creating market signals and responding to them. Kimball produces grain, milk, lumber, and biomass within the context of a particular landscape using management practices and activities that he considers optimum for the particular growing season and market conditions. In this effort of generating provisional ecoservices, he simultaneously generates regulating ecoservices, but only a few of the regulating ecoservices are accounted for and valued. In Kimball's natural resource summary, he meets conservation compliance on his 60 acres of highly erodable lands and for having not drained the wetland. What is not known is the erosion rates on the remainder of the farm, what type of tillage system is used in relation to water quality, what is the potential for habitat, what are the carbon-sequestration rates, and numerous other issues related to the sustainability of both the production resource and natural resources of the farm operation. Table 3.3 lists the production resources and their economic values alongside natural resources and their economic values. The conundrum is that if society and government entities desire natural-resource outcomes, but there is not a system in place to express that value, then how do Kimball and other resource managers develop a strategy that meets these ill-defined and unvalued goals?

Table 3.3	Comparison of Outcomes and Values				
Production Resources	Desired Outcome	Value ($/unit)	Natural Resource	Desired Outcome	Value ($/unit)
Crops	Increasing Yield	$/bushel	Plants	Diverse Populations	$0
Soil	Fertility	$/Acre	Soil	Tilth	$0
Water	Meets Crop Needs	$/gallons	Water	Meets human and ecosystem needs	$0
Nutrients	Sufficient	$/pounds	Nutrients	Sequestered & cycled	$0
Organic Material	Soil Tilth and nutrient release	$/ton	Carbon	Sequestered	$0.15/ton
Micro-organisms	Build Soil and cycle nutrients	n/a	Micro-organisms	Build Soil and cycle nutrients	$0
Genetics	Growth and Production Traits	$/seeds	Animals	Diversity	$0
Air	Minimum Impact	n/a	Air	Clean	$0

If the economic values in Table 3.3 provide the basis for the market signals in Table 3.1, then one would expect the market responses listed in Table 3.2. Table 3.3 illustrates that most production-resource outcomes have well-defined units and only one natural-resource outcome has a defined unit. If government, industry, and society desire natural-resource outcomes but do not have an efficient and transparent means to express or place value toward this demand, then this must be the source of this economic conundrum. Applying these values toward a provisional and regulating ecoservice-production strategy would create a production-possibility frontier graph illustrated in Figure 3.3. Point A ($Q_{9.9}$) on the PPF illustrates that ~ 99 percent of the valued outcomes are provisional ecoservices and about 1 percent ($Q_{0.1}$) is regulating ecoservices. Since only the Environmental Benefits Index is represented as a measurable regulating ecoservice benefit, other regulating ecoservice benefits provided by Kimball's production systems are not accounted for and are not included on the PPF or within the economy. The regulating ecoservices that are not included are positive economic externalities. Due to the ability of others to *free ride*, that is, not to pay for the benefits and still enjoy them, there is often no concern to address these positive externalities. The result is often that, over time, management systems that do provide ecoservices are either neutral or at a disadvantage to those systems that do not produce ecoservices and the production of those ecoservices diminishes.

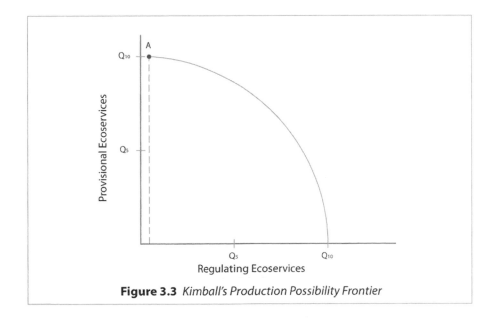

Figure 3.3 *Kimball's Production Possibility Frontier*

Paths to Formalizing Ecoservices in the Economy

If the production of regulating ecoservices entails thought and management strategies similar to the production of provisional ecoservices, then the strategies that produce ecoservices must also be valued. For ecoservices to be generated at a consistent and desired level, their production must be accounted for, a value established, and a portion returned to those that have the capacity to generate ecoservices. This valuation of ecoservices must be formalized into the economy as either a direct incentive applied to the ecoservice, or as an attribute of a good or service. This valuation should also be applicable to the development of natural-resource accounts, perhaps at multiple levels beginning at a locally definable area, such as a watershed and culminating to the level of a national account. Accounting for the potential ecoservice values generated by Kimball would result in a PPF that represents a greater production frontier as illustrated in Figure 3.4. In Figure 3.4, Point A represents the same point and quantity as Point A on Figure 3.3. Point A_1 on Figure 3.4 also represents the amount of provisional ecoservices as represented in point A, but in a context of a frontier is shifting outward to represent greater total production, as Point A_1 now represents a regulating ecoservice quantity of Q_5 (rather than $Q_{0.1}$). In this example, a growth in the economic system is occurring because positive economic externalities are being brought into the system. Point A_2 on the graph represents both an increase in provisional ecoservices ($Q_{11.5}$) and regulating ecoservices ($Q_{6.5}$). This scenario could occur if an increase in soil health generated better water quality and higher crop yields.

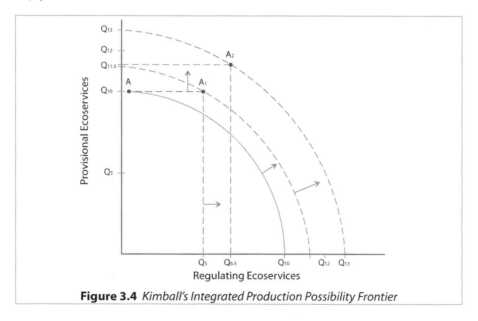

Figure 3.4 *Kimball's Integrated Production Possibility Frontier*

The outward shift of agriculture's PPF can be accounted for using strategies within a centrally planned economy, a market economy, or through a hybridized version of the two. If ecoservice markets are to succeed, it will be due to a well-defined process that integrates natural capital management to the extent that its value can be accounted for within the market logistics used today. In addition, a signal, consisting of a defined unit and price, will need to be developed to allow the marvel of the market to be expressed. The following two chapters explore two paths: the well-defined path of the centrally planned conservation economy of the USDA and the wandering path of the immature ecoservice markets of recent decades. EcoCommerce recognizes that the ecology, which is the natural economic system that contains the natural capital of the economy, has significant value relative to the manmade economies on earth. With that said, the man-made economy decides how and how much value is transferred and resources applied to maintain the natural capital and its services. This connection to the economy has been attempted through the development of a centrally planned conservation economy with its roots in the Dust Bowl and the New Deal. The following chapter explores the successes of that effort and its 21st-century limitations.

in the United States. The 1905 survey of Louisa County, Virginia, in particular, profoundly affected Bennett. He had been directed to investigate declining crop yields. As he compared virgin, timbered sites to eroded fields, he became convinced that soil erosion was a problem not just for the individual farmer, but also for rural economies. In November 1934, Bennett recommended that states be encouraged to pass legislation authorizing (a) cooperation with the federal government in erosion control; (b) the organization of conservancy districts or similar legal sub-divisions with authority to carry out measures of erosion control; and (c) the establishment of state or local land-use zoning ordinances where lack of voluntary cooperation make such ordinances necessary (Helms 2009).

Coincidently, when Bennett testified on April 2, 1935 to the Senate Public Lands Committee on a proposal to create a new national soil conservation program, Washington, DC was inundated with windblown clouds of soil blotting out the sun. The Soil Conservation Service (SCS) was created in the USDA by an act of Congress on April 27, 1935. Over the course of its 75 years, the NRCS and its centrally planned economy has evolved under the forces of legislation, congressional appropriations, interpretation of rules, and the omnipresent constituency groups that represent the interests of industrial agriculture, sustainable agriculture, agribusinesses, agri-industry, environmental groups, conservation organizations, and landowners and operators.

Today the NRCS remains the lead agency in providing technical and financial assistance to agriculture to manage its production and natural resources. In tow are the nearly 3,000 local conservation districts, numerous state agencies in every state, and a well-funded crop of non-profit organizations that promote environmental, conservation, and wildlife goals.

Creating a Centrally Planned Economy

The development phase of the SCS did not go through without opposition. Bennet's recommendations created concern by the American Farm Bureau Federation, and the Committee on the Extension Organization and Policy made common cause against the New Deal's Department of Agriculture and attempted to "decentralize" the Department's soil-conservation program. Bennett and the New Deal policies prevailed. The states began to act on the recommended legislation in early 1937. The federal soil-conservation effort began to shift from a program of demonstrating conservation techniques to one of reaching out to involve farmers and others in the design and operation of the program itself. Perhaps, more importantly, in terms of the ultimate directions the program would take, USDA was promoting the creation of a new set of operational and political allies at the local and state levels. The new program would not be just an experiment in conserving natural resources; it would be an experiment in the application of government to natural-resource problems in a democracy (Sampson 1985).

The first soil conservation district was chartered August 4, 1937, in the Brown Creek District of North Carolina, which included Hugh Bennett's native home. The Brown Creek District also provided the first conservation plan based on the nine-step process:

Phase I – Data Collection and Analysis

1. Problem Identification

2. Determine Objectives

3. Inventory Resources

4. Analyze the Resource Data

Phase II – Decision Support

1. Formulate Alternatives

2. Evaluate Alternatives

3. Client Decisions

Phase III

1. Client Implements Plan

2. Evaluate the Plan

This conservation-planning process was criticized by some for not including an economic analysis and by others as being too complex. Regardless, it is still the planning framework that is used today. The basis for this success was quite simple. NRCS staff met with farmers on-site to assess their resource needs, discuss options, and then technically and financially assisted farmers in implementing a conservation plan that was compatible with their production system. By 1940, more than 300 districts covering 190 million acres had been organized and "Billion Acre Day" was achieved on June 9, 1947. By 1950, the number of districts climbed to 2,164. By this time, legislation enabling state agencies was developed and the progression of the organization of conservation districts led to the National Association on Conservation Districts. A broad-based, centrally planned economy, the now-called "conservation delivery system" was in place.

By many accounts, this centrally planned conservation-delivery system is considered to be extremely successful in improving the soil-resource base of agriculture and the farming economy. In hindsight, the success of the USDA Soil Conservation Service may have been its singular control on policy and programs, a singular focus on the soil resource and the relatively evenly dispersed, national, skilled workforce employed to address this concern. With the SCS being the primary stakeholder, policies and programs that needed to be passed by Congress seldom met political resistance to the extent that derailed their attempts. And the customers of the SCS, the farmers, while always unique in their nature, were contained within an agricultural economy that was relatively simple in comparison to today's economy that has few financial, trade, and transportation limitations. A centrally planned conservation-delivery system was, perhaps, the ideal vehicle to initiate and support a soil-conservation ethic to the countryside in the period of 1930 and for several decades.

Expansion of the Centrally Planned Conservation Economy

The centrally planned conservation-delivery system has matured and expanded in its 75 years of existence. Today, the USDA NRCS employs approximately 12,000 employees, of which 10,000 are critical to the mission of providing natural-resources support such as soil scientists and related field staff. Approximately 3,000 locally based conservation districts, each having board members and/or staff, have been a major partner. State agencies related to the function of the USDA and the EPA exist in every state. In addition, watershed districts, water-management organizations, and joint power boards have been created to address natural-resource concerns. This organizational structure has political inertia and, to a large degree, has been given a social license to continue forward with their work.

During these seven decades, non-profit and private organizations have emerged and evolved to access the human, financial, technical, and social resources of this centrally planned economic structure as well as to expend significant resources to influence its movement. In addition to the government staff, the NRCS developed TechReg (USDA NRCS 2009), an on-line program that allows agriculture and conservation professionals to become certified as technical service providers (TSP). These TSPs provide both technical and administrative assistance in the delivery of conservation programs and are based within the private and public sectors.

In the 1985 Farm Bill and each succeeding Farm Bill, the scope and funding for conservation programs expanded. Major pieces of legislation have included significant advances (USDA 2006):

1. The 1985 Farm Bill established the Conservation Reserve Program (CRP), which provided payments to producers to put environmentally sensitive cropland into conserving uses for 10 to 15 years.

2. The 1990 Farm Bill created a Federal program to restore and place conservation easements on wetlands—the Wetlands Reserve Program (WRP). The 1990 Farm Bill also authorized the Water Quality Incentives Program (WQIP) that signaled the emergence of water quality as a primary environmental objective of conservation programs.

3. The 1996 Farm Bill created the Environmental Quality Incentives Program (EQIP) by consolidating the Agricultural Conservation Program, WQIP, the Colorado Salinity Program, and the Great Plains Conservation Program. In addition, the 1996 Farm Bill authorized the Farm and Ranch Land Protection Program (FRPP) and the Wildlife Habitat Incentives Program (WHIP).

4. The 2002 Farm Bill vastly increased funding for conservation on lands in crop and animal production, or "working lands," by authorizing increased spending for several programs authorized under prior Farm Bills and establishing the Conservation Security Program (CSP) and the Grassland Reserve Program (GRP) for the long-term protection and restoration of grasslands

Today, there are four basic approaches to address conservation and environmental concerns on farm and ranch lands:

- Education and technical assistance
- Economic-incentive payments
- Conservation compliance
- Regulatory requirements

A key difference among these approaches is the degree to which producer participation is voluntary. These congressionally funded compliance and incentive programs affected the NRCS in two profound ways. First, they changed the perspective that farmers had on the agency from one of a technical-assistance agency to one of a compliance agency. Second, the program and the requirement to manage them began the evolution from a resource-driven organization to a program-driven organization.

Without going into the precise statistics for each government, non-profit, and private sector entity, it can be inferred that the conservation delivery system, including the regulatory aspect, is truly an extensive system. Between 2008 and 2012, an estimated $25 billion dollars will be spent on USDA conservation programs. This, of course, does not include budgets of the hundreds of non-USDA conservation programs and environmental agencies. One could estimate that $50 billion dollars will be spent in this time frame and probably remain in the ballpark. If the case for government involvement in [natural-resource management] is greatest when farmers and landowners have no private incentive to take action, then it could be assumed that the current state of ecological economics is nearly non-existent (Claassen 2009).

2010 Centrally Planned Conservation Economy

The mission of the USDA's Natural Resources and Environment (NRE) area is to promote the conservation and sustainable use of natural resources on the nation's private lands and to sustain production of all the goods and services that the public demands of the national forests. The mission area includes two agencies, the Natural Resources Conservation Service (NRCS) and the Forest Service (USDA OBPA 2009).

The NRE mission area, primarily through NRCS, also has responsibility for implementing most of the Conservation Title of the 2008 Farm Bill, which in 2010 will enroll more than 280 million acres at a total cost of about $2.7 billion. The President's 2010 budget for NRCS supports partnering with landowners to conserve land, protect wetlands, improve wildlife habitat, and promote a variety of other conservation initiatives. The President's budget also reflects a proactive strategy to increase the ability of conservation programs to address and meet critical national needs such as energy conservation, renewable-energy production, and reductions in greenhouse gas emissions. Working with local partners remains important to efficiently implement conservation programs and initiatives, and the NRCS will continue to direct financial and technical assistance programs to landowners and users through the USDA Service Centers and through local conservation districts.

Key performance measures for NRCS include:

• comprehensive nutrient-management plans applied (number of plans)

• cropland with conservation applied to improve soil quality (millions of acres)

• grazing land and forest land with conservation applied to protect and improve the resource base (millions of acres)

• wetlands created, restored, or enhanced (acres)

The Forest Service, with more than 30,000 staff years, is the largest employer in USDA. For 2010, the total request for the service's ongoing discretionary activities is $5.2 billion, an increase of $474 million over 2009. This budget will enhance the mission of the Forest Service as a protector of clean air, clean water, and wildlife habitat; a provider of recreation opportunities; and a key player in reducing greenhouse gas emissions.

The Forest Service's key performance measures include:

• percentage of total National Forest System land base for which fire risk is reduced through movement to a better condition class;

• total acres treated by the Forest Service that achieved fire objectives;

• acres of hazardous fuels treated outside the Wildland-Urban Interface (WUI);

• acres of WUI fuels treated to reduce the risk of catastrophic fire;

• percentage of acres treated in the WUI that have been identified in Community Wildfire Protection Plans.

Other objectives in the 2008 Farm Bill include the promotion of conservation through Environmental Services Markets (Claassen and Nickerson 2008).

This objective requires the USDA Secretary to establish technical guidelines for measuring environmental services from conservation and other land-management activities. Specifically, it requires the Secretary to develop:

• procedures for measuring environmental services benefits;

• a protocol to report these benefits;

• a registry to collect, record, and maintain information on benefits measured;

• a priority to be given to establishing guidelines for participation in carbon markets;

• guidelines to be established for a process to verify that farmers have implemented conservation or land-management activities reported in registry;

• a role of third parties in verification to be considered.

Emerging Constraints of the Conservation-Delivery System

This centrally planned conservation economy has become vulnerable to the changes in the economy, agriculture, ecology, and the expectations of society. When it emerged in the 1930s, its focus was to solve the singular problem of soil erosion. Since that time, the NRCS has expanded with the expansion of society's demands and congressional appropriations. Despite this expansion, it has not been able to meet all the expectations of citizens and congress. This shortfall is not just a problem of bureaucracy, in that it cannot evolve fast enough to acquire all the traits and abilities needed to successfully deliver conservation in the 21st century. It is that the solution resides in a broader context than what a centrally planned economy can control. This is illustrated by the context of *Key Performance Measures* listed in the previous section. The measures are based on the number of plans, acres of treatment, and percentage of land addressed. These are important measurements that must be generated to understand the efficiency of the USDA programs and staff, but they are not adequate in understanding what is occurring with the nation's land resources in a comprehensive perspective. When this data is presented to describe the level of management of natural and production resources in the United States, it excludes all the management activities that farmers, ranchers, and foresters engage in that do not involve government assistance. It assumes that resource-management goals are not being met, unless resource managers are engaged within the centrally planned conservation economy. In reality, a significant percentage of technical and financial assistance is provided to the resource managers by the private sector under a process that is not directly tied to federal, state, and local programs (Gieseke 2009). This myopic perspective is the result of a program-driven sightline, rather than a resource driven viewpoint.

Erosion of its Resource-Driven Foundation

The Soil Conservation Service was built with the intention to assess the resources of the farm operation and provide a conservation plan that identifies the practices and the technical and financial assistance needed for the farmer to meet their goals and the USDA goals. This resource-driven process provided a whole farm-resource assessment that would be the basis for management recommendations. By providing the farmer with a whole-farm-resource assessment, the farmer was able to incorporate the recommendations of the government staff into the farmer's production plan. As a conservation technician at the Carver Soil & Water Conservation District in the 1990s, I viewed hundreds of file folders that showed cropping rotations and other land uses that would improve the resource base of the farm. Many of these were drawn up in the 1960-1970s.

In the 1985 Farm Bill, conservation compliance and the Conservation Reserve Program emerged. Conservation compliance required farmers to manage their highly erodable lands (HEL) to reduce soil erosion and placed restrictions on draining wetlands.

Both of these provisions could be considered reasonable, but it did cause the centrally planned conservation-delivery system to move from a voluntary program to that of one that mandated conservation in some circumstances. The apparent and actual loss of soil on highly erodable fields and drainage of wetlands occurred under the dynamic processes of the market economy and the centrally planned economy of the commodity support programs. Regardless of the exact cause and motivation, it was deemed necessary to prevent the market economy from "externalizing" both the soil and wetland losses any longer. As the focus on the whole-farm-resource assessment waned and a new focus on conservation programs and conservation compliance was established, the conservation-delivery system evolved toward a program-driven delivery system and away from a resource-driven delivery system.

This perspective can be illustrated by a discussion I had with NRCS staff when we were discussing the merits of a Conservation Planning Course that I had provided in 2006 to 32 agriculture and conservation professionals in both the public and private sector. The well-respected and seasoned staff asked, somewhat rhetorically, "Why would anyone want a conservation plan?" This question was asked by a career NRCS employee who thoroughly understood the technical merits of a whole-farm-conservation plan. I deduced that he did not see the value of a conservation plan because the program-driven conservation-delivery system of the NRCS placed little or no value on it. Enrolling in certain conservation programs required that a conservation plan be written, but the primary value of the partial-farm-conservation plan was that it met the program requirements, not that it would identify other resources of concern. If the resource assessment did identify other resources of concern and there were not an existing program to be applied toward the resource concern, there is a high probability that no activity would be conducted toward that issue. That was not because the NRCS staff was not committed to their work, but that there were few or no tangible incentives for that staff and their field office to commit resources toward it. When insufficient value is placed on a good or service, it will create insufficient motivation to produce that good or service. As Adam Smith (1952) described, "There would be sufficient absolute demand [in that many people would like the resource concern corrected], but there would be insufficient effectual demand, the demand that brings with it enough incentive to encourage the entrepreneur to produce it."

It is these types of scenarios that seem illogical to the casual observer, but the actions are very logical to those who are compelled to live by the rules of the invisible hand. Regardless of the type of economy, a centrally planned conservation-delivery system or an outcome-based, market-driven process, the participants learn what actions and activities are rewarded within the system parameters and react to those rewards. These so-called "unintended consequences" become very "apparent consequences" of the invisible hand.

This loss of the resource-driven process did not go unrecognized by the National Association of State Conservation Agencies (NASCA 2007). In an NRCS-sponsored multi-year effort (2005-2007), the NASCA along with dozens of public and private partners evaluated the nation's conservation delivery system. The participants of the effort were from a broad-based network of agriculture, conservation, government organizations. In the 2007 NASCA report titled, *Evaluation of the Nation's Conservation Delivery System*, it was stated that a program-driven focus is a key obstacle to successfully delivering the resource-management needs to farms and farmers.

NASCA's five recommendations to be taken by or in partnership with others included:

• simplifying program rules and regulations and allow greater state/ local decision-making;

• simplifying conservation-program-delivery processes;

• reversing the current trend of program-driven conservation, toward more flexible resource-driven conservation;

• developing a single working-lands conservation program, with resource-protection targets and applying aggregated federal, state, and local resources;

• keeping decision-making local, within a nationally set framework.

In the discussion on how to reverse the current trend of a program-driven process toward a more resource-driven process, the resulting conversation often led to a cyclic mentality without solution. The logic imposed consisted of the following attributes of the current condition:

• The conservation-delivery system needs to be more resource-driven.

• Congress allocates dollars based on constituencies' goals and objectives via programs.

• The USDA distributes dollars based on program rules and guidelines.

• Federal, state, and local staff must abide by the rules and guidelines and are obligated to deliver program dollars to landowners and operators under these circumstances.

• The conservation-delivery system remains program-driven.

Unable to Decouple Resource Assessments from Programs

Many of the conservation professionals at the NASCA workshops stated that they would prefer to conduct activities that promote a resource-driven conservation-delivery system rather than program-driven process. In a program-driven process, one assumes that the government programs and staff are the singular method for addressing resource concerns. In a resource-driven process, all the resource concerns are identified and options are provided to address these concerns. In many cases, these resource issues can be addressed by the farmer in an efficient and cost-effective manner. A 2009 report to the Minnesota Department of Agriculture on the Livestock Environmental Quality Assurance program stated that up to 40 percent of the technical and financial assistance to implement conservation practices may be derived from the farmers themselves and nearly 40 percent was derived from the private sector. In this particular program report, NRCS and state/local governments provided 21 percent (Gieseke 2009). In the LEQA model, the intentions are to assess the resources relative to management standards developed by a consortium. It is in the interests of the consortium for the farmers to meet these standards in the most efficient manner. The manner that the farmer chooses can be via private sector, government programs, or themselves. In this process the resource assessment is conducted in a manner that is decoupled from any one particular process on how to achieve those objectives.

The participants in the NASCA effort recognized the short-fall to having a program-driven process in that some resource concerns were not addressed. And I think they recognized the scenario that they would have a difficult time in becoming unbiased resource assessors as long as their agencies administered conservation programs. Since they viewed themselves as the primary resource assessors and did not give consideration to the agricultural private sector, they could not see any reasonable avenue to take to revert back to a resource-driven process.

Non-scalable Assessments

Soil quality is often managed at the field or management unit scale, water quality at the watershed and basin scale, carbon at the regional, national or global scale, and animals and birds on the scale of migratory patterns. An assessment that cannot be used at multiple scales is limited in value.

Using the traditional conservation-planning procedures on an individual farm, the final product is generally a three-ring binder containing extensive compilation of resource-management data, schedules of implementation plans, and narrative descriptions of how these outcomes can be achieved. This farm-level conservation plan cannot efficiently be applied at the watershed or basin scale, or for carbon credits at the regional, national, or global scale, or habitat needed for animals and birds on the scale of regional or national migratory patterns. This is especially revealing when one could speculate on the number of individual plans that would be needed for each of these scales. Any resource-management outcome that is assessed and planned for outside the immediate area of a handful of farms becomes overwhelming in the attempt to sort and collate these assessments and plans. Today's resource-management plans developed for the purpose of delivering technical and financial assistance through conservation programs cannot be utilized at any scale other than the planning-unit scale.

Tsunami of NRCS Retirements

If the solution to the program-driven process is to employ and engage more government conservation professionals as on-the-ground whole- farm resource assessors and planners, then the timing of that solution is flawed.

According to the 2006 NRCS Human Capital Strategic Plan, the NRCS employs a total of 13,000 persons of which approximately 10,000 are mission-critical staff. Of those 10,000, 80 percent will be eligible for retirement by the year 2010. Of the 28 in senior executive service positions, the average length of service is 28 years and nearly half of those were eligible to retire in 2006 with 79 per cent of those eligible to retire in 2011 (USDA NRCS 2005).

Dana York (2006), the 2006 interim NRCS Chief spoke at the 2006 Soil & Water Conservation Society Annual Meeting in Keystone, Colo., and further elaborated on the situation. She stated that of those 8,000 that will be eligible for retirement, they can be generalized as a group that has agricultural experience, as many grew up on farms; they have a fairly conservative perspective on career mobility; and they have relative lower computer-related technological skills. These are basically NRCS career employees and have been with the NRCS for two and three decades. Those who will replace these several thousand employees come from much different spectrum of society. Of this new group, 70 percent will not have on-farm experience, many of them have a much more liberal career mobility perspective than the previous group, and they generally have a high-level technological skill base.

To assimilate these employees into the NRCS structure so that they may provide the same services as those leaving the agency will require a steep educational and experiential learning curve. The NRCS currently employs a 10-day boot camp to familiarize new recruits with agricultural systems, but that is a time-consuming and expensive venture. In addition, only so much agricultural experience can be absorbed by the new recruits in a boot camp scenario; if they cannot apply this experience early and often, much of that knowledge is lost. Understanding agricultural systems, like most all occupations, requires a certain level of regular activities associated with the occupation.

State and local agencies, while not experiencing the degree of retirement eligibilities, will experience a similar trend that will be an additive burden to the centrally planned conservation delivery system. This tsunami of retirements could, conservatively speaking, be cycled through in 12 years when the average age would be 66. In that time, it would be assumed that the senior executive service position would be replaced by those in mission-critical positions and nearly 80 percent of mission-critical positions would also be replaced. If Dana York's statement that the new work force personal and professional traits contrasts the retiring workforce to such a significant degree, it would be hard to accept that the agency, its strengths, and its roles would not also be significantly altered. It could also be assumed that if the NRCS leadership, and as importantly, its broad-based political and professional partners, try to maintain its role as it was envisioned by Hugh Bennett 70 years ago, it would endure obstacles and challenges that would presumably be too large to address.

Missing "Conservation Intelligence"

"Conservation intelligence," as described by Cox (2005), is the most up-to-date information about how landscapes are being managed "and is used to direct government policy and programs." He also states that the conservation-delivery system does not generate it.

Intelligence can be defined as the process of assembling facts and turning them into knowledge of what might happen and what we are able to do about it. The advantage of having outcome-based intelligence is so great that it is difficult to identify a government, business, industry, or economy, other than the conservation-delivery system, that does not rely heavily on the acquisition and analysis of data to further the cause at hand.

At the onset, the NRCS (then SCS) relied on the 9-Step Conservation Planning process to gather intelligence through its resource-assessment and inventory process. Both farm and "area-wide" conservation plans are based on the USDA NRCS National Planning Procedure Handbook Amendment 4 with detailed steps on how these "intelligence" gathering efforts are vital to the planning and eventually the outcome of the resource-management activities. With the movement away from a resource-driven process and a significant reduction in seasoned conservation professionals at the NRCS, the interest and capacity to conduct resource assessments has been greatly diminished. This has also greatly diminished the available conservation intelligence at the individual farm level.

Under a program-driven conservation-delivery system, farm-level conservation intelligence becomes vital to be able to target conservation programs to the farms and to the site-specific locations on the farm that need the application of conservation practices. This loss of on-farm conservation intelligence must be recovered if targeting conservation programs is desired. In addition to this on-farm conservation intelligence, conservation intelligence at the level of landscapes, watersheds, basins, and the nation is needed. In the early days of the NRCS, the focus was managing the soil resources on individual farms to improve the farm operation and the local and regional economy. This focus must remain or perhaps be regained, but today the focus also needs to be on how the individual farm is being managed to improve the local, regional, national, and global ecology. And not only the various scales of ecosystems need to identifiable, but also the components and the types of ecoservices must be identified and quantified. Without conservation intelligence, the government programs and policies cannot be directed, or perhaps, more importantly, the resource managers cannot understand what strategies are needed to improve the resources at the scale that is desired. Without conservation intelligence, neither the NRCS nor other stakeholders have the ability to fully communicate to partners, legislative bodies, and other state and federal agencies on the progress that is or is not occurring.

In September 2009, the USDA announced (USDA MRBI 2009) a new initiative to improve water quality and the overall health of the Mississippi River Basin. The Mississippi River Basin Healthy Watersheds Initiative (MRBI) is slated to provide approximately $320 million over the next four years for voluntary projects in priority watersheds located in 12 key states. Participation in this initiative, which will be managed by USDA's Natural Resources Conservation Service (NRCS), will be made available through a competitive process for potential partners at the local, state, and national levels.

This investment will probably improve the condition of the Mississippi River Basin, but it will be implemented without a "conservation intelligence" process that provides an on-farm resource assessment that is integrated with the farmers' production plans or is cognizant of EPA water quality requirements, Walmart's Sustainability effort, the USDA Biomass Crop Assistance Program, the Chicago Climate Exchange's carbon credit processes, or the myriad of natural-resource issues that are emerging regularly. The lack of conservation intelligence limits the ability to communicate and cooperate among common stakeholder goals and even among programs within the same government organization.

Narrow View of the Resource-Management Arena

Since the early days of the SCS, the NRCS has greatly expanded their vision on what constitutes natural-resource management, and their name change in 1990 exemplifies that broadened view from soil resources to all resources under their SWAPA & E (soil, water, air, plants, animals and energy) planning process.

But the resource-management arena is quite larger than the realm of NRCS resource-management programs. There are state-level, industry-led programs such as the mentioned Livestock Environmental Quality Assurance program that was initiated by Minnesota Milk Producers Association, adopted by a consortium of agricultural stakeholders, and accepted by Minnesota NRCS as an acceptable resource assessment process. There is the global-level effort that was recently announced by Walmart Stores, Inc. to develop a common "sustainability index" to determine the impact their products have on the world's resources. The bio-industry is searching for standards that address the resource impact that cellulosic-based energy would have on the soil, water, and wildlife resources. The Chicago Climate

Exchange and dozens of water-quality-trading markets are emerging.

The list of related efforts is much broader in scope and scale from local up to global models. The NRCS, once the sole leader in how private lands resource management is funded and implemented, could assume a new role as a peer partner in the vastness of the multi-scope and scale arena of global resource management.

With that said, NRCS should remain as one of the leaders in resource management, but more so as a servant manager rather than remaining the central planner. In the Mississippi River Basin Healthy Watersheds Initiative, a centrally controlled system consisting of government agents allocates project dollars via a winnowing process and eventually to the land managers. If NRCS recognizes that they are part of an evolving ecoservice market economy, and not the conductor of a centrally planned economy, they will no doubt lose some control of their designed smaller arena, but they may gain more influence in the larger resource-management arena.

Box 4.1 Economic-System Mindsets

It is difficult for any individual, let alone a consortium of individuals within a government agency, to invite players into their home arena. In Friedman's *Market Mechanisms and Central Economic Planning*, (Friedman 1981) he discussed, with a Chinese audience in 1970, the process of incorporating market components within centrally planned economies and how services and goods were distributed by the invisible hand of the market economy. One member of the audience, the Chinese minister from the Ministry for Materials Distribution, then visited the United States and on arriving he was asked who he would like to see. In his interest to understand how the goods were distributed in the United States he replied, "Tell us, who in the United States is responsible for the distribution of materials?" For us engaged in the market economy, it is nearly unimaginable how such a distribution would occur or to think it could occur with any level of efficiency. But if they were to ask what government office in the United States is responsible for allocating funds to implement conservation practices on our nation's landscape to improve our natural resources, it could be answered as the USDA NRCS. Much like the inquiry of the Chinese Minister for Materials Distribution seems foreign to us, so would an inquiry of who is responsible for distributing the resource-management allocation seem odd in the EcoCommerce future. Just as the invisible hand is responsible for the distribution and price of "widgets" in our economy, individuals and the invisible hand will be responsible for land-management activities that produce ecoservice outcomes.

Lacking an Enduring Stakeholder Engagement Strategy
With the evolution from the SCS to the NRCS in the early 1990s, the service expanded its goals and programs beyond the traditional focus of the soil resources. The environmental movement created a broad-based awareness of global issues and has created an extensive network of organizations in government, non-profit, and the private sector. Farmers, who own most of the land in the United States, are now only a small percentage of those who are engaged in some aspect of natural-resource policy.

The larger percentage includes those who are willing to provide support in some manner to improve the nation's natural resources. NRCS has reached out to those groups and individuals through funding programs that support cooperation among each other. Since participants of a centrally planned economy act as agents for others, rather than the voluntary cooperation one finds in a market economy, the controller must pay individuals and entities to engage in commerce. This does have value in the very early stages of developing an economy, but after everyone has been introduced, and they fulfill that particular project's goals, the individuals return to their normal tasks until additional funds that provide the incentives for more cooperative meetings and tasks become available.

Using the Mississippi River Basin Initiative as an example demonstrates that there are many procedures that must be prescribed to generate economic activity within a centrally planned economy. In comparison to the tasks listed below, the market economy only needs to provide a price and a unit for the desired outcome. With an outcome-based process that is void of a unit/value relationship, the following process is required to motivate [centrally planned] economic transactions (USDA MRBI 2009):

How will the Mississippi River Basin Initiative work overall?

Step One: Making Watershed Selection
Step Two: Selecting and Implementing Cooperative Projects
Step Three: Adding Other Programs to the Effort
Step Four: Implementing Conservation Practices
Step Five: Measuring Outcomes

The Role of Partners
In addition to providing input for watershed selection criteria and the

processes used to implement, the project partners will have a crucial role in encouraging and supporting producer participation. Partners' involvement will be important in a variety of ways:

- Providing information and conducting education and outreach activities

- Forming agreements for technical assistance and education activities

- Joining the State Technical Committee to provide input

- Submitting proposals for projects

- Targeting organizations' programs toward the project

- Assisting with monitoring, evaluation, and assessment

The $325 million will provide a significant amount of conservation, but the funding process will not create an enduring process or sustain a level of management of the land resources in the Mississippi River to meet the program's long-term objectives. The long-term process of humans' use of such ecosystems is guided by the economic forces such as the invisible hand. The funding used in this process will provide the glue to hold the network together for as long as the funding is there. The process will not sustain.

Human Capital Costs and Resource-Management Markets
This financial allocation of the Mississippi River Basin Initiative will consume an immense amount of human resources toward developing proposals to distribute these funds, and then an immense amount of human resources to act as agents of the centrally planned economy to decide how the funds should be allocated. Since it takes a significant commitment of time to engage in this process to receive funds and then to allocate funds, the vast majority of the participants in this type of economy must be subsidized by similar entities such as local and state governments and non-profit organizations. Resource managers, such as farmers, ranchers, and foresters do not engage within this resource-management economy until the funds have been allocated and then the agents encourage their involvement to apply for funds for conservation practices to be implemented on the land. The farmers, for the most part, have not had an on-farm resource assessment completed as the NRCS

has evolved away from on-farm assessments. And since the application of these funds toward conservation practices are not in relation to a comprehensive farm, watershed, or basin scale outcome process, no one will be directly motivated to determine outcomes on these scales in any uniform manner. Before, during, and after the project, no conservation or landscape intelligence will be accessed or added to. Since there are not a significant number of farm assessments to begin with, there really is no way to determine what the status of the resource management was before, during, or after the investment.

Inability to Integrate Production-Resource and Natural-Resource Management

Farmers generally have a whole-farm production plan that is developed within the context of their resource capacities and production goals, and are integrated within the policies and programs of the federal Farm Bill commodity title. Farmers generally do not have a whole-farm natural-resource plan and have not completed a resource assessment that includes conservation goals that are integrated within the programs of the federal Farm Bill conservation title. Until there is an integrated process and motivation to follow, NRCS's natural resource objectives will not be integrated and will remain unrealized. Due to the significant success of food production in the United States and the loyalty that many farmers have to the commodity title of the federal Farm Bill, it should be noticed that objectives of the commodity title are being met and the objectives of the conservation title are not. Competition for the farmers' resources is often won by the commodity title over the conservation title, but that should not be used as an excuse for failure, but as a plan for success. The $320 million Mississippi River Basin Initiative is an effort without a plan to integrate production-resource management and natural-resource management. The effort will cause farmers to implement conservation practices on the land, but it will not motivate the integration of production resource and natural resource management to any extent, and if it does, there are no methods for accounting for that progress.

Agriculture Technologies Transcended Agency Capacity

The technological improvements made in agriculture in the last decade are quite extensive and include the use of monitoring and global positioning devices for farm equipment, improved crop genetics, and tools for of precision agriculture. In addition to these controllable features, agricultural commodities have entered a larger arena of use, such as bio-based industries and market penetration that requires greater financial sophistication. In many cases, the agricultural professional has far more resource-assessment tools than the agency conservation professional. Agriculture's resource-management capabilities and needs have transcended the financial, technical, and human capacity of the traditional conservation-delivery system. This new knowledge base can be utilized either as an asset in an EcoCommerce structure or as a detriment to a system whose structure caters to centralized decisions.

Inability to Value Natural-Resource Outcomes

Farmers, ranchers, and foresters operate in a market economy that values production in quantity and quality. It provides little or no guidance for specific activities that are conducted to reach those outcomes. A centrally planned economy also has the ability to value natural-resource outcomes, but it does not necessarily have to. As farmers and other resource managers are being asked to provide the relatively long list of resource-management outcomes (water quality, biomass supplies, air quality, carbon sequestration, habitat improvements for game and non- game species, endangered and at-risk species, recreational and scenic opportunities) and maintain the productive capacity of the land, NRCS does not have a system to value those outcomes for themselves or other stakeholders of natural resources. In the past, there was not a need to value resource-management outcomes. A conservation plan was conducted for the wants and needs of the individual farmer or a group of farmers and communities meeting common goals. As *NRCS Planning Handbook* states, the farmer is the client of the NRCS. Today, those roles are being reversed in that the client can be defined as the government agencies, nonprofits, political organizations, communities, and even individuals who are requesting resource-management outcomes from the farmers and other resource managers. The farmer is the supplier, and, therefore, a means to determine what they are supplying becomes a necessity for the NRCS as well as for all others who want to engage in EcoCommerce or ecoservice markets.

The USDA Economic Winnowing Tool

To allocate limited financial resources to improve the agro-ecology, the USDA uses an economic tool described as a winnowing process (SWCS 2007, 92). This process begins with *all* agricultural producers and land, and then uses various mechanisms to narrow the set of possible producers and land down. In most conservation programs, the process begins with a request for proposal (RFP) often referred to as a "sign-up notice." The first step in the winnowing process is to determine which producers, land, and practices are eligible. The second step is producer application where the producer decides what land, practices, and perhaps, payment the producer is willing to accept in exchange for the conservation practices. In the third and final step, the government decides which bids or applications to accept or reject.

Using this system makes apparent that there is a high probability that the winnowing process will not allocate financial resources to address the natural resources in an efficient manner. First of all, the initial step of the winnowing process—going from all producers to those willing to sign up—excludes a significant number of transactions that would have benefited the natural resources significantly. Part of this reasoning is that many of the producers who enroll in government conservation programs already practice some level of conservation on their land and are interested in expanding their conservation. Those who have neglected to practice conservation and are perhaps in the greatest need are often not willing to participate in the centrally planned conservation economy. Second, a significant amount of effort is often put into the process of enrolling into conservation programs by farmers and by government staff assisting farmers to enroll. Those who are not accepted may have gained some information and knowledge, but for the most part, signing up for conservation programs is more often an administrative task that has little enduring value for the farmer to use in future conservation activities. Third, the RFP winnowing process is not a procedure that farmers can accept any ownership in. They realize they are in a winnowing process and feel somewhat removed from controlling their fate. The process is often a mystery, and as programs gets more specific and complicated, the eligibility process is often contained within the computer software in the government office. Even the recent Conservation Stewardship Program sign-up that is designed to reward farmers for their natural-resource management outcomes requires farmers to submit a questionnaire that is entered into a software system that is beyond their reach. The rational for this is that it is a new program and farmers will not be able to handle this process on their own without specific guidance from the federal government staff. And that is mostly accurate, but that will be true for any program developed under a centrally planned economy. By design, in a centrally planned economy, an agent acts on behalf of the economic participants and must do so in a winnowing process.

The challenges to efficiently applying the winnowing tool can be further appreciated by the number of land-management possibilities that exist for a relatively small watershed (Ruhl 2007, 208). If there are 1,000 fields and 10 possible land uses for each field, there are 10^{30} possible land-use patterns. This is due to the mathematics of permutations, in that the number of land-use patterns in a watershed is equal to the number of land-use units, such as fields, *raised to the power* of the number of possible uses. If there were 1,000 units and four uses it would equate to 10^{12}. Considering these large "economies of configuration" reveals the tremendous challenges that are posed to a centrally planned conservation economy as it pertains to identifying how to most efficiently allocate limited financial resources to improve the natural-resource base. While the number of these landscape possibilities is truly mind-boggling for a winnowing process, it is a perfectly natural process in a market economy in which people express their self-interest with the guidance of the invisible hand, a marvel indeed.

USDA Transitions Toward a Market-based Economy

One form of a transition economy is an economy that is changing from a centrally planned economy to a market-based economy. A traditional definition of transition economies includes economic liberalization (letting market forces set prices and lowering trade barriers), macroeconomic stabilization, and restructuring and privatization in order to create a financial sector and move from public to private ownership of resources. A transition process is usually characterized by the changing and creating of institutions, particularly private enterprises; changes in the role of the state, thereby, the creation of fundamentally different government institutions; and the promotion of private-owned enterprises, markets, and independent financial institutions (IMF 2000).

In all fairness, USDA NRCS is aware of the limitations of their organization and the centralized system they employ. And it is not always within their ability to amend the process in which they are heavily invested. The NRCS and many government agencies receive great pressure from legislators and constituency groups that benefit from the programs that are in place. An agency does not exist and grow for 75 years without a tremendous amount of support from long-term advocates from the public, non-profit, and private sectors. A transition from a centrally planned economy in which few people and organizations ultimately decide how funds are distributed can only occur gradually from within the organization, or if the existing system is recognized by a critical mass that it is not meeting its objectives, or if another system can emerge that carries far greater value, at far less cost and that resides outside the immediate control of the government. It is the intentions of this book to highlight the significant efforts outside the direct control of the federal government, such as Walmart's "sustainability index," the carbon markets, bio-energy markets that could benefit from the EcoCommerce structure and that could assist the USDA to transition toward an outcome-based market system.

Government Programs in the Transition

It is probably correct to state that the leadership in NRCS and its congressional constituents have never lost sight of the fact that a resource-driven process is essential to the proper distribution of funds and proper management of the land. Two significant efforts in the last decade or so have illustrated a transitional attempt.

Environmental Quality Incentive Program

One of the first major efforts to reinstitute a resource-driven process occurred in the 1996 Farm Bill with the Environmental Quality Incentive Program (EQIP). The EQIP was initially designed to replace the singular practice-based program of the Agricultural Conservation Practice with a whole-farm planning effort in EQIP. The EQIP required farmers to submit a conservation plan and expressly allow non-agency people to develop EQIP plans. The program intentions were to encourage the producers to assess the areas of their operations that face the most serious problems associated with soil, water, and related resources, including grazing lands, wetlands, and wildlife habitat. The plans were also to be designed, to the extent practicable, to help producers comply with local, state, and federal laws. The EQIP, as described, was never implemented as it was quick to revert back to a single-practice program. But the USDA presented the direction toward a whole-farm resource assessment and allowed the private sector to enter this transitory market.

Conservation Security/Stewardship Program

In May 2004, the draft rules for the USDA NRCS Conservation Security Program were made public. The CSP was touted as the new way to address on-farm natural-resource management "By Rewarding the Best and Motivating the Rest." This was in contrast to the traditional conservation programs that identified resource concerns and then provided the farmer with funds to address that problem. The CSP was to pay for ecoservices that were being provided by the farmer to the public.

This vision was put into practice by the USDA Natural Resources Conservation Service (NRCS), the agency charged with CSP implementation. In 2004, Bruce Knight, then chief of NRCS, said that CSP would have a profound effect on NRCS and its conservation partners. He said, "CSP will revolutionize the way we work, the way we operate and the way we think. Since CSP is a resource-based enhancement program, producers of all types of agricultural uses and agricultural operations will be eligible to enroll. The CSP revolution will reverse our growing emphasis on program-driven approaches and lead us back toward a conservation planning approach that is resource driven" (Knight 2004). Unfortunately, this vision was not yet been realized.

The basis of the program was to develop eligibility requirements based on how the farm operation was being managed. Management indices and ratings such as the Soil Conditioning Index, Soil Tillage Intensity Rating,

Program Costs and Distribution of Benefits

The paper also stated that federal costs of promoting private sector environmental markets may be less than the costs of direct payments and cost-sharing. Federal costs would be limited to the costs associated with rule-making, research and development of methods for quantifying benefits, and investments in activities to foster emerging markets. The private sector would bear the major costs of implementing actions. Moreover, the costs to firms of purchasing environmental benefits under market systems would be lower than their costs under traditional command-and-control approaches.

Office of Ecosystem Services and Markets

On December 18, 2008, the USDA, under a mandate in the 2008 Farm Bill Section 2709 Environmental Services Market to promote incentive-based conservation formed an Office of Ecosystem Services and Markets (OESM) (USDA FS 2008). The office is currently headed by Sally Collins, a USDA Forest Service veteran. The OESM will also support the Conservation and Land Management Environmental Services Board, an oversight board comprised of the Secretaries of Interior, Energy, Commerce, Transportation, and Defense – as well as the Chairman of the Council of Economic Advisors, the Director of the White House Office of Science and Technology, the Administrator of the Environmental Protection Agency, and the Commander of the Army Corps of Engineers.

This is a significant change in how the NRCS views a successful resource-management process. And as with all bureaucracies, it could be assumed that the changes will be attempted to be implemented at a pace that provides both progress in the movement and assurance that the organizational culture and norms are respected. The policy and program changes by the USDA to engage its employees and constituents in a transition from a centrally planned resource-management economy to one that contains features of a market-based economy will take time according to Collins, head of the OESM. Collins predicted it will take five years to complete sufficient research and build the infrastructure needed to put this type of comprehensive environmental market in place.

A Transitory Economy

Choosing specific programs, policies, and actions of the USDA over the last decade or so illustrates that the USDA has pursued additional directions other than the single-practice program-driven process that has dominated much of its past and current activities. A transition process is usually characterized by the changing and creating of institutions, particularly private enterprises; changes in the role of the state, thereby, the creation of fundamentally different government institutions and the promotion of private-owned enterprises, markets and independent financial institutions (IMF 2000). Applying this characterization to the 2008 Farm Bill proposal to encourage private markets to develop for ecoservices reveals that many of the traits that the USDA described would meet the criteria of a transitory economy. In this case, the USDA proposed policy alternatives that would compel a transition to occur, but few emerged as formidable options. Perhaps the creation of the OESM falls under the category of the "creation of fundamentally different government institutions" is the one aspect that saw the light of day.

CHAPTER 5

Immature Ecoservice Markets

Ecoservice Markets Moving Forward
Carbon and Greenhouse Gas Markets
Water Quality Markets
Retail Eco-Labels
Market Incentives for Wildlife
Analyzing Market Maturity
First-Generation Ecoservice Market Lessons
Obstacles to Overcome
Attributes of an Ideal Ecoservice Market

Ecoservice Markets Moving Forward

This chapter reviews a few of the ecoservice markets such as carbon, water, wildlife, and consumer-driven. Designing and implementing an ecoservice market is not an easy task, and, as will be discussed in Chapter 6, ecoservices pose many more "unnatural" challenges than that of a traditional economic market. So with these markets being the first generation of ecoservice markets, many relatively minor successes need to be appreciated. First-generation market successes include the creation and administration of the market structure, making trades within the market, pricing of ecoservices, and, in some cases, even an improvement of the natural resources. Regardless of these challenges and relatively small successes, the number of ecoservice markets has expanded in the last decade in their attempts to capitalize on providing ecoservices. In forestry alone, 287 ecoservice markets around the world were in existence in 2002 (Landell-Mills 2002).

Most of these ecoservice markets exhibit characteristics of an immature market. These include payment mechanisms that are often bilateral trades and lack the fluidness of a commodity market; the government is a major participant in most or all of the activities; the institutions that are nested within the market are often compilations of existing institutions and have not yet evolved into a unique organization; and most of these markets are considered immature just due to the few numbers of years that they have been trading.

Carbon and Greenhouse Gas Markets

Due to the global dispersion of carbon dioxide and other greenhouse gases (GHG), these ecoservice markets could operate on a global scale. Most other ecoservice markets' supply-and-demand interactions are based on geographical limitations such as watersheds and wildlife corridors. But, to date, GHG markets have emerged from a regional perspective. These carbon markets have two primary scenarios for creating demand:

• Regulatory cap and trade markets that set emission limits

• Voluntary markets driven by consumer willingness to pay to reduce their carbon "footprint," by firms wishing to show themselves as responsible environmental actors and, by firms wishing to gain control of low-cost alternatives that may be used to comply with future emission limitations (Butt 2004)

Regulatory markets create a property right for greenhouse gas (GHG) reductions in the form of tradable credits, much like the discharge allowance in water quality markets that will be discussed in the next section.

Trading Units

Trades are made in units of 1 ton carbon dioxide equivalent (CO_2 e). All major GHGs are sold within carbon markets, not just carbon dioxide. The other gases are converted to their CO_2 e using their global warming potential which compares the ability of different GHGs to trap heat in the atmosphere (i.e. 1 ton methane = 23 tons CO_2 e credits and nitrous oxide = 296 tons CO_2 e credits). There are two types of credits: (1) regulatory credits that are auctioned or allocated to GHG emitters based on a regulatory formula and (2) project-based credits are generated from projects that sequester carbon or reduce GHG emissions. The Kyoto Protocol sets legally binding emission reduction targets for 37 industrialized countries and the European Union to reduce their GHGs by 5 percent against 1990 levels over the period of 2008 to 2012. To date, 180 have ratified the accord (Williams, J. 2009).

Trading Protocols

Under the Kyoto Protocol, each country must create a national registry to track credit ownership and transfer, which in turn must be linked to the International Transaction Log. While becoming popular (at least 10 formalized markets exist), credit markets are not the only avenue to reduce GHG emissions. Each country is free to implement a mix of policy tools to meet their commitment, which may also include persuasion, regulations, incentives, and taxes, among others (Williams, J. 2009).

In the United States, several state and regional cap and trade programs have recently been approved to reduce GHG emissions. Voluntary markets are currently the greatest source of demand for GHG reductions credits in the United States. The Chicago Climate Exchange (CCX) is a voluntary cap and trade program covering emission sources from the United States, Canada, and Mexico and offset projects from these countries and Brazil. While joining CCX is voluntary, members make a legally binding commitment to meet annual GHG emission-reduction targets (Ribaudo 2008). The CCX trades carbon financial instruments that come in allowances and offsets that are similar to the regulatory and project credits of the Kyoto Treaty. Allowances are issued to emitters and offsets are generated from emission reduction, including agriculture.

Individuals sequestering less than 10,000 t CO_2 e must be enrolled through a CCX-registered aggregator. The Kyoto rules are more stringent than CCX and must demonstrate a reduction of emission additional to businessas-usual. CCX does not. Therefore the 1 t CO_2 e is not interchangeable, and therefore prices are different. The CCX offers five-year contracts and, depending on the geographical location, sequestration ranges from .2-.6 t/acre for cropland and .12-.52 t/acre for rangeland. So about 16,000 acres would be the minimum needed to trade in the CCX.

In addition to the CCX, the Oregon CO_2 Emission Standards, the Regional Greenhouse Gas Initiative, California Global Warming Solutions Act, and the Western Climate Initiative are either in the development stage or are making trades. The voluntary market in 2006 was 23.7 million t CO_2 and approximately 43 percent of the transactions were through the CCX. Agriculture accounts for 6% of US GHG emissions Methane and nitrous oxide are the primary GHG emitted by agriculture. Enteric fermentation and manure management account for 30 percent of U.S. methane emission and NOx account for 72 percent of U.S. NOx emissions (Williams, J. 2009).

Agriculture and Carbon

CCX issues tradable contracts to owners or aggregators of eligible projects on the basis of sequestration, destruction, or displacement of GHG emissions (Ribaudo 2008). Eligible projects include management impairment. States then were required to provide a listing of all impaired waterways to the EPA and also establish Total Maximum Daily Loads (TMDL) for the limiting of pollutants in each impaired waterway. TMDLs are designed to achieve applicable water-quality standards of uses such as swimming or fishing that a waterbody must be able to support. A complete TMDL analysis includes two major components. The first is the calculation of the maximum amount of pollutant that a water body can receive and still meet the water-quality standards. The second component divides the total maximum daily load between point and non-point sources. Establishing and implementing TMDLs has been difficult from the scientific, technical, social, and political aspects, and relatively few have been completed since the passage of the CWA in 1972. One reason is the difficulty in choosing the appropriate policy instrument with respect to non-point-source pollution. First, non-point-source pollution involves diffuse sources, meaning it is difficult, if not impossible, to identify the exact point or location that the pollution is entering the waterway. Second, random events such as weather can affect the runoff load. Third, site-specific factors may also affect loading. The combination of these factors makes measuring, monitoring, gathering, and analyzing information on each and every site impossible. Therefore, regulatory approaches to address this type of pollution are equally challenging.

Water-Quality-Restoration Markets

Due to these insurmountable regulatory challenges, a market-based approach has grown in popularity as a potential means to address water-quality problems. A March 2009 report, *Water Quality Trading Programs: An International Overview*, the World Resources Institute identified 57 water-quality-trading programs worldwide with 51 of those residing in the United States and less than a fourth of them active (Selman 2009). Those considered active were programs that have finalized their trading program design and are allowed to trade. They were not necessarily having active trades.

In a 2003 review of 37 U.S.-based water-quality-trading programs by the Environmental Law Institute, only three programs were identified as having experience with any trading activity. Also, the few trades that have taken place have been primarily regulator-approved bilateral agreements negotiated between point-source dischargers and not the market-style trades that the EPA and USDA have promoted (King 2003).

The motivation to develop these U.S. markets included three government factors (Selman 2009):

1. Increased enforcement of the Clean Water Act's Total Maximum

Daily Load in the late 1990s

2. The EPA's endorsement of water-quality trading via its 2003 Water Quality Trading Policy

3. Funding support from the USDA and the EPA to cover water-quality-trading program start-up costs and fund any initial scoping or communication activities

These government factors create a potential economic incentive for dischargers with high abatement costs, such as wastewater treatment plants to purchase pollution discharge reductions from sources that have lower abatement costs such as agricultural producers. This emission trading is organized around the creation of discharge allowances, which is a time-limited permission to discharge a fixed quantity of pollutant into the environment. The trading credits may be established by using performance-based criteria (e.g. actual measures of nutrient discharges) or activity-based criteria (e.g. changes in practices that have an expected effect on water quality discharges) (King 2003). These credits or a discharge allowance have characteristics of a private good and property rights and are enforced by the regulatory agency managing the program (Ribaudo 2008).

With property rights established, trades can be legally defined and can occur in four primary methods. First, bilateral agreements are used where buyers and sellers directly interact to carry out a transaction. The second-most-popular market, following bilateral agreements is that of a clearinghouse, in which the government or third-party broker acts as an intermediary between those that generate credits and those that demand credits (Nguyen 2006). The third type of trading allows for sole-source offsets in which trading *per se* does not take place, but emitters are given the opportunity to find alternative ways of reducing their environmental impact. The fourth market type is that of an exchange in which market-style trading is based on standardized units and large number of buyers and sellers. Such fluid markets have yet to arise for the case of water quality.

In addition to the types of trades allowed, the EPA's 2003 Water Quality Trading Policy Statement (EPA 2003) stated the following general elements are necessary:

1. Markets must have clear legal authority and mechanisms.

2. Units of trade must be clearly defined.

3. Credits should be generated before or during the same period they

are used to comply with the specified period of the limit.

4. Standardized protocols are necessary to quantify pollutant loads, reductions and credits. (*see Box 5 .1)

5. There must be compliance and enforcement provisions.

6. There must be public participation and access to information.

7. Markets must provide periodic assessments of environmental and economic effectiveness.

Box 5.1 Addressing Water-Trading-Credit Uncertainties
*Due to the difficulties in quantifying credits and addressing the uncertainty of non-point-source pollution due to precipitation, variable land-use practices, time lag between complete practice performance and the effects of soil, cover, slope on the pollutant load delivery, the EPA provides further approaches for meeting the uncertainties of #4. The EPA supports a number of approaches that include monitoring to verify load reductions, the use of trading ratio greater than 1:1 between point source and non-point source pollution, using demonstrated performance values for conservative assumptions in estimating the effectiveness of non-point-source-management practices, using site-specific or trade-specific discount factors, and retiring a percentage of non-point-source reductions for each transaction or a predetermined number of credits. The site-specific procedures and protocols used in water-quality-trading programs that involve agriculture and forestry operations should estimate nutrient and sediment load delivery. Numerous methods are available that have been developed or used by the USDA agencies. An example is the Revised Universal Soil Loss Equation that can determine sediment yield at the end of a slope, and this information coupled with an appropriate method to estimate sediment loading would be acceptable (Abdalla 2008).

Despite the high interest in water-quality trading, a defined structure and significant financial assistance provided by government agencies, particularly the EPA and the USDA, the experience so far with actual water-quality trading is very limited with most of the trades categorized by bilateral agreements that were based on ad hoc criteria and direct negotiations. These trades do not provide many insights to help guide the development of the kind of market based trading system that will be needed to significantly reduce the cost of achieving water quality goals in most parts of the country (King 2003).

Based on the findings of these water-quality-trading programs, it does not seem probable that market-based systems will be successfully used for the purpose of restoring public waters. This is despite having several dozen programs in existence and a high level of desire for them to function. There are, however, some successful water-quality markets that do exist, and two of the most-often-cited examples include the New York City Watershed Region and the Nestlé Waters - Vittel program in France.

Potable Drinking Water: New York City Watershed Region
    In New York City, where the quality of drinking water had fallen below standards required by the EPA, authorities opted to restore the Catskill Watershed that had previously provided the city with the ecosystem service of water purification (WAC 2010). New York City and an ad hoc task force on agriculture reached consensus on a comprehensive program for farming in the New York City watersheds that satisfactorily addressed the city's objectives for drinking-water-quality protection and compliance with federal and state rules and standards, as well as the farm community's concerns for sustaining and enhancing the agricultural economy and way of life. In return, the city withdrew proposed regulations for agriculture in its discussion draft relating to agriculture. Except for a general prohibition to safeguard against individual farm operators who exhibit a willful and irresponsible intent to pollute in a manner that threatens to significantly increase pollution levels and degrades the source waters of the city's water supply, the program will be entirely voluntary.

With financial incentives in place of regulation, farmers were encouraged to work with their soil and water conservation district, Cooperative Extension, and NRCS to develop individual farm plans to control point and non-point sources of pollution. These plans will cover the entire spectrum of farm management, including practices to improve farm profitability and sustainability. It is the intention of the task force and New York City that not one farm will be put out of business by this program. While actively participating in the development and implementation of their farm plans, farmers will not have to pay for the planning, implementation, maintenance, or operation of best-management practices recommended to meet the water-quality objectives of New York City outlined in the plans.

The Council will develop and be instrumental in evaluating the program, advising the environmental protection agency commissioner, reviewing individual farm plans, providing liaison to the larger group for agriculture, and disputing resolution.

The preferred approach to reduce potential pollution from farms is use of management practices developed to meet water-pollution-control policies under New York State law and Section 319 of the Clean Water Act amendments of 1987. The mechanism of choice for selecting the best-management practices is preparation of a Whole Farm Plan for each farm. A collateral objective for each Whole Farm Plan is to sustain and improve the economic viability of the farm. The cost of this investment in natural capital was estimated between $1-1.5 billion, which contrasted dramatically with the estimated $6-8 billion cost of constructing a water-infiltration plant plus the $300 million annual running costs.

Retail Bottled Water: Nestlé Waters - Vittel

Vittel, a mineral water product of Nestlé Waters, was facing legislative problems and a risk to their reputation when its source waters were increasing in nitrates (Perrot-Maitre 2006). The French legislation is very strict as it pertains to "natural mineral water" and water quality must be achieved naturally other than the removal of unstable elements of iron and manganese. The waters for the Vittel brand had been captured from the Vittel catchment since 1882. In the early 1980s, the de la Motte family, then the owners of the Vittel brand, realized that the intensification of agriculture in the Vittel catchment posed a risk to the nitrate and pesticide levels to the water supply.

In the Vittel catchment, as in many places in France and in Europe, the traditional hay-based cattle ranching system has been replaced by a corn-based system. Free range was limited while stocking rates increased. The increased nitrates were caused primarily by the heavy leaching of fertilizers from the corn fields in the winter when fields are barren, overstocking, and poor management of animal wastes.

This led Vittel to consider five options and the feasibility of each:

1. Do nothing. This option carried too much risk of further contamination of the water and potentially closing the business;

2 . Relocate to a new catchment . This would cause the business to lose the Vittel label and the premium price associated with it;

3. Purchase all the lands in the catchment area. This was not feasible due to French law that does not allow the sale of agricultural land for non-agricultural use. Vittel would need to obtain the capacity to manage the land and due to its social ethics, a sale of that much farmland may cause a social protest;

4. Require farmers to change their practice through legal action. There are no legal grounds to pursue this because these waters met acceptable public standards. In addition, it would not technically be feasible to demonstrate which individual farmers were liable for the impairment;

5. Provide incentives to farmers to voluntary change their practices. This was the only feasible alternative left. The challenge is to make Vittel and farmers' interest coincide so that it was in the farmers' interest to cooperate.

Vittel developed an incentive package for farmers to alter their agricultural practices and consequently reduce water pollution that had affected Vittel's product. For example, Vittel provided subsidies, labor, and free technical assistance to farmers in exchange for farmers' agreement to enhance pasture management, reforest catchments, and reduce the use of agrochemicals. The final agreements were extensive and relatively costly, but the benefits that were provided to both Nestlé Waters and the farmers were acceptable.

Water-Quality-Markets Summary
In the cases of Nestlé Waters - Vittel and the New York City Watershed Region, it was relatively straightforward to determine a value of the watershed ecoservices being provided. New York City and Nestlé wanted the best quality of water that could be provided, and farmers managed the land that provided a certain level of water quality. And in both instances, the non-point-source pollution could not be traced back to individual farmers so a voluntary approach accompanied by various support and incentive mechanisms were the most effective means to achieve the water-quality levels desired. These ecoservice markets, or rather bi-lateral business transactions, emerged because the economic value of the ecoservice (natural capital) being provided was greater than the economic costs associated with cleaning the water using man-made treatment facilities (man-made capital). Both of these watersheds have specific and definable characteristics that allow these markets to function in the manner that they do. These specific and definable characteristics have not emerged in markets to restore public riparian waters, and that is the primary reason that most, if not all, of these immature water-quality-trading programs and markets could be considered unsuccessful. Due to this, it does not seem feasible to apply this system in the broader view of water-quality-trading markets, but it certainly could be compatible. Another market failure that is often overlooked in these two "successful" water-quality-trading markets

farm operation. Depending on the individual and the landscape scale and features that are available to them, specific species could be promoted and some secondary income could be garnered from the land. Beyond the recreation component, wildlife and habitat types do provide ecoservices that promote genetic diversity. Pollination of crops by bees is required for 15-30 percent of U.S. food production, and most large-scale farmers import nonnative honey bees to provide this service (Ribaudo 2008).

Analyzing Market Maturity

Market structures vary between locations and goods. Economists concerned with efficiency have traditionally been preoccupied with the degree of market competition. However, when examining markets that are dynamic, that involve varied participation, and that are embedded in a wider institutional framework, it is important to examine an array of features. Seven market features will be used to highlight some of the market traits and how those traits identify market status or maturity. It should be noted that these features are not independent, and a change in one is likely to be linked to changes in others. For instance, immature markets are likely to have higher levels of public-sector participation (reflecting government efforts to promote institutional development), simpler payment mechanisms, and lower level of competition than fully established markets. As competition picks up, governments are likely to become less interventionist and payment mechanisms more sophisticated (Landell-Mills 2002). To apply these seven features to ecoservice markets, the four types of markets listed in this chapter will be used and a brief analysis will be given for each market. The intentions of this are to illustrate the types of characteristics ecoservice markets have and how these early attempts at trading ecoservices have evolved toward certain levels of growth.

The Commodity

The key ingredient in any market is the commodity that is being bought and sold. The carbon and GHG markets use commoditized, tradable units. The carbon and GHG does have a system that uses a commoditized unit, and the production of that unit is based either on a direct measurement of methane capture, for example, or on identifying particular agricultural practices, such as no-till, that would be expected to generate commodity units. The challenge with this market is that it is voluntary with the expectation of a regulatory control. As an immature ecoservice market, it does not have the database to determine the status and condition of the landscape to sequester carbon or what activities are occurring that will cause the inventory of sequestered carbon to increase or decrease.

The water-quality markets use bi-lateral agreements that negotiate price, usually for a type of practice to be implemented rather than a commoditized unit. The eco labels identify procedures that have the probability of causing a desired outcome and the price is incorporated in the food commodity. The wildlife markets contain the Environmental Benefits Index; a number along with a price may act, in a manner, as a commodity that is then delivered via a bi-lateral type of agreement.

Characteristics of Participants

Participants include those demanding environmental services, those supplying services, and intermediaries involved in facilitating transactions. Participants may include the private sector, the public sector, non-government sector, civil society, or a combination.

The GHG markets allow for a wide range of participants, but primarily have a fairly narrow involvement at this point as relatively few land managers are aware of the market or feel like it is a sustainable market. Companies, organizations, and government units can act as aggregators and brokers to facilitate the trades. The water-quality markets operate on much smaller geographical scales, and, therefore, each market has fewer potential suppliers within the market. Buyers for water-quality credits are also quite limited to processing facilities, waste-water-treatment plants, and perhaps some watershed districts. The eco-labels involve the most consumers or buyers of the ecoservice compared to the other markets, but they participate in dozens, if not hundreds, of separate individual product markets. The advancement of the Walmart "sustainability index" would greatly expand the characteristics of the participants and could cause a full integration of ecoservices within the food and product industry. The wildlife markets are primarily government agencies and non-profit as the buyers and land managers as the sellers.

Level of Competition

The level of competition determines the extent to which individual market players can influence prices—often referred to as market power. Conventionally, competitiveness is measured by the number of players in a market: the fewer the players (e .g. in the case of monopolies), the greater each participant's market power and the less competitive the market. Competitive markets involve several participants. However, it is critical to distinguish between explicit and effective competition. Even where markets are highly concentrated, if there is a credible threat of entry by competitors, the market may be competitive.

The GHG market prices for carbon sequestration fluctuate, but those are often not based on a certain supply-or-demand process in the traditional sense, but are highly correlated to political influences at this time. The water-quality markets have not matured to a level that allows competition to influence prices as most are based on negotiated bi-lateral agreements. The eco-label market has a high level of competition in relation to foods not labeled for ecoservice outcomes as well as among the eco-labeled foods. The wildlife market, using the EBI, does allow farmers to compete with each other, creating a pricing influence. However, since farmers are not privy to what other bids are, the level of competition has little influence on the transaction of the moment but may have influence on the next sign-up period when the market participants have the information based on the last sign-up.

Payment Mechanism

Several options exist for transferring funds from buyers to sellers, including direct negotiation, broker-based markets, auction systems, and exchange-based markets.

The GHG markets use an exchanged-based market along with contractual agreement to provide assurance for both parties. The water-quality markets are usually based on bilateral agreements. The ecolabels vary on how payments are determined depending on how the grower and processor interact. The wildlife markets use a price-discover method in the EBI process and then a bilateral contract is developed.

Geographical Extent of Trading

Trades may be local, national, regional, or international depending on the market and its location in relation to political boundaries. The GHG markets vary on geographical scale, depending on the policies, and operate on a national and regional level. As these markets mature, it is conceivable that trading units will become compatible and a global market will develop. The water-quality markets would presumably operate in the geographical boundaries of the watershed, but various markets could exist at scales within those boundaries. The eco-labels would exist within the boundaries of distribution of those goods as defined by the retailer. It may be local criteria, or globally as it pertains to Walmart's network. The wildlife markets using the EBI have included geographical considerations and could be adjusted to meet certain geographically related goals.

Nested Nature

Markets evolve in a context. Not only may markets replace existing institutional arrangements, but they build on institutional arrangements which will influence the form they take. It is important to understand this context and the nature of inter-institutional relationships.

The GHG markets probably represent the creation of new institutions to manage ecoservice markets. The development of a trading platform initiated new businesses, such as aggregators, to develop as well. The water-quality markets have struggled with creating new institutions and have often relied on government agencies or private consulting firms to manage trades. Eco-label markets have created or have used organizations to act as a certification agent. The wildlife markets have relied extensively on the USDA to manage the CRP program.

Each of these markets has, to some degree, experienced growth toward a mature market framework, but none has reached that state or established a path that will bring it to a mature state.

Level of Maturity

Market maturity may be defined in a number of ways. Four useful criteria include: the time period since transactions were first initiated (i.e. the age of the market), the degree of price discovery attained to date, market participation and liquidity, and the level of sophistication in the payment mechanism employed.

Time Period: The GHG markets are all relatively young due to the limited time that policies have existed to motivate market stakeholders. The water quality markets of Nestlé-Vittel and the New York City Watershed Region have been in existence since the 1990s. The eco-label markets have existed for decades as well at some locations. The wildlife markets of CRP came into existence in the 1985 USDA Farm Bill.

Market Sophistication: The GHG markets are most advanced as it pertains to how the commodity is traded and how payment mechanisms have developed if compared to traditional markets. It is not mature, however, on its price discovery, the breadth of market participants, and the liquidity of the market. The water-quality markets, for the most part, rely on bi-lateral trade agreements, a low level of sophistication. The eco-labels usually rely on a certification process that is cumbersome by market standards. The CRP market and its use of the EBI have evolved to incorporate more attributes and allow for a weighing process depending on the market desires.

First-Generation Ecoservice Market Lessons

The insight gained from these first-generation ecoservice markets will lay the foundation for EcoCommerce and other ecoservice markets. Successes include identifying transactions, valuation, audit, oversight and, other needs associated with bilateral trades, things that are often taken for granted in mature markets. Some of these market paths could be considered dead ends, but at this developmental stage of ecoservice markets, the only choice for understanding how to move forward, is to move forward. This is stated well by Govindarajan (2004): "Never is execution more important than when innovation is at the heart of a strategy. That is because innovation always involves treading into uncertain waters. And as uncertainty rises, the value of a well-thought-out strategy drops. In fact, when pursuing entirely new business models, no amount of research can resolve the critical unknowns. All that strategy can do is give you a plausible starting point. From there you must experiment, learn and adapt." Without this strategy, many efforts get struck with *analysis paralyses*, a condition that prevents any further action until all is known about the task at hand. These first-generation ecoservice markets have provided a plausible starting point, and some basic components. If these efforts are valued from that perspective, further evaluation can determine how these or the next ecoservice markets can adapt.

Open Dialogue

Ecoservice markets, such as the Nestlé-Vittel and New York City Regional Watershed examples, are unique in that the ecoservices being provided by the landscape and its management is a highly valued commodity whose property rights are distinct and identifiable. The land-management activities that provide this regulating ecoservice (water quality) can be identified to a high enough degree that negotiations that led to a contract have occurred. But these, too, were bilateral type of trades, and are costly and not considered a true market in which traditional commodities are traded with ease. It is not conceivable that these examples of ecoservice markets will exist in many other areas, except those that have a very definable geographically area and a very definable "commodity." In essence, these were nearly "perfect" conditions to make ecoservice trades. This model, therefore, is not a model that should be expected to be applied in a generic fashion. Perhaps the greatest applicable success of both the Nestlé-Vittel and the New York Regional Watershed examples were that the buyers of the ecoservices understood that the success of the negotiations was not just a financial solution. The Nestlé-Vittel experience illustrated that even with generous financial incentives and scientific knowledge, the success of the effort has as much to do with understanding farmers, establishing a permanent dialogue with them, and recognize their perspectives – not only in terms of farming practices but also in terms of life choices. The methodology used in this process was the key to success, not the funds injected into the program (Perrot-Maitre 2006). This same revelation also occurred in the New York City Regional Watershed project. The conclusion is that when the solution is beyond a dollar figure, dialogue must occur, and respect and trust must exist prior to effective dialogue. In these types of bilateral trading markets, the level of dialogue and respect may need to be higher than if the trades were conducted in a more commodity-type trading atmosphere, since, in those cases, the buyers and sellers do not usually know each other. But the lesson learned from these two relatively successful markets is that dialogue and respect should exist in the development stage of any ecoservice market to provide the foundation to define the ecoservice commodities and the processes "correctly."

Identify and Manage Transaction Costs

Transactions costs associated with trades are often viewed as the components of paperwork, verification, auditing, commissions, and other activities surrounding the sale of an item. A major set of transaction costs that are often overlooked are those associated with the creation and operation of markets. Costs of market creation include, among other things, defining property rights, setting up exchange systems, educating market participants, establishing monitoring and enforcement mechanisms, and building confidence in the system. Market operation includes costs of information gathering, negotiation, contract formulation, monitoring, and enforcement. These include:

- Ex-ante costs associated with obtaining relevant information needed to plan, negotiating agreements, making side-payments to gain agreement and communicating;

- Ex-post costs associated with monitoring performance, sanctioning and governance, re-negotiation when the original contract is unsatisfactory;

- Strategic costs associated with shirking, free-riding, and corruption.

Transaction costs are not only financial. Time and other in-kind contributions should be measured and, wherever possible, monetary values of these inputs calculated. In most economies, trades increase as transaction costs are decreased. The water-quality trading appears to have the most challenging transaction costs, but all the ecoservice markets are vulnerable to these costs to some degree. Separate ecoservice markets exasperate the obstacle of transaction costs. Trading in any market will not occur if the transaction costs exceed the benefits of a potential trade. Water-quality credit-trading programs that involve agriculture non-point-source pollution are characterized by higher transaction costs than programs involving point-source pollution only. They are higher because

steps are taken, there are numerous obstacles that can create inefficiencies or failures in the markets. The following are brief descriptions of those potential obstacles.

Valuation Process

An uncoordinated ecoservice-valuation process leads to miscommunication among potential participants. As in a commodity market, the price of one commodity carries so much information to allow the invisible hand to begin the process to allocate resources as long as the proper price "signal" is given. If multiple methods and processes are used for the valuation process, signals may get confusing.

Limited Professional Capacity

Due to immaturity of the markets, the available workforce has had limited time to gain the knowledge, skills, and abilities to conduct the activities that support the market components. Professional niches will need to be established to conduct activities that may be similar to other markets. Relationships between government and the various bio-economy factions will need to be developed.

Practice-based Contracts

The CCX, water-quality-trading markets, and the USDA incentive programs are generally practice-based rather than management-based outcomes. A practice-based process may be considered easier to account within the processes of each individual market, but it lacks the comprehensive perspective that is needed to demonstrate how ecoservices are generated and how agriculture operations function. An agriculture operation has a management strategy that consists of a menu of practices, but the management practices are used as needed and are not considered as absolute in any given year. It is understandable that these ecoservice markets find that multi-year practice-based contracts seem efficient, but a fully accessible carbon or water-quality market must function within a more complex interaction with agriculture-production realities.

Pursuing Permanence

Since ecoservices are produced by specific land-management activities, it is apparent that when these land activities change or stop so, too, would the quantity of ecoservices. This issue of permanence, depending how "permanence" is defined, is an issue for all ecoservices that involve land-management activities that are not in permanent easement or ownership of a government body. Instead of accounting for ecoservices as a permanent item, ecoservices may be viewed as a rate of effect.

Ecosystems are not static and neither are any of the land-management activities of agriculture.

Non-Contextual Supplies and Demands

Ecoservice markets that are not operating within the context of what the supply of the ecoservices is cannot determine the value of ecoservice in any sense of a typical economic system. Agro-ecosystems continually provide ecoservices that the markets are not aware of. Market-based systems that do not have access to an adequate amount of information are destined to have some level of failure, and the immature markets have limited capacity as well. Even the more mature markets, such as the centrally planned conservation economy, do not have the capacity to apply the ecoservices they purchase within an ecosystem context.

Lacking Landscape Knowledge

Broad-based information on how the landscape is being managed is required for watershed organizations to achieve goals, bio-refineries to understand their ecological impact, and ecoservice markets to evolve. Acquiring, compiling, and organizing this level of data may seem like a market luxury, but without this data, ecoservice markets cannot be integrated with either ecological or economic realities. Efficient markets are predicated on the basis that full information is available to buyers and sellers. The full information criterion requires that producers and consumers both know all relevant information about the product, including factors such as quantity, quality, time, and location of supply, price, and so on. Bhatia (2005) states that if you can't measure something, you really don't know much about it. If you don't know much about it, you can't control it. If you can't control it, you are at the mercy of chance.

Accounting for Additionality

Accounting for additionality is determining what ecoservice was generated for a specific trade and to be able to provide proof that those activities would not have occurred in the absence of that particular project investment. Morris (2009) states that if other ecosystem markets link-up with the carbon market on a piece of land, the landowners will likely need to show that actions that can earn other types of credits would not have occurred without additional investment. This requirement may significantly increase transaction costs as well as the cost of individual ecoservices.

Double-counting

Double-counting is the process of a landowner's attempt to obtain multiple revenue streams for the implementation of a singular activity. Morris

(2009) states that selling water-quality credits from land that is only being managed for carbon will not generate the correct incentives for landowners and will undercut the effectiveness of the water-quality market. The added value of different services must be established well enough to avoid multiple payments going to one specific type of action. This requirement may significantly increase transaction costs as well as the cost of individual ecoservices. For many transactions that involve non-monetary benefits, or indirect monetary benefits, it may be most advantageous for all market participants and beneficiaries to accept double-counting as a reasonable occurrence in an ecoservices market. If the transactions are succinct and transparent, the market purchasers would be able to create an effectual demand for their ecoservice at a cost less than the whole price. In effect, not allowing double-counting provides incentives for management activities that only provide singular ecoservices, or perhaps provides disincentives for management activities that provide multiple ecoservices.

Summary of Obstacles

Many of these first-generation ecoservice markets have experienced a low level of success beyond the actions of establishing various trading networks and managing some trades. That is probably not surprising when the list of obstacles is considered. But ecoservice markets can overcome these obstacles if a new perspective is applied. In the early 1990s, the Nestlé-Vittel circumstance had few real-world experiences to refer to when developing their ecoservice market. The entire program was essentially a "learning-by-doing" experiment, and it was the ability to "think outside the box" brought by the multidisciplinary team and the active participation of farmers in identifying and testing alternative practices that brought success to the experience (Perrot-Maitre 2006).

With these first-generation ecoservice market experiences and insights, the ecoservice box is much bigger, and stepping out of that box will allow an even greater ecoservice market potential to emerge. What may be learned is that ecoservice markets, such as water-quality trading, carbon trading, and habitat cannot accomplish what they desire on their own. That is, if their intentions are to improve the resource, they must co-exist and be closely coordinated with all other ecoservice markets. Developing these ecoservice markets in unison will demonstrate that several of the obstacles are not insurmountable and others have been artificially created.

Attributes of the Ideal Ecoservice Market

An ideal market for any good or service would contain attributes that allow the total economic value to be accounted for and distributed fairly. Neither free markets nor centrally planned economies of government agencies have demonstrated that those attributes can be supported independently. The ideal ecoservice market would combine the efficiency of the tree market while recognizing the economic externalities, a task often left to government regulations or centrally planned economies. The first-generation ecoservice markets attempted to bridge the valuation gap between the agro-economy and agro-ecology. The combined strategy of making this connection one ecoservice market at a time, each with individual processes and contracts dilutes the values, raises transaction costs, and causes a higher market-entrance burden to be placed on ecoservice producers.

To bridge this gap and address the obstacles, the ecological values of the economy and the economic values of the ecosystem must be correlated. In other words, human activities that improve the natural capital need to be valued and the natural capital itself must be valued. To construct the ideal ecoservice market the following attributes will be listed and briefly explained and are categorized by the attributes of valuation, logistical, process, and support.

Valuation Attributes

1. Transparent Valuation Process. An ideal market will allow the participants to determine the value of ecoservices under a system that is transparent to the buyers, sellers, brokers, and third-party verifiers. An ecoservice market cannot operate efficiently when the values of the ecoservices are determined within the context of a centrally planned market.

2. Rate and Mass Value Calculations . An ideal market would allow the calculation of ecoservices using both rates of production and mass determinations. Ecological and economic systems function in a cyclic manner that is often measured by rates of change, in addition to the ability to measure certain parameters by mass calculations.

3. Proximity Valuation. An ideal market would have the capacity to recognize the additional outcomes that are produced from land-management activities that are implemented in proximity to landscape features that generate additional outcomes. In other words, a native grass planting may generate more wildlife values if it is adjacent to a wetland complex rather than isolated from other features.

4. Multi-scale Valuations. An ideal market would allow the values generated by land-management activities to be expressed at the local, regional, national, and global scales, if the market deems that to be

an efficient process to distribute the costs and benefits of producing ecoservices.

5. Hierarchy of Values. Ecoservice values should be applicable to how the values are used. Industries, non-profits, government, and consumers may each have a different rationale for providing incentives for certain ecoservices. Some may be interested in sustainable production methods and others in tradable resource credits. Each requires a different level of precision that is needed to accommodate transactions and different levels of value. For example, meeting Walmart's "sustainability index" criteria may require certain land-management activities to occur, whereas making a water-quality trade between a point-source discharger and a non-point provider may require a precise measurement that is exclusive to that transaction.

6. Bundled Ecoservices. Land-management activities that produce one ecoservice often produce other ecoservices. Ideally, the market would be able to process each value separately and allow individual purchasers to participate. This would have two significant consequences. First, it would allow the ecoservice producers to market more ecoservices to more buyers. Second, it would allow the buyers to individually spend less to acquire the ecoservices since they would only need to provide a portion of the financial incentive needed to persuade a producer to conduct the activities that it took to create the ecoservice. Two types of bundled ecoservices are used, basket bundled ecoservices that can be separated, and merged bundles that are inseparable. While merged bundles do not permit services to be subdivided and sold individually, they offer a useful control on transaction costs. The basket approach is more sophisticated, permitting the sale of individual services to different purchasers. The result is likely to be a more efficient allocation of resources and higher returns to sellers (Landell-Mills 2002).

Logistical Attributes
1. Integrate Production Resource and Natural Resource Management. The ideal agro-ecoservice market would begin by recognizing the inseparable characteristics of production-resource management and natural-resource-management outcomes. The agro-economy's primary objective today is to provide abundant food, feed, fiber, and fuel stocks, and that will remain the primary objective even when the ideal ecoservice market is functioning. The difference is that in an integrated market both the positive (wildlife, cleaner water) and

negative (soil degradation, non-point-source pollution) externalities will be accounted for within the context of the value of the production outcomes.

2. Integrate Biomass, Bio-food and Bio-fuels Policies. An ideal ecoservice market would compel the natural resource policies associated with the production of agricultural products to be integrated whether they are fruits, vegetables, grains, or cellulose.

3. Direct Measurements. An ideal market would use techniques to directly measure the desired outcomes such as the gallons of water with identified characteristics, tons of soil created, number of ducklings hatched, tons of carbon sequestered, etc. These techniques could provide measurements with a high degree of reproducibility.

4. Precise Measurements. An ideal market would use techniques that measure the desired outcomes in a uniform manner that is reproducible to an acceptable degree.

5. Standardize Measurements. An ideal market would use standardized-measurement techniques for each parameter and these measurement techniques could be equally applied to the resource by the producer, broker, auditor, or buyer as long as each had the capacity and information to generate the measurement.

Process Attributes
1. Single Resource Assessment and Assurance Template. To reduce transaction costs and to provide a means to reduce the market-entry burden, a simplified resource-assessment template would be applied uniformly. This template would provide an identification and quantification of ecoservices that could be or are being provided and would be universally accepted by the various entities and valuation types.

2. Standardized Ecoservice Units. An ideal market would utilize ecoservice units that are standardized so that their scales would be coordinated. For example, a score of 50 for any particular ecoservice unit would mean that the quantity, rate of production, or quality of the parameters would correlate with other parameters.

3. Flexibility in Market Entrance and Exit. An ideal market would allow participants to enter and exit the markets in a fairly efficient

SECTION 2
ECOCOMMERCE COMPONENTS

CHAPTER 6

Generating Effectual Demand

Value of Use
Creating Value in Exchange
Identifying Marginal Ecoservice Values
Ecoservice Property Rights
Ecoservice Market Relationships
Trading Mechanisms
Trading Elements
Creating Effectual Demand

Ecoservice markets are emerging for the same reason any other market emerges: a scarcity of a resource increases the value of that resource in proportion to the producers and consumers. This then develops demand and motivates the production of that resource, and trade ensues. For these trades, there needs to be a method to process the transactions and to address the marketers' concerns. These ecoservice values also have to be associated with property rights for both parties to recognize and exchange values. Ecoservice values can be expressed in various manners and through various trading methods. Within these processes, the trading programs or markets must provide confidence that the transactions are fair and legitimate.

Perhaps the fundamental obstacle that has prevented ecoservice markets from emerging is the inability to measure ecoservices and its (negative externality) counterpart, non-point-source pollution. For this chapter, it will be assumed that ecoservice "units" are identifiable, standardized, and measurable. This critical aspect will be addressed in detail in Chapter 8.

Value of Use

As more economic participants are moving away from the misconception that ecoservices are infinitely available, ecoservices are moving from the category of "value of use" to "value in exchange." As Adam Smith (1952) observed, the word "value" has two meanings. The "value of use" is the things that have the greatest value in use and have frequently little or no value in exchange. On the contrary, those that have the greatest "value in exchange" have frequently little value in use. Nothing is more useful than water, but it will purchase scarce anything, Smith states. A diamond, on the contrary, has scarce any value of use, but a very great quantity of other goods may be exchanged for it.

Identifying ecoservice value is actually more complex than just identifying the provisional ecoservices that are generated by natural capital such as water and others. Smith understood the value of natural resources as he identified them as a significant source of the wealth for nations, but he may not have been able to envision the day that an economic system would be needed to convert things of "value of use" to "value in exchange." In many locations in the 18th century, there were water resources still available for the taking. It should be noted that a resource converted from "value of use" to "value in exchange" only changes how it is viewed economically as it still has the same ecological value and the same "value of use." Water was as important to life in the 18th century as it is today. Water, which in Smith's era "will purchase scarce anything," is now the source of several ecoservice markets. But ecoservices are defined as not just the provisional "thing" of clean water or abundant wildlife, but the regulating and supporting ecosystem processes and functions that continually provide these provisional "things." In the case of EcoCommerce, ecoservice "units" of value are those functions that are generating soil fertility, habitats for wildlife, and purifying air and water. As noted, this concept of ecoservice units is further elaborated in Chapter 8.

Creating Value in Exchange

Creating markets for this type of ecoservice units is no simple task. A key measure of a well-functioning market is how well it facilitates interaction between consumers and producers to improve the utility for both partners in the exchange, which involves much more than simply the sale of ecoservices (Ribaudo 2008). The challenge of ecoservice markets is determining the value of these ecoservices and to create the effectual demand that motivates people to generate additional ecoservices.

Effectual and Absolute Demand

An effectual demand is created when a sufficient price is applied toward a commodity to entice entrepreneurs to produce it. The effectual demand is different from the absolute demand, in that the absolute demand is the total demand whereas the effectual demand is only the portion of demand that has sufficient funds to entice the production of the commodity (Smith 1952). Historically, as it pertains to ecoservices, they may have or may not have been provided in a manner that meets the absolute demand, but the willingness or ability to pay was below the marginal cost of producing the ecoservice. Or more likely, there was not an economic system in place to be able to account for and assign value to the regulating ecoservices. If in the recent centuries and decades the ecological capacity to supply ecoservices has been reduced while the absolute demand has risen, then these ecoservices will become scarcer and the value of these ecoservices will presumably rise.

Market Equilibrium

If this scenario occurred with traditional goods and services, then this could be illustrated by Figure 6.1, the economic supply-demand graph. The demand has increased along with a diminishing capacity to supply and the two shifts cause the market equilibrium (E_1) to migrate to a new market equilibrium (E_2) at a new higher price (P_5 to P_7) providing the quantity (Q_5).

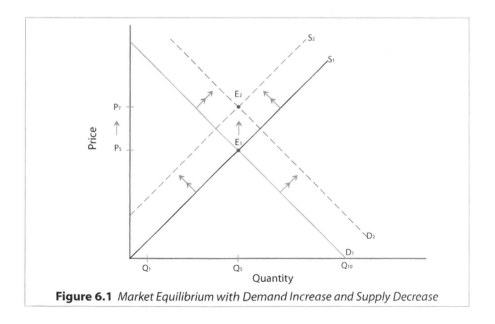

Figure 6.1 *Market Equilibrium with Demand Increase and Supply Decrease*

The creation of this new equilibrium is set by the increase in price. The same quantity is being produced but at a higher cost.

Ecoservice Market Disequilibrium

The great challenge with ecoservices is to instate a price that generates an effectual demand that motivates entrepreneurs to create a greater supply. Since demand for ecoservices is not elastic, that is there are no alternatives to them, demand is seldom reduced. With a growing population that is striving toward a higher standard of living, a reduction in the demand for ecoservices seems remote. Using an EcoCommerce graph to illustrate this, a reduction in the ecological capacity-to-supply and an increasing shift in economic demand (without price controls) would lead to the scenario in Figure 6.2.

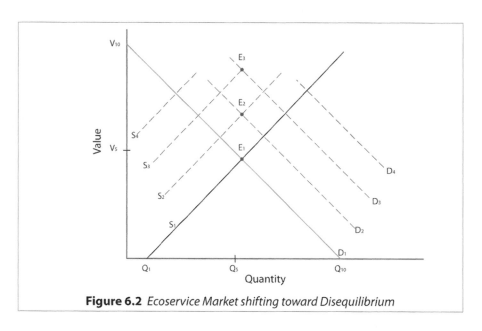

Figure 6.2 *Ecoservice Market shifting toward Disequilibrium*

In Figure 6.2, the economic-demand curve advances to the right (D_1, D_2, D_3, D_4) and the ecological-supply curve advances to the left (S_1, S_2, S_3, S_4). Since there isn't an applicable economic value, and because ecological and economic systems cannot interface, the scarcity of the ecoservices does not create a signal for the ecological-supply capacity to be increased or the economic demand to be decreased. In economic theory, the supply-and-demand curves always have a theoretical point-of-market equilibrium. But without the information and motivation for the market to strive toward a point of equilibrium, the economic demand curve could represent a greater quantity than the ecology's capacity-to-supply. The separation of the supply-and-demand curves would represent disequilibrium then can no longer seek a market-equilibrium point. This event may be nonsensical from an economic viewpoint, but it represents an advancing economic demand and a dwindling capacity of an ecosystem to supply. At point E_3, the demand of D_3 can be addressed by the supply of S_3. As the shifts move into the fourth stages of D_4 and S_4, the demands on the ecosystems are far greater than the ability, capacity, and "will" of the ecosystems to supply. A worst case scenario is an ecological collapse that would lead to a full or partial economic collapse or social upheaval. Even if a tremendous amount of financial capital would be available to the economy, it cannot create an effectual demand to generate an increase in supply if the capacity to supply no longer exists. An analogy to manmade capital would be if all the automobile factories burned down. No matter how much financial capital you apply to generate a demand, the capacity to supply does not exist. For this worst case scenario to be prevented, people and businesses would need to act outside their economic self-interests, significant macro-economic forces would need to be imposed, or ecoservice markets that can generate an audible market signal must exist. Of course, today's economy relies primarily on macro-economic forces to maintain the integrity of the ecology, although the ability of regulations, taxes, subsidies, and other macroeconomic forces to continue to maintain this into the future is in question. The ability of the government and other institutions to impose additional macroeconomic forces is also in question if the climate legislation is indicative of the trend. In summary, if the economy fails to convert a significant portion of the absolute demand for ecological services into an effectual demand, then the ultimate limits of the ecological systems will become known.

Absolute-Demand Effects
   A main feature of Figure 6.1 includes the market-equilibrium point. It is at that equilibrium point that no excess supply or unfulfilled demand occurs. A main feature of Figure 6.2 is that as demand increases, the capacity of the ecological system to supply ecoservices may decrease. Those occurrences in Figure 6.2 are somewhat related in that the capacity of the natural capital to produce is often diminished or consumed as ecoservices are used.
   To further illustrate the effect of an ecological market in disequilibrium, Figure 6.3 depicts the diminishing quantity of natural capital as an increasing amount of absolute demand (Demand$_{Ab}$) or consumption is applied toward it. In a traditional market economy, an absolute demand, less the effectual demand, would have little or no effect within the economy. Since absolute demand, less effectual demand, only exists as wants and not in their ability

to motivate others to produce goods, and therefore, the absolute-demand portion can be ignored by the economic system. In an ecological system, absolute demands are often appeased by access to water, air, habitat, and other features that are considered rights by many. As absolute demand increases, as it may do with a growing population, the ecological capacity and the supply of ecoservices may also diminish.

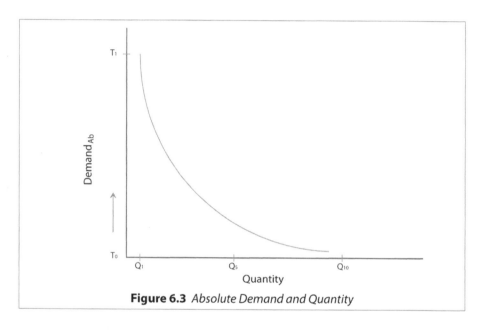

Figure 6.3 *Absolute Demand and Quantity*

Figure 6.3 illustrates the simple scenario of the reduction in natural capital or ecoservices as the absolute demand increases. In this scenario, the line approaches near zero as time passes, as it implies an increase in population and the standards of living.

Instating Effectual Demand
If the intentions of EcoCommerce are to instate a value on ecoservices, then applying EcoCommerce to Figure 6.3 should have an economic and ecological effect as depicted in Figure 6.4. At T_1, EcoCommerce begins and allows an effectual demand to be applied toward ecoservices generating a willingness-to-supply using a certain land-management strategy that, in turn, generates ecoservices. The $Demand_{Ab}$ portion is the scenario without price but with participants having access to the ecoservices. The $Demand_{Ef}$ (effectual demand) portion of the graph is where price is applied and the resulting curve resembles a more traditional economic-supply curve (S_1). $Demand_{Ef}$ is price and S_1 is, in this case, a quantity supplied that will increase with an increasing price. Instating EcoCommerce or an ecoservice market

within the economic activities that impacts the natural capital would cause a market signal and a response toward a generation of ecoservices.

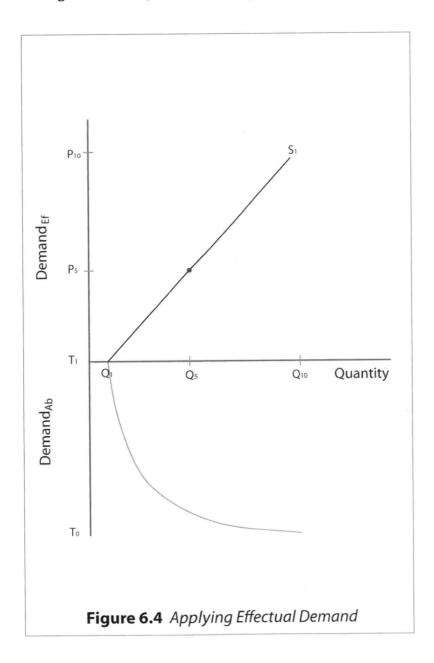

Figure 6.4 *Applying Effectual Demand*

Applying Effectual Demand

A challenge of applying an effectual demand toward ecoservices is determining at what level of landscape management the incentives should be applied. Ecoservice markets are unique from traditional economic markets because, even without an effectual demand, agro-ecological landscapes will sequester carbon, water will be transpired and cleansed, and soil microbes will provide nutrient cycling; all are positive externalities. As long as these ecosystem functions and processes occur at a level that appeases absolute demand, no effectual demand needs to be expressed. For example, if a watershed provides an adequate supply of water to a river and that river can naturally assimilate all the pollution that is being discharged into it, then it could be stated that those ecosystem functions and processes are in equilibrium with the level of demand. This could be illustrated by the EcoCommerce graph in Figure 6.5 with the center point (E_1) representing the equilibrium between the quantity (Q_5) of clean water and a presumed value. If the amount of water that is shed into the river is reduced, then the capacity of the river to supply an assimilation function is also reduced. This is shown by the shift in the supply curve to the left ($S_0 - S_1$). If it is presumed that the demand (pollution assimilation) remains the same, then a reduction in a quantity of clean water to Q_3 would occur, resulting in a supply shortage of Q_2. If the amount of pollution that is being discharged into the river is increased, then the demand on the river to assimilate pollution is increased. This is shown in Figure 6.6 by the shift in the demand curve to the right ($D_0 - D_1$). If the water supply does not increase, then an increase in demand for pollution assimilation would increase from Q_5 to Q_7 resulting in a demand excess of Q_2.

To bring that river system back into equilibrium, the river's capacity to supply an assimilation function needs to be increased (more or cleaner water) or the demand on the river's assimilation capacity needs to be decreased (less pollution) or a combination of these effects that could bring the equilibrium to Q_5.

Box 6.1 Odum's Thoughts on Integrating Ecology and the Humanities

In the two scenarios described (in Figures 6.4 and 6.5) the EcoCommerce graphs represent the relationship between the ecological (natural economy) capacity to supply and the combined demand (ecological and economical). According to Odum (1971), understanding these relationships is essential for humankind. He stated that success or failure in applying the principles of ecology for the benefit of man may depend not so much on technology and environmental science, but on economics, law, politics, planning, and other areas in the humanities that have had very little ecological input. It is man the geological agent, not so much man the animal, who is too much under the influence of positive feedback, and therefore, must be subject to negative feedback. The positive feedback involved with the expansion of knowledge, power, and productivity threatens the quality of human life and will continue to do so unless adequate negative feedback controls can be found.

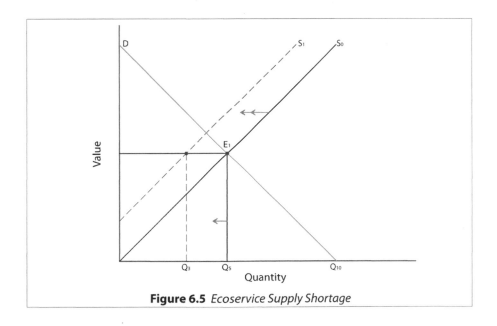

Figure 6.5 *Ecoservice Supply Shortage*

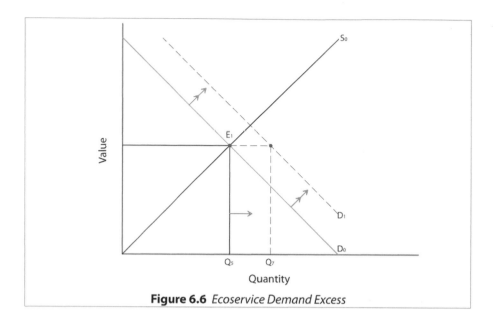

Figure 6.6 *Ecoservice Demand Excess*

This is a challenging aspect for ecoservice markets. To be efficient, an effectual demand needs to be expressed so land managers create the circumstances for the watershed to deliver more water to the river and less pollution. This will cause an increase in the river's assimilation capacity and a decrease in the demand on the river. In essence, the intention of the ecoservice market would be to reverse the arrows on Figures 6.5 and 6.6 and increase the river's capacity to process and assimilate a quantity of pollution to provide a quantity (Q_5) of clean water. To identify that point, landscape intelligence (explained in detail in Chapter 9) must be available. Without landscape intelligence, ecoservice markets may be vulnerable to pay for all resource-management activities with no regard to a baseline management. If individual and uncoordinated ecoservice markets do demand a baseline, but do not develop a comprehensive landscape-intelligence system, then each market's objectives may be not coordinated with the activities of the other land managers and markets within the particular ecosystem that is being addressed. For ecoservice markets to be efficient, they will conduct transactions that return the river system to a point that it is in an ecological equilibrium at the ecoservice market clearing price. The ecoservice markets have to "know" when that occurs, to what degree, and allow the market to find out what the marginal costs are to produce these ecoservices.

Box 6.2 Ecoservice Market Baseline Management and TMDL Background Levels

As mentioned, a challenge to ecoservice markets is to determine what minimum level of landscape management should be considered as a market-entry point and for ecoservices payment. This is somewhat related to the TMDL challenge of determining what the natural background levels of certain pollutants are. Nutrients, of course, naturally cycle through the river systems and some nutrient level would exist regardless of land-management activities. A TMDL plan that states that nutrient levels must be reduced below the natural background level is not economically or ecologically feasible. Agreeing to an accepted natural background level is a point of contention in TMDL plan development as opposing sides of the debate benefit from different standards, and water-quality analysis to determine natural background levels prior to European settlement did not occur. Agreeing to a baseline of land management that allows entry into an ecoservice market is a slightly different scenario. Rather than a regulatory framework to determine the standard, a market-based framework is used. In this manner, it may be less contentious, as the standard does not force someone to do something, but gives them the option to determine if certain land- management activities can be integrated within their production plan of the operation at a reasonable cost and benefit.

Identifying Marginal Ecoservice Values

The carbon-and-water-quality-trading markets of today are attempting to develop an effectual demand while having little knowledge of what is currently being provided by the agro-ecosystems. Government programs, policies, and regulations have also created an effectual demand—that is, enticed the production of ecoservices. However, the mechanisms used may or may not have been very efficient because there is not a process within the transaction that generates the information to determine the marginal value in relation to the marginal cost. Perhaps the Conservation Reserve Program with the use of Environmental Benefits Index and a price-bidding process has a higher enough level of maturity that allows land managers and the USDA to come near to a market-clearing price. Beyond this government program, the ecoservices that are currently being provided are done so, somewhat coincidently, within the context of the agro-economy and commodity-production outcomes. These ecoservices fall under the category of positive economic externalities and are part of the agriculture landscape, both literally and economically. But due to the lack of ecoservice units and pricing, this information is hidden and the market has no knowledge of the quantity of ecoservices being generated. This knowledge is important, because generating an effectual demand without having an understanding of what ecoservices are being provided will create a market that inefficiently allocates resources. In other words, we may pay too much and get too little for it or vice versa. In either case, the markets become unsustainable.

To be efficient, this effectual demand must provide payment, not to the total ecoservice value generated by the ecosystems, but to the additional value generated above an ecological threshold. To properly identify this marginal value, the ecoservice inventory on the landscape is needed. An ecoservice inventory could only be generated by having the landscape intelligence that describes the landscape characteristics and management strategies. This type of database would be based on consistent and extensive data, rather than focusing on exact data, as the immeasurable nature of ecoservices will not allow that to happen. But a "reasonable" attempt to collect this information as a starting point will be necessary. Without "agro-ecosystem intelligence," that is data on what ecoservices are being produced, markets can only operate in the dark on what is needed. This would result in a low level of confidence in all aspects of the market. If ecoservice markets are based on a regulatory framework without landscape intelligence, they become politically fragile. As regulations change, are challenged, or are adjusted, market stakeholders sense their values can evaporate quickly.

This is where the ecoservice markets are now. Establishing "agro-ecosystem intelligence" has the potential to allow the market to value resource-management outcomes that are woven into the economy. For this to occur, a comprehensive EcoCommerce structure is needed that is accountable to an ecoservice inventory and can transform agriculture's environmental liabilities into ecological assets. It is only under these circumstances that the agriculture community can effectively engage in the ecoservice markets. To expect participation by any other means other than economic engagement, is expecting a new paradigm in socio-economic interaction other than one's self-interests and the invisible hand. Agriculture, as a whole, has never consciously provided ecoservices in regard to an agro-economic system, but ecoservices have been provided, *ad hoc*, in response to an economic system that has demanded provisional ecoservices. The expanse of haying, grazing, and small grains in the middle of the 20th century was the result of the political and economic systems, just as corn and soybeans across the nation and world is in response to those same systems. These different sets and levels of ecoservices produced by these two types of farming systems are primarily the result of economic decisions, set in motion, in part, by political decisions. The provisional ecoservices of the agro-economy in the mid-20th century were generated by a broader mix of perennials within a more diverse crop rotation. Likewise, so were the regulating ecoservices. The rate and quantity of those provisional ecoservices were tabulated using bushels, pounds, tons, and bales. No organized effort existed to account for the regulating ecoservices that were produced. As we fast forward to the 21st century, the provisional ecoservices are generated using fewer perennial systems with a crop rotation that is much less diverse. Likewise, the regulating ecoservices are produced under this agro-ecological system. No organized effort exists to account for the regulating ecoservices produced.

To create a market-driven "value in exchange," an organized effort to account for the regulating ecoservices that are being provided by the agro-ecological landscape must be created. The ability to obtain a reasonable level of landscape intelligence is not as remote as it initially appears. These agro-ecosystems are fairly well mapped out as it pertains to soil, topography, and land use, and determining the general quantities of ecoservices that are being generated is actually a relatively reasonable task. Nearly every acre of farmland in the United States has landscape-production intelligence verified each year by the USDA Farm Service Agency, and this data is then analyzed by the public and private sector to determine the production level of provisional ecoservices. The free market digests this information, and the invisible hand guides producers, buyers, and sellers. This system is applicable to determining production of regulating ecoservices and is explained in further detail in Chapter 9.

Ecoservice Property Rights

To be exchanged for value, the ecoservice unit must be owned. This ownership must be recognized by government institutions and their courts of law. This ownership issue is often cited as the reason that ecoservice market cannot or will not emerge. Without recognized property rights and access to markets, assets become "dead capital" unable to generate returns over and above that associated with their direct use. This ownership issue arises because ecoservices have the characteristics of being defined as a "public good" rather than a "private good." Public goods lack of a clear definition and allocation rights (Lindell-Mills 2002).

Public goods are a special class of externalities distinguished by their non-excludability and non-rivalry. Non-excludability means that consumers cannot be prevented from enjoying the good or service in question, even if

ecoservices provide the foundation for this trend.

What Ruhl confirms about the legalities of ecoservices is that the concern is not who owns the land where the natural capital produces the services or the land where the benefits are enjoyed —that is usually perfectly clear—but rather what the respective owners can do with their property and can reasonably expect of each other in return. Defining the relationship between property owners is the far more complex aspect of any property system. And in the domain of law, any question of relationship between people is ripe for developing a set of rules and liabilities designed to lead to desired behavioral outcomes.

Ecoservice Market Relationships

It is apparent that ecoservices have unique aspects that have prevented functioning and open ecoservice markets to emerge. Consequently, the relationships that are needed or that could be developed in an ecoservice market to secure value will also be unique. Direct monetary incentives are often the first type of value that individuals associate with any transaction, but for ecoservice markets to be successful, transactions with various types of values and relationships between parties will be needed. There are five ecoservice market valuation types that vary with market relationships.

Monetary Payment

In this case, the market is created by a buyer placing a sufficiently high value on the ecoservice. These consist of monetary benefits provided to producers that meet predetermined outcomes. Examples could include the New York City Regional Watershed market, the Nestlé-Vittel water bottling business, the USDA Conservation Stewardship Program, or state or local stewardship tax breaks.

Resource-Credit Trading

In these cases, the demand for ecoservices is created by a regulatory structure that states a certain threshold must be met. These consist of monetary benefits that are paid by one party to another party to mitigate discharges. Transactions may occur in water-quality-trading markets where a water-treatment plant trades pollution credits with an agriculture operation. This also occurs in GHG markets where corporations that emit GHGs trade with agricultural producers or other entities that sequester carbon.

Regulatory Assurance/Compliance Protection

These cases are created by the demand that is articulated through a regulatory structure similar to credit trading. These consist of non-monetary benefits, but provide the producer with the knowledge that their operation meets the goals of the regulatory agency. Examples could include EPA's TMDLs, USDA Farm Bill conservation-compliance provision, feedlot permit provisions, or a local watershed district's land-use planning criteria such as an environmental-impact statement.

Market Access/Participatory Benefits

These cases consist of access and recognition benefits and provide the opportunity for producers to be eligible to access markets or gain prestige. Examples could include meeting sustainability criteria such as the Walmart Sustainability Initiative, providing biomass by meeting a bio-refinery's cellulosic production standards, recognition from an agricultural industry, or selling corn to an ethanol plant with a carbon-footprint reduction goal.

Liability Protection

This consists of immunity benefits such as acquiring some level of protection from suits brought by private parties under state or federal environmental statutes, or a monetary benefit through the reduction of environmental liability or crop-production insurance premiums.

Any of these relationships and exchanges could occur independently from each other or in conjunction with other values. For example, an insurance company may provide a rebate on the premium if the farm-management plan produces ecoservices that reduce the potential of a fish kill occurring. This same resource-management strategy may also meet a government incentive program, allow the producer to meet a bio-refineries' sustainable criteria, or make the producer eligible to participate in the CCX carbon trades or a water-quality-trading program. Applying these resource-management outcomes toward multiple valuations and market relationships may be, at face value, considered a detriment to a successful ecoservice market or even considered that ecoservice producers are "double-dipping" and are receiving too much value in exchange for their ecoservices. But with a transparent and open market system, allowing ecoservice producers to engage in commerce with multiple relationships will cause greater market efficiency. This efficiency will be created as those purchasing ecoservices will not have to pay the "whole value of rent, labor and profit," but only the portion that is not being paid by the other market participants.

In each of these types of market relationships, resource-management goals or ecoservice commodity(s) can be identified along with the stated value whether that is monetary or non-monetary. These values can then be exchanged using predominantly six trading mechanisms.

Trading Mechanisms

Once the ecoservice right has been established and an incentive has been identified, a transaction can occur to exchange values. Depending on the valuation type that the ecoservice provided, the following market mechanisms can be applied to transactions. A combination of these trading mechanisms can be applied toward a singular transaction.

Bilateral Agreements

These agreements are where buyers and sellers directly interact to carry out a transaction through voluntary contractual agreement with property rights and enforceable contracts as clear key elements (Nguyen 2006). These deals tend to emerge when transaction costs hinder private initiatives, for example, involving numerous small landholders or when the private parties lack the authority to implement plans. For example, payments by Nestlé-Vittel to upstream landowners for improved land-use include individual negotiations to obtain the desired level of ecoservices (Perrot-Maitre 2006). The vast majority of ecoservice markets function in this manner rather than an open market.

Public-Payment Arrangements

These arrangements involve resource-incentive payments by governments to either encourage or discourage certain activity. For example, farmers may receive annual payments to install a grassed buffer or, as in the New York City Regional Watershed effort, the farmers received financial support for nutrient-management plans. The USDA Conservation Stewardship Program provides payment to farmers who meet a management threshold. The difference in these examples is that the first two focus on cost of individual practices and the CSP attempts to pay for outcomes based on a spreadsheet-type questionnaire.

Tax Credits

These credits involve reducing the tax liability of an ecoservice producer in lieu of public payment. The benefits of this transaction depend on the level of tax credit in relation to the conservation payment and the tax-rate implications. An example is tax deduction for taxpayers who take voluntary measures to aid in the recovery of species that are either listed as threatened or endangered under the Endangered Species Act (Nickerson 2009) or forest owners who adopt a forest stewardship plan and receive a tax rebate in return.

Clearinghouse

This mechanism provides facilitation or a third-party broker that acts as an intermediary between those that generate credits and those that demand credits (Nguyen 2008)

Sole-source
This mechanism is used as offsets in which trading per se does not take place, but emitters are given the opportunity to find alternative ways of reducing their environmental impact.

Market-style Trading
This mechanism is based on standardized units and large number of buyers and sellers. Open trading schemes are created by the government when it establishes caps or targets on ecoservices and pollutants. Although the caps are regulatory in nature, they create a market mechanism. The imposed caps create a new market for trading allocated quotas, whereby an entity that exceeds the quota may purchase additional quota rights from an entity that has a surplus quota. Examples include wetland banking in the United States, and carbon emission off-set markets. Market-style trading could occur within an industry or business. If a corn-ethanol processing plant required that the corn used by the processor must meet some production standards (a cap in a sense) then corn producers may be able to trade ecoservice units to meet the processor's overall production standards.

In any of the markets described, the trade of these ecoservices may be established by using performance-based criteria, (e .g. direct or indirect measurements) or activity-based criteria, (e .g. changes in practices) that have an expected effect on water quality [or ecoservices] (King 2003).

Trading Elements

With property rights, incentives menu, and trading mechanisms established, certain trading-program elements must be contained within the market to maintain its credibility and success. The EPA (2003) lists the following elements to be used for water-quality trading and could be utilized for other ecoservice markets:

1. Clear legal authority and mechanisms;

2. Clearly defined units of trade. Pollutant-specific credits are examples of tradable units for water-quality trading. These may be expressed in rates or mass per unit time as appropriate to be consistent with the related time periods;

3. Creation and duration of credits. Credits should be generated

before or during the same period they are used to comply with a monthly, seasonal, or annual period. Credits may be generated as long as the pollution controls or management practices are functioning as expected;

4. Quantifying credits and addressing uncertainty. Standardized protocols are necessary to quantify pollutant loads, load reductions, ecoservices, and credits. (Where trading NPS pollution, methods should account for the greater uncertainty in estimates of NPS pollution loads, see Box 5.1);

5. Compliance and enforcement provisions. Mechanisms for determining and ensuring compliance are essential for all trades and trading programs;

6. Public participation and access to information. Information related to trading, prices, credit generation, and other data related to the trades should be available electronically and to the public. This information is necessary to identify opportunities, to allow easy aggregation of credits, to reduce transaction costs, and to establish public credibility;

7. Periodic assessments of environmental and economic effectiveness should be conducted to include ambient conditions and costs associated with the trades.

Creating Effectual Demand

As stated earlier in the chapter, "creating markets for the ecoservice units is no simple task" as one of the primary issues is how to create an effectual demand for ecoservices that have never had a market much beyond government programs. Ecoservices have been supplied relatively "free" to the public, and the public has often assumed that ecosystems will meet an always-present absolute demand. Moving the economy from a point that ecosystem services are not even acknowledged to a point that costs and benefits are applied is a significant step. This step can be taken if buyers are compelled to bring forth a sufficient value. This value (money, market access, tax credits, regulatory assurance) must be significant to generate an effectual demand, and, for the markets to sustain themselves, the transactions and their costs must be manageable and transparent. To develop an ecoservice market, units and prices of ecoservice must lead to a commoditization of ecoservices. For a commodity market to function, data must be available and data sets must be manageable. And because ecoservices are spatially bound, the agro-ecological landscape must be understood to a high enough degree to generate confidence in the market. Ecoservice units must be assessed and accessible via a smart ecoservice-assessment process.

CHAPTER 7

A "Smart" Ecoservice Assessment

Resource-Assessment Types
Resource-Assessment Attributes
Building a "Smart" Agro-Ecological Assessment
EcoCommerce-Assessment Approach

The essence of any market is, of course, the item or commodity that is being exchanged and how that commodity is quantified. And as Hayek stated, the commodity and its market becomes a "marvel" because this one indicator, the market price of a commodity, spontaneously carries so much information that it guides buyers and sellers to make decisions that help both obtain what they want (Gwarty 2005). Of course, this "marvel" is much easier to create when the commodity can be directly measured in pounds, gallons, or acre-feet. Ecoservices and diffuse sources of pollution cannot be measured with any accuracy in quantity or in relation to their sources. As mentioned previously, this has been one of the primary reasons that ecoservice markets do not function at an adequate level. So to move ecoservice markets forward, a reasonable surrogate is needed that can assess the status of the resources and a method to assess how land-management activities impact the resources. Ideally, the assessment process would generate a similar outcome as the price of a measured commodity, in that the assessment becomes a "marvel" and carries enough information that it guides buyers and sellers to make decisions that help them both obtain what they want.

Resource-Assessment Types

The four assessment types or approaches listed provide varying degrees of information related to the condition or status of the resource.

These assessment types can be used singularly or in combination (multi-method) if the data is applicable. During the Millennium Ecosystem Assessment (2003) project, these types were identified as a means to assess the global state of resources. Understanding the state of resources is a primary objective of an assessment, but an assessment should also be applicable throughout the ecoservice market to integrate the process and make efficient use of the information. The information gathered from an assessment is the source of the market "marvel" as it brings key information as to how ecoservices may be valued.

Remote Sensing
      The use of satellite, aerial photographs, or LiDar (Light Detection and Ranging) can assess the condition or existence of land use or land-use responses such as the extent of forest cover and cropland, or the level of productivity of those land uses. LiDar is a remote-sensing system used to collect topographic data. This technology is being used by the National Oceanic and Atmospheric Administration (NOAA) and NASA scientists to document topographic landscape changes. These data are collected with aircraft-mounted lasers capable of recording elevation measurements at a rate of 2,000 to 5,000 pulses per second and have a vertical precision of 15 centimeters (six inches). After a baseline data set has been created, follow-up flights can be used to detect landscape changes (NOAA 2010). All remote-sensing techniques are useful for covering large tracts of land and can determine physical states as well as bio-physical and chemical functions such as evapo-transpiration and photosynthetic rates. An example of such use was conducted by Thoma and Gupta (2005) to quantify sediment sources in relation to upland versus riverbank erosion. Detailed topographical data can be collected on an annual basis and compared.

Geographical-Information Systems
      Geographical-Information Systems (GIS) is any system that captures, stores, analyzes, manages, and presents data that are linked to location. Technically, a GIS is a system that includes mapping software and its application to remote sensing, land surveying, aerial photography, mathematics, geography, and tools that can be implemented with GIS software that spatially maps and analyzes digitized data. This software can analyze temporal changes in ecosystems that correlate trends in ecoservices with land-use changes. These data maps can also overlay social and economic information with the ecosystem information.

Ecological Models
      Ecological models are simplified mathematical expressions that

represent the complex interactions between physical, biological, and socioeconomic elements of ecosystems They can be developed at different scales, for different ecoservices, and for differing time frames. These models can quantify the effects of management decisions on the condition of ecoservices and can project long-term effects of changes in ecosystems. Watershed models and agricultural-management indices are examples of ecologic modeling. Agricultural-management indices are a core component of EcoCommerce and will be explained in further detail in the next chapter. In brief, the calculations are based on site-specific static characteristics such as soil type, topography, and climate as well as how management strategies can affect the resource outcomes. The outcomes may include the condition of the soil, the quality of the water, the amount of carbon sequestered, and the potential for wildlife.

Participatory Approaches

This method relies on stakeholder groups, resource managers, agro-ecological professionals, and scientific experts to supply resource information. It can be highly valuable as this approach collects knowledge not currently available in scientific literature and community. This information adds new perspectives, knowledge, and value to the assessments. The participatory approach is also the most challenging as there may be significant diversity in the capacity of the individuals supplying the information. All assessment systems must be funded in some manner, and the participatory approach, by nature, often involves the largest number of people, and therefore, often the most costly of the four approaches described.

Multiple-method Approach

These assessment-approach options can also be combined with each other to provide a more extensive measurement and analytical system. For example, the participatory approach could include gathering information from farmers on how they manage their production and natural resources. If this information is consciously gathered to be incorporated in ecological models, then both farm and watershed-scale assessments may be able to be completed. Both GIS and remote sensing could complement these initial participatory assessments.

Resource-Assessment Attributes

The Millennium Ecosystem Assessment project also stated that a good assessment must be scientifically credible, politically legitimate, and useful for responding to the needs of decision makers. If these attributes are combined with the intentions of building an enduring process for assessing, planning, and implementing management activities to address resource concerns, then an intelligent ecoservice marketplace may emerge.

An assessment process should include five key attributes (MEA 2003):

- Proper scale and scalable data

- A flexible framework

- Knowledge generated for multiple stakeholders in the assessment process

- An ability to create resource-management capacity with the population

- An ability to apply the assessment in multiple manners

Assessment Scale

It may seem to be an obvious statement, but the scale of the assessment must be applicable to the scale that improvement is desired and within the scale that the ecoservice market must function. A multi-scale approach (farm, watershed, region) will focus assessment findings on the needs of decision makers at the scale of each component assessment. A regional-scale report may be more a cost-effective level of effort and relevant to regional or national decision-makers, but it will not necessarily speak to stakeholders interested in a more local scale. For assessments to be meaningful to local decision makers, assessment approaches that gather their perspectives and identify their issues may have to be adopted.

Since there are multiple scales over which ecological processes take place, and there are multiple scales over which ecosystem-management decisions are made, there can never be a single "correct" scale at which to conduct an assessment. But the least "correct" scale is one that creates a mismatch between the assessment scale and management scale, in that the information is not applicable to scale that the resource management decisions are going to be made. (MEA 2003).

The choice of scale for an assessment is not politically neutral, because that selection may intentionally or unintentionally privilege certain groups. The adoption of a particular assessment scale limits the types of problems that can be addressed, how they are expressed, and what types of generalizations are likely to be used in analysis. For example, users of a global assessment of ecosystem services would be interested in some issues such as carbon sequestration on a biome-level scale that may be of relatively little interest to users of a local assessment.

Incorporating multiple assessments in a single process may provide a balance to the various approaches and could help mitigate potential structural biases associated with the choice of scales. For example, an assessment conducted at the national level may or may not be as useful to local people as an assessment conducted at the local level. The unique contribution of the multi-scale framework is that it enables the use of multiple knowledge systems, including knowledge held by resource users, practitioners, decision makers, and researchers. Ideally, local knowledge that creates locally relevant information for both markets and implementation could be added or scaled up to higher levels of assessments.

Assessment Flexibility

Resource conditions and resource managers' needs are not static, even over short time periods. Therefore, resource assessments need to provide opportunities for users to engage with the assessment at regular intervals to accommodate this dynamic process and to re-assess user needs as necessary. Irrespective of how carefully an assessment is designed, new information, technologies, or changes in objectives will emerge that will require the assessment to be flexible in adapting to these changes. The need for active user engagement increases as assessments become more fine-grained and are more intimately involved with the needs, aspirations, and dynamics of local communities. This process of user engagement is also extremely time-consuming and resource-intensive, but local assessments are important sources of innovation in that they prompt new analytical tools and new institutional-response mechanisms (MEA 2003).

The experience with local assessments emphasized the need for tools and approaches to deal with issues at widely differing scales, as well as for integrating across scales. The MEA findings also suggest that it is feasible to develop analytical methods that not only are consistent with the goals of a multi-scale assessment, but that it can also significantly enhance the multi-scale assessment process over space and time.

Assessment Knowledge

The MEA (2003) explicitly valued local-level knowledge and recognized that local and traditional ecological knowledge provides information that is often not documented by the science community. In the agro-ecosystem, this local-level knowledge would consist of daily and seasonal activities that may impact the resources, or historic data that does not have a formal repository. The assessment should also be designed to be policy-relevant and operated on the premise that assessments should be conducted at the level where decisions are made. The assessment should empower local resource users through the assessment process itself. By linking local and traditional ecological knowledge to decision-making at higher levels, land managers will have a well-informed opinion on the processes. The gain in knowledge should consist of bringing local resource-management information into the assessment process, and, in exchange, the local resource managers will gain insight into the objectives and goals of the regional and national decision-makers.

Creating Capacity

Since assessing is doing, and doing is learning, those who participate will naturally gain some knowledge in the process. A farmer and their advisors who assess the soil and water resources on the farm operation will gain knowledge that benefits himself as well as a watershed manager. While that has value in itself, the assessment and the new knowledge should also generate a level of capacity that allows the farmer to conduct resource-management activities to reach the local and regional goals (MEA 2003). The assessments must also compel the development of the knowledge, skills, and abilities needed by the local participants to implement the management strategies that produce the desired ecoservices. The resource-assessment process must build the many skills to implement resource improvements, but also to fill the niches that will be created by the market to market the resource outcomes.

Assessment Applicability

A challenge for all local assessments is to conduct an integrated assessment with a focus on both ecosystems and human well-being, and communicating the results to a set of users prepared to use the findings that are relevant to them. This requires a multidisciplinary team and a governance structure to integrate the findings from different fields. The MEA (2003) learned that ideally, assessments would have met the needs of local users, while at the same time enabling those analyzing the data at larger scales to locate the interactions among the components of the global assessments and various sociopolitical and environmental contexts. This could be translated that an ideal assessment process would be completed by local decision makers, and that the information generated could be useable and compatible at the scales that other decision makers desired. An assessment should create data and knowledge that allows well-informed decisions to be made. This process must have a well-defined framework that is flexible enough so that, as innovation in assessment techniques and ecoservice knowledge is increased, these benefits can be incorporated into the process to allow a natural evolution of the assessment process to occur.

Building a "Smart" Agro-Ecological Assessment

A smart assessment implies that the assessment process and product accomplish much more than communicating the condition of a resource. Since an assessment can be an extensive and expensive process that relies on human, technical, and informational resources, it should also be considered as a means to achieving the overall ecoservice market or sustainability objectives. Resource assessments are far too expensive to have just the single result of the knowledge of the condition of that resource in that particular moment in time. The assessment should be transferable to the various scales and phases of assessment, planning, assurance, and valuation.

In evaluating the key attributes of an assessment from an agro-ecosystem perspective, the following components emerged as a foundation for a smart assessment. A smart agro-ecosystem assessment would consist of stating the condition of the resource, communicating the resource condition to multiple stakeholders, providing a basis of a plan to improve the resources, measuring the resource benefit of the activities, and being used as a valuation foundation. When utilizing these attributes, the resource manager would gain the knowledge and capacity to improve the resources or meet a particular ecoservice market goal. To create a smart assessment it was necessary to integrate the assessment types mentioned earlier in the chapter.

The "participatory approach" is considered an essential component of the foundation for a smart assessment due to its ability to bring new information to the scientific, government, or economic community. This information is not attainable by any other means as it is generated by the land-management activities of the farmers and land managers. The effect of these land-management activities are directly related to the context in which these activities and practices are applied. Soil types, topography, and climate are non-controllable variables that affect the ecoservice outcomes that are further influenced by variables included within the menu of activities that farmers apply depending on the cropping system. To capture the effect of these site-specific variables, the "ecological model" is also used. A large number of ecological models have been created for the various levels of ecological function. For a farmer, land-management indices developed and used by the USDA, universities, and institutions are often based on site-specific resource data and allow for detailed cropping-system inputs. This data can be compiled and used to analyze resource outcomes at scales larger than the farm.

This database naturally lends itself to be incorporated into a geographical-information system that can correlate the assessment outcomes in a spatial and temporal format. This spatial database can then be compared, or even validated under some circumstances, using remote-sensing techniques. This combination approach was chosen as it meets many of the positive attributes sought by the MEA for an assessment process, it integrates very well within the production aspect of the agro-ecology system, and its components were developed and accepted by government and land grant universities. The core of the assessment is the use of agriculture-management indices, which are described in more detail in the next chapter. When these indices and ecological models are applied to an agro-ecosystem, they can deliver the following values.

New Knowledge

Information that has not previously been made available to the scientific community or any community could become available. The USDA currently acquires extensive crop-management information from farms in the United States through a process that certifies the type and quantity of crops planted. It does not acquire information on the resource-management strategies used to produce those crops such as their tillage practices. An ecoservice market would not necessarily want to know how many times and when a farmer cultivated a corn field, but it would want to know what ecoservices were generated as the direct result of land-management activities.

Multi-scale Capabilities

It utilizes assessment processes developed by regional and national institutions and applied at the local level. Agricultural-management indices have been developed by the USDA, land-grant universities, and institutions to provide resource managers a method to account for their management strategies. Local resource professionals can acquire the skills to utilize these ecological models, and the results can be recognized by entities at multiple government and institutional levels and often can be applied at multiple geographical scales.

Address Local Concerns

The indices are based on the local resource base and the local resource-management activities and can be efficiently integrated within the agricultural-production systems. This integration allows the collection of this local and extensive data set to be done relatively cost-effective by a trusted, professional workforce currently employed and knowledgeable in the agricultural community. By using a local assessment process, local ownership in the process will allow their concerns to be addressed.

Increase Local Capacity

The assessment process provides a significant amount of information needed to develop a site-specific resource-management plan and communicates the resource status and plan in a succinct and transparent manner. This collection process increases the local capacity for implementing the necessary practices and activities that will be needed to improve the resource base and market the ecoservice.

Flexible Process

Since these indices use basic resource information, any new models or advancements made in current index models will be applicable and will allow the process to evolve as new technology and information is generated.

Broad Applicability

The assessment template, with resource-management objectives or standards applied, can be used as a resource-planning tool, an assurance process for regulation, or as a structure for ecoservice payments.

Integration of Values

The assessment and assurance process can be conducted somewhat cost-effectively on an annual or regular basis and could be readily integrated within the USDA Farm Service Agency process that "certifies" production-based land-use information or channeled through an entirely different entity. Both production capacities and natural-resource integrity will remain a high priority and should not be viewed as competing interests.

Commoditized Data

The assessment and assurance process and the resulting data can be readily sorted, compiled, and queried to provide specific resource information needs to varying government, non-profit, and the private sector. Therefore, the management data itself becomes a value above and beyond the value of resource-management outcomes. This occurs because the resource-assessment data generates a landscape intelligence that can be utilized with the supply-and-demand dynamics of ecoservice markets.

EcoCommerce Assessment Approach

Regardless of what particular ecosystems or ecoservices are assessed, it is imperative to engage the on-the-ground resource managers into the process. Their participation in the assessment is the only feasible approach that will also involve them into the planning, implementation, and valuation phases of EcoCommerce or any ecoservice market. Using agro-

and communicating information about something that is of importance to decision makers or stakeholders.

In this chapter, the use of indices will be the primary type of indicator that is examined. An "index" is a single number derived from two or more indicators. Ott (1979) located six purposes for which indices were used:

• Resource Allocation: indices applied to decisions to assist managers in allocating funds and determining priorities

• Ranking of Locations: indices applied to assist in comparing conditions at differing geographical locations

• Incentives/Enforcement: indices applied to specific locations to determine the extent to which legislative standards are being met

• Trend Analysis: indices applied to data at differing points in time to determine changes in quality (degradation or improvement)

• Public Information: indices applied to inform the public about conditions and trends

• Scientific Research: indices applied as a means to reduce large volumes of data to a form that provides insight to the researcher

EcoCommerce incorporates the purpose of each of these indices into the process of understanding the supply-and-demand forces and in determining the capacity of the natural capital to generate ecoservices.

Optimally Inaccurate

Indices and other indicators are imperfect representations of reality. They represent compromise designs, involving trade-offs between ease and cost-of-data measurability, scientific validity, transparency, and relevance to users. At best, they may be "optimally inaccurate" (OECD 1999, 124). This does not mean that indices have no value; rather their value depends on how they are applied and interpreted. The next section in this chapter, *Familiar Indices in Use*, discusses the wind chill, heat, and consumer price indices that are representations of reality, which have been accepted and therefore could be considered "optimally inaccurate." The use of an optimally inaccurate index may provide a better sense of what is occurring on the landscape, in a lake, and within an agro-ecosystem than using direct measurements. Minnesota State University – Mankato limnology professor Dr. Henry Quade (1992) cautioned the interpretation of direct measurements as it pertained to water quality. He stated that a direct measurement of dissolved oxygen within a eutrophic (nutrient-rich) lake could vary greatly depending on whether that measurement were taken at noon or midnight or at the hours in between. To illustrate the point, he stated that someone without regard to the internal and external inputs of the lake could "get you the water quality you wanted" from many lakes. If you want a high oxygen reading in a eutrophic lake, they would take the measurement during high noon when the algae were actively generating oxygen through photosynthesis. If a low oxygen reading were desired, the measurement would be taken during relatively high respiration rates around the midnight hours. Direct measurements that provide an erroneous assessment of the lake are not solely caused by unethical practices. Due to the dynamic nature of ecosystems, and the monitoring constraints (inconvenience, inability, unfeasibility, uneconomical, or impractical conditions) scientists face significant obstacles in acquiring timely and accurate measurements. A stakeholder purchasing an ecoservice outcome, in fact, may be more assured by an "optimally inaccurate" index, rather than a direct measurement whose accuracy lends itself to the wide range of physical constraints of being at the right places at the right times, all or enough of the time. Directly measuring ecoservices and non-point-source pollution (that are generated from agricultural management activities) as it pertains to source and quantity is impossible. "Optimally inaccurate" measurements via indices fall within the realm of possibility and reasonability.

Familiar Indices in Use

In addition to ecosystem indices, the use of index-based systems is common throughout our society to describe many complex systems including weather conditions, economic trends, human body condition, tooth decay, and chemical-reaction potential. As stated, the purpose of an index is a relative numerical value to describe and communicate a rate, trend, a comparison, or movement in how a situation is being affected.

Two very common weather-related indices are the heat index and the wind-chill factor. The heat index uses the measurement of the temperature and the humidity to describe how the combination of those elements may affect humans and animals. The wind-chill factor uses temperature and the wind speed at six feet above the ground surface to describe the potential harm the combination of those elements will have on exposed skin.

Economic indices are another type of index that is common to many people. The Consumer Price Index (CPI) is a measure estimating the average price of consumer goods and services purchased by households. A consumer price index measures a price change for a constant market basket of goods and services from one period to the next within the same area (city, region, or nation). It is a price index determined by measuring the price of a standard group of goods meant to represent the typical market basket of a typical urban consumer. It is one of several price indices calculated by most national statistical agencies. The percent change in the CPI is a measure estimating inflation. The CPI can be used to make adjustments to wages, salaries, pensions, and contracts to account for the effects of inflation.

Each of these (heat index, wind chill factor, and inflation) is "non-measurable" in the traditional sense of the word, but each index contains factors that are measurable. And since indices are developed, not by using a direct measurement methodology, but by individuals and organizations who want to communicate information for their needs, indices are subject to disagreements, evolution, and adjustments.

Wind-Chill Index

The need or desire to adjust an index, even an index with just two variables whose measurements can be obtained with a high degree of certainty, does occur. Siple and Passel first measured the combined impacts of varying wind speed and freezing temperatures in 1945. They did this by estimating heat loss from water as it froze in a plastic container suspended from a tall pole (NWS 2008). It was on Siple and Passel's work that the wind-chill index used by the National Weather Service and the Meteorological Services of Canada was based. The wind-chill factor historically used the wind speed at 20 feet aloft until the early 2000s. Beginning in 1999, there were discussions between the United States and Canada's weather services about updating the wind-chill index. In 2000, a weather specialist consortium evaluated the existing wind-chill formula and made changes to improve it. The group's goal was to internationally upgrade and standardize the index. The new wind-chill index makes use of advances in science, technology, and computer modeling to provide a more accurate, understandable, and useful formula for estimating the dangers arising from winter winds and freezing temperatures. In addition, clinical trials were conducted, and the results of those trials have been used to verify and improve the accuracy of the new formula. With these changes, the wind- chill temperature includes specific threshold values that provide specific warning of time-to-frostbite at given levels of wind chill. For example, a temperature of 5 degrees Fahrenheit and a wind speed of 30 mph equal a wind chill of -19, which will produce frostbite in 30 minutes. The chart also shows how frostbite will occur sooner if the temperature is lower or the wind speed higher. Since it is the responsibility of the National Weather Service to help protect lives, this is an important service to the American people.

The point of this wind-chill index discussion is that indices are not direct measurements but are methods to measure the "immeasurable" and therefore are exposed to opinions on what methods and core measurements should be used in the calculation. But in developing the index and utilizing it to make judgments that can better serve people, the index was refined over time and will, presumably, be refined again. Perhaps in 1945, when Siple and Passel first developed their measurement, they assumed that someday an instrument much more refined than their plastic water bottle would be able to directly measure the wind chill. But even 55 years later, in 2000, further refinement came to an index rather than an instrument that could make direct wind-chill measurements.

Air-Quality Index

The Air-Quality Index (AQI) is an index for reporting daily air quality (EPA 2009). It tells how clean or polluted the air is, and what associated health effects might be a concern. The AQI focuses on health effects that a person may experience within a few hours or days after breathing polluted air. The EPA calculates the AQI for five major air pollutants regulated by the Clean Air Act: ground-level ozone, particle pollution (also known as particulate matter), carbon monoxide, sulfur dioxide, and nitrogen dioxide. For each of these pollutants, the EPA has established national air-quality standards to protect public health. Ground-level ozone and airborne particles are the two pollutants that pose the greatest threat to human health.

The AQI could be seen as a yardstick that runs from 0 to 500. A higher AQI value indicates a greater level of air pollution and the greater the health concern. For example, an AQI value of 50 represents good air quality with little potential to affect public health, while an AQI value more than 300 represents hazardous air quality. An AQI value of 100 generally corresponds to the national air quality standard for the pollutant, which is the level the EPA has set to protect public health. When AQI values are above 100, air quality is considered to be unhealthy for certain sensitive groups of people, then for everyone as AQI values get higher. The purpose of the AQI is to help you understand what local air quality means to your health and is divided into six categories from Good (0-50) to Hazardous (>300).

In this case, policy makers do not need to know all the scientific components of the AQI to make decisions regarding air quality, but they need to have a "language" that allows them to communicate to scientists and an avenue to seek out detailed scientific information if they have the desire and capacity to utilize it.

Index Types and Formats

Indices have had their own evolutionary track moving from simple to more complex organizational structures (Burk 2005).

Simple Indices

Simple indices utilize specific data sets for focused decision making and communication. The examples of the wind-chill, heat, and air-quality indices are simple indices whose calculation is for just one component. As a simple index, the AQI only shows the reader if the air quality meets a certain standard, and does not show the reader what actions are needed to improve the air quality. From a policy perspective, this simplicity may provide for better decision making for a policy maker who lacks a comprehensive understanding of air pollutants and may not be able to determine which pollutants at which levels pose an environmental hazard. The simple index does not incorporate values, preferences, and politics, but can lead policy makers to ask questions of the consequences of certain AQI levels. Such relative questions may be how other regions compare relative to the AQI; does certain ranges of the AQI pose a hazard to humans, animals, and plants; and what are some of the activities that can significantly raise or lower the AQI scores.

Examples of simple indices that are relevant to land-management ecoservices will be discussed later in the chapter including a soil conditioning index and a phosphorus index. Simple indices cannot illustrate the effects or the comparative value that the one component has relative to other measurements. A high soil or phosphorus index may be related to water quality, but a simple index does not show the relationship among other parameters.

Compound Indices

When used appropriately, simple indices are valuable tools, but since they are one-dimensional, they may be deficient for use when several environmental components need to be described. Compound indices combine simple, one-dimensional indices into a measurement capable of addressing many [environmental] issues at once. It allows aggregation and integration of dissimilar indices to present data into a tool capable of accommodating multiple data sets, adjusting weights, and being used to represent multiple stakeholder interests. The compound index is constructed so that the data sets are fixed and the weighting of values is implicit. In other words, the developer of the index inserts weighting and values within the structured index, rather than allowing the user to define these characteristics. The Environmental Benefits Index of the USDA Conservation Reserve Program (CRP) is a common example that has had significant acceptance and success. The EBI contains five environmental components as well as a cost variable. The EBI functions as a static instrument for each CRP sign-up, but parameters and weighting can be and are adjusted prior to each CRP sign-up to accommodate new scientific findings, social interests, and political desires.

In the 1995 CRP sign-up, the EBI evolved toward placing more weight, thus emphasis, on water-quality protection, habitat development, soil erodibility, and tree planting rather than just focusing on soil erosion. The sums of these criteria were then divided by the cost to determine its ranking. In 1996 and 1997, emphasis was given to air quality in relation to erosion and to lands within a targeted region. This process illustrates how the EBI and other indices can evolve to address new scientific findings and changes in society's values.

Matrix Portfolio

The matrix portfolio is not an index, but a structure to gather indices and to present them in different formats. It can represent information comprehensively without compromising the flexibility to develop different types of indices for different users. The matrix portfolio is able to accommodate many different data sets, as well as yielding different visual formats for indices depending on what the user values and is considering during the decision-making process. It avoids implicit or internal weighting to allow decision makers to explicitly provide weighting of values. In other words, it allows the users of the indices, rather than the developers, to apply values.

The EcoCommerce Matrix Portfolio (Table 8.1) is an example of the matrix portfolio that allows a farmer to compile both simple and compound indices in a framework that meets the particular ecoservice market in which he wants to engage. The interchangeability of indices and weights allows a unique and marketable product to be sold. This matrix portfolio could also be used as a foundation for developing a compound index. If Walmart's "sustainability index" eventually includes soil, water, air, habitat, and energy components, it could opt for a compound index developed from a landscape-portfolio matrix. This process would allow for more transparency on what parameters are being addressed and would also allow flexibility for the farmers who use a landscape portfolio for other markets to customize their matrix for a particular market.

Table 8.1	EcoCommerce Portfolio					
Management Unit	Ecoservice Parameters					
	Simple Indices					Compound Index
	soil	water	air	habitat	energy	Sustainability
Farm ID						
Farmstead						
Feedlot A						
Forest						
Field						
Pasture						
Range						

Policy-Possibility Frontier

The policy-possibility frontier (PPF) provides the newest generation of indices that can facilitate cooperation to attain a common goal (Burk 2005) and generate agreement between disparate stakeholders in achieving management objectives. It was developed from the production-possibility frontier in economic study that was discussed in Chapter 1. In EcoCommerce, it is envisioned that the policy PF will have a role in providing stakeholders the ability to define "sustainability" for the landscape relative to its production capacity.

Burk (2005) describes a *disparate stakeholder-management process* to develop a policy PF applied by Cauglin and Hoag (2002). Their stakeholder-management process is a strategy or structural tool that explicitly includes stakeholder preferences for group negotiations and decision-making by including indices about stakeholder preferences. They demonstrated the process in collaboration of the National Park Service and the U.S. Fish and Wildlife Service and used an *analytical-hierarchy process*.

Box 8.1 Analytical-Hierarchy/Network Process

A rationale for the use of this process is that the number of things we don't know how to measure is much larger than the things we know how to measure, and it is highly unlikely that we will ever find ways to measure everything on a physical scale with a unit because, unlike physical things, most of our ideas, feelings, behavior, and actions are not fixed once and for all, but change from moment to moment and from one situation to another (Saaty 2008). Actually, we measure and decide things in this manner all the time without thinking about it. The analytical-hierarchy process makes this natural thought process more transparent by using a structured means of modeling the problem at hand. It consists of an overall *goal*, a group of options or *alternatives* for reaching the goal, and a group of factors or *criteria* that relate the alternatives to the goal.

In the Caughlin and Haug study, stakeholders completed a survey to quantify their preference for elk and bison management. This raw data was then used to develop a policy PF that illustrated the range of interests on the continuum of management practices ranging from "natural" to a "human-managed" land-use approach. This type of index illustrated the interests of the government, environmental, economical, and tribal interests in relation to each other and along the continuum of land-management activities.

The probably role of the policy PF in EcoCommerce is to establish a level of land-use management as it pertains to differing ecoservice markets. The ecoservice markets of government incentive programs, Walmart's "Sustainability Index," and biomass-production standards for a bio-refinery may all have differing thresholds of acceptable land-use-management standards. A policy PF process may assist in developing these standards. The relationship of the indices and formats can also be described in a reverse-logic process. Once the policy PF process defines a level of sustainability (a point on a PPF arc similar to Figure 3.3), a matrix portfolio (such as Table 8.1) can be used to present the ecoservice types and any weighting factors that are used to define a particular level or brand of sustainability. The matrix can then be populated with both compound and simple index ratings that are generated from land-use strategies. Resource managers can develop their unique EcoCommerce Portfolio to participate in the markets as they deem appropriate.

Criteria for Ideal Indices

As Ott (1979) explained, an index should reduce a large quantity of data down to its simplest form, retaining essential information for the questions that are being asked of the data. In short, an index is designed to simplify. In an effort to advance agricultural indicators, the OECD (1999) derived a list of attributes that would describe an "ideal" indicator. These attributes were listed under three categories.

Policy Relevance and Usefulness for the User
An agri-environmental indicator should:

• provide a representative picture of environmental conditions and pressures;

• be simple, easy to interpret, and able to show trends over time;

• be responsive to changes in the environment and related human activities;

• provide a basis for international comparisons;

• be either national in scope or applicable to regional issues of national significance;

• have a threshold or reference value against which to compare it.

Analytical Soundness
An agri-environmental indicator should:

• be theoretically well-founded in technical and scientific terms;

• be based on international standards and international consensus about its validity;

• lend itself to being linked to economic models, forecasting, and information systems.

Measurability
The data required to support the indicator should be:

• readily available or made available at a reasonable cost/benefit ratio;

• adequately documented and of known quality;

• updated at regular intervals in accordance with reliable procedures.

Multi-functional Challenges
The OECD explains that environmental indicators, designed to capture the relationship between humans and the natural world, face a greater challenge than indicators applied toward social and economic issues that are often concerned with monetary measurements. These "ideal" indicators must also function in respect to spatial and temporal scales that identify the economic, environmental, and social linkages with some weighting factor such as a cost/benefit framework. The OECD concluded that if a cost/benefit framework is used, then there may be a need to develop indicators that use a common monetary unit rather than [just] physical measures.

To further elaborate on the spatial and temporal scales, the indicators should address measurements from the field, farm, watershed, ecosystem, and national levels. From the OECD perspective, data need to be captured at as detailed a level as possible and then aggregated to the national level with some explanation of the variation around the national average value. The variations in the time scales of different environmental effects range from the short-term, such as the impact of the use of tillage or pesticides, medium-term such as the depletion of groundwater reserves, and the long-term such as soil erosion.

Presentation Characteristics

The OECD (1999) concludes that these criteria and challenges describe what would be met by the "ideal" indicator and would not expect all of them to be met in practice. Even if the indicators meet those objectives, it must also meet two presentation characteristics to be accepted. There must be transparency in how the index was chosen and the process by which its result is derived from available data. This places the onus on designers of indicators not only to be competent scientifically, but also to be able to argue or present indicators to a (possibly) non-technical audience. This poses difficulties where the underlying science may be complex. It also poses difficulties where the degree of processing of underlying data is significant.

In addition to transparency, the index must be relevant to decision makers. Moreover, the decision maker has to perceive some self-capability to monitor the indicator and/or influence the value of the indicator through (positive) action. If an offered indicator does not appear relevant to a decision maker, or is perceived to be beyond the decision maker's sphere of influence, the decision maker is unlikely to feel ownership of the index or process and it is unlikely to be accepted.

A Classification Scheme for Indices

One of the common issues related to creation of indices is that many of them were developed independently and their use is not coordinated. In hindsight, this is a rational result of the emergence of any language, as words and syntax evolve out of a necessity to communicate specific needs beginning from a simple format and gradually becoming more complex. As these indices were developed, they took on different characteristics and forms. This diversity was documented by Ott (1979) when he devised and applied an index classification system for air pollution indices based on four criteria. Those were based on the *number of variables* included in the index, which means how many air pollutants would be considered in the index. The second included the *calculation method* used to compute the index. The calculation method denotes the manner in which the overall index—sub-indices plus aggregation function— is calculated. The third category is the *calculation mode,* which describes how the sub-indices are combined or aggregated. The fourth is the *descriptor* category that related to the use of "words" to report or describe the different ranges of the index. For example, 0-100 is "good," 101-300 is "poor," etc. The types of descriptors were based on government standards, episodic criteria, or an arbitrary description.

To provide an illustrative example of Ott's classification system, an index may be classified using the code $5A_3A$. This code describes an index has 5 variables; A_3 denotes the type of calculation method and mode; and A refers to the basis for the descriptor categories. The details of how Ott generated the classification code are not the intent of this discussion, but that a classification system for resource indices is a requirement to allow clarity in discussing resource condition and potential. To develop an EcoCommerce classification system, it would seem advantageous to review Ott's scheme and perhaps adjust and build on his insights.

When Ott (1979) applied the classification system to the air pollution indices, it revealed a great diversity and a lack of consistency in the way air-quality conditions are reported to the public. Indices cited in literature differed from indices used by metropolitan areas. In fact, no two indices were exactly alike in the 35 U.S. cities that were surveyed. An index value of 100 reported in Washington, D.C. means something entirely different from a value of 100 reported in Cleveland, Ohio.

The lack of uniformity among different indices creates serious problems. Not only do the differences raise questions about the meaningfulness of the indices, but an interested individual or stakeholder would become confused about what scale the value is associated with. If a national, regional, or local picture is to be drawn of resource conditions and trends, compiling these values would be inefficient at best. This lack of uniformity itself suggests that no consistent scientific rationale has been employed in developing these indices. This then creates three undesirable consequences:

- It creates confusion;

- It raises questions of the technical validity;

- It prevent indices from being used to gain insight into resource problems at local, regional, national, and global scales.

A uniform index as proposed by Ott should include certain characteristics:

• It should use a non-dimensional number that the public can relate to.

• It should include the parameters for which standards have been or will be established.

• It should be flexible enough to evolve as new issues arise or more scientific information is gathered.

• It should be calculated in a simple manner using reasonable assumptions.

• It should be based on reasonable scientific premise.

• If addressing multiple parameters, it should be possible to report each parameter separately, if necessary.

• It should be spatially meaningful, in that high concentrations of either desirable or undesirable parameters should not be "averaged out" for specific locations.

• It should allow for noticeable variation over a reasonable period of time whether that is hourly, daily, monthly, seasonally, or yearly.

For ecoservice markets to function, a process needs to be in place that allows communication to occur with ease. An EcoCommerce structure will use a type of a classification scheme to identify commonalities and differences in describing ecoservice units. A classification scheme would also assist in developing new indices and ensure that there is an identifiable relationship among indices.

Value of Standardized Indices

In a May 6, 2009 *Resources for the Future* panel discussion on "New Directions for Managing Our Ecosystems," the need to standardize indicators was recognized by the four panelists: Iris Goodman, U.S. Environmental Protection Agency; Jim Laity, Office of Management and Budget; John Kostyack, Executive Director, Wildlife Conservation and Global Warming; and Sally Collins, Director, USDA Office of Ecosystem Services and Markets (RFF 2009).

In addition to standardization, Jim Laity said that the indicators must also be scientifically valid, quantitative, and limited in number – perhaps as many as 12, but no more. These indicator qualities must be able to answer the question, "Is it a good or bad idea to make more or less of a particular ecoservices?"

With these qualities, the indicators could then be applied and have relevance to government performance assessment, non-market or "green" welfare accounting, natural-resource valuation, conservation planning and priorities, and trade in ecosystem services. The lack of indices with these values has slowed the advance of addressing ecoservices, both scientifically and in public policy. A "Resources for the Future" workshop concluded that if standardized units of accounting would be adopted it would advance the following policy and scientific objectives (RFF 2006).

Resource Welfare Accounts

Conventional welfare accounts, such as Gross Domestic Product (GDP), do not measure nature's contribution to well being. The measurement of non-market benefits in these accounts is thwarted by a lack of units consistent with those used to measure conventional economic outputs.

Conservation Planning and Priorities

Resource-management plans are necessary at field, farm, watershed, basin, and nation and need to be compatible to be effective. Generation and protection of ecoservices, for example, require resource managers and stakeholders to account for and communicate a much broader set of objectives. Standard units of account will make this task easier.

Government Performance

Agencies are increasingly being asked (by Congress, OMB, and others) to demonstrate the public benefits of environmental regulations, programs, and expenditures. Since ecoservices are about the benefits of nature to the public, measuring and communicating ecoservice outcomes could support important trustee and regulatory activities.

Ecosystem Markets

Systems for trading habitats, ecosystem services, water quality, and other heterogeneous environmental goods have been slow to develop. This is largely due to the difficulty of judging and monitoring the qualities of what is traded. Standardization will foster more transparent and defensible rules for such environmental markets.

Environmental Valuation

Ecosystem valuations have been conducted for decades. The comparability of these analyses, and the ability to transfer benefits from one location to another, is limited, however. A part of the problem is that valuations do not employ standard units to foster comparison and analysis. If units are standardized and incorporated into an economic system, then commerce conducted by the economic participants can define sustainability through their actions.

Summary

This list of objectives covers the scales at the field level (if the farmer is engaging in an ecoservice market or is conducting conservation planning activities) through to the global level if countries want to describe and compare resource welfare accounts. In applying standardized provisional ecoservice units, the farmer grows bushels of grain, produces hundred-weights of milk, pounds of meat, and tons of forage. These differing units allow for economic valuation, open markets, government policy performance, agronomic planning and priorities and they are incorporated into the nation's GDP. These production units are converted into a common currency unit that allows communication to occur both in physical and financial outcomes. A standardization of ecoservice indices would allow communication to occur on the bio-physical and ecological outcomes, and eventually these quantities could be converted into financial outcomes by many of the same economic participants as those that participate in the provisional ecoservice markets of grain, milk, beef, forage, etc. Since provisional and regulating ecoservices are all derived from site-specific land characteristics and management strategies, it would be advantageous and efficient if all these ecoservices were considered within the context of both the agro-ecological and economical systems wherein they reside and by which they are influenced.

Why Use Indices on the Farm?

The Need Arises

Historically it has been neither necessary nor feasible to apply ecoservice indices toward farm-management systems. It was not feasible due to the lack ecological information and technologies needed to create and use indices. And it was not necessary as farm-management systems had relatively less impact on the environment, and the agro-economic systems were in a relative rapid evolutionary phase. The OECD (King and Parris 2002) recognized farm-management evolution can be characterized in four phases:

through both the land cover and how that land cover is managed. For example, a particular cropping system in a particular region can generate off-site impacts. And therefore, monitoring land use may provide a reasonable measure of various aspects of the agro-environment. This data is currently available in many regions, as agricultural crop-cover data is collected in many countries, either from Farm Bill requirements, regular censuses of agriculture, or, more recently, from satellite imagery (OECD 1999). These data do not, however, reveal land management such as fertilizer usage rates, crop varieties, and field-tillage practices. These management data or rather their outcomes could be obtained through the application of site-specific indices. This index data would then be correlated with land-use data that could be used as a partial, superficial verification process. Combining land-use data and management indices is further described in Chapter 9 as landscape intelligence.

Management Flexibility

Producing provisional ecoservices (food, fiber, fuel, and feed stocks) is a dynamic and capital-intensive endeavor. When attempting to provide regulating ecoservices in conjunction with provisional ecoservices, it is necessary that the same level of flexibility is afforded to both to achieve the optimum return for each ecoservice. That flexibility will allow decisions to be implemented at the will of the producers and assure that those decisions will be accounted for in the outcomes. This is demonstrated by the use of a phosphorus index to determine crop-management needs rather than a prescriptive method. The following is a summarized excerpt from the *Phosphorus Indices to Predict Risk for Phosphorus Losses* (Maguire 2005) written by a university and USDA staffed task force.

Box 8.2 Flexibility is Key to Ecological and Economical Phosphorus Management

A comprehensive P-Index considers individual site and management characteristics instead of soil test P value alone and is far superior for determining potential runoff risk. P-Indices can show that some fields with high soil test P have little risk of P losses due to minimal risk of transport from the field, and therefore do not strictly limit P additions to these fields. Limiting P applications on soil test P alone is therefore generally more restrictive than implementing a P-Index. In situations where livestock producers have access to manure, a P-Index would be less restrictive than application of manure based on a soil test P-threshold. This may be a benefit to the producer in the short term, but may lead to problems in the long run as soil test P may increase further in these fields until it causes the site to be ranked "High" by the P-Index. Flexibility in management is a key asset to implementation of P-Indices. With the soil test P threshold approach, P application would be restricted once soil test P values reach the threshold. However, P-Indices allow producers or other land users to select from many strategies that will reduce the risk for P loss, including changing the method and/or timing of fertilizer or manure application, changing crop rotations and tillage practices to reduce erosion, or installing vegetated buffers or application setbacks to increase flow distances. This flexibility will help the producers search for the best methods to maintain profitability while protecting the environment (Maguire 2005).

Demonstrated Use of Indices on the Farm

Performance-based Environmental Policies for Agriculture

Ag-management indices are a viable option in the short list of options of measuring the immeasurable. In a quick review, if ecoservice markets are ever able to materialize, there are several obstacles that must be addressed (Maille 2009). First, agriculture non-point-source pollution and [ecoservices] from a farm or field are diffuse and difficult to measure. Leaching and runoff into ground and surface waters occur in many places making monitoring difficult and expensive. Second, random events such as rainfall have a large impact on the delivery of non-point-source pollution to waterways. Such events cannot be accurately predicted. Third, the linkages among agriculture-production decisions and practices (i.e. inputs and technologies), non-point pollution, water quality, and social damage costs tend to be site-specific and poorly understood. Finally, implementing performance-based policies may greatly increase the information needs and administrative burdens placed on farmers and the implementing agencies.

Due to these obstacles, the Performance-based Environmental Policies for Agriculture Initiative implemented by the University of Vermont and Winrock International attempted to bridge the gap between economic theory and the current implementation of non-point-source pollution control programs by exploring the use of field and farm-level management indices to be used as proxies for performance measures.

These proxies have important advantages over directly measuring "immeasurable" components of non-point-source pollution and ecoservices. First and foremost, farm-level proxies are much easier for farmers to respond to. As such, farm-level performance measures may be able to provide a usable link between farm business decision making and environmental performance through appropriately designed incentives. In this way, farm-level proxy measures can serve as the missing link for successful implementation of [TMDL] water-quality improvements.

Additionally, current approaches to water-quality trading involving agricultural non-point-source pollution are generally focused on the use of a certain, limited set of best management practices (BMPs). Using farm-level performance indicators could bring an increased level of confidence to potential purchasers of water-quality credits from agriculture, relative to the purchasing of credits based on a static co-efficient associated with a BMP. Second, farm-level performance measures that are not tied to a given set of practices will allow the farmer much greater flexibility in meeting the performance measure in the least costly manner, relative to the current, BMP-focused approach. This is an extremely important characteristic that differentiates a performance-based approach from design-based or practice- based approaches.

If applied correctly, performance-based incentives may be more likely to reduce the farm-level costs per unit of non-point-source pollution reduction [or ecoservice increase] than will practice-based approaches. An analysis by the Economic Research Service estimates that performance-based conservation programs can generate more than two times the environmental quality per dollar spent compared to practice-based programs (Weinberg and Claassen 2006).

Conservation Planning Training for Private-Sector Agronomy Service

A USDA Sustainable Agricultural Research and Education grant funded the non-profit Minnesota Project effort in 2006 to identify the cost-effectiveness of agricultural advisors to assist farmers in calculating their environmental performance using management indices. This project, Conservation Planning Training for Private Sector Agronomy Service and Local Conservation Agencies, was based on the knowledge that farmers receive much of their management-decision support from agricultural advisors who provide them with advice on how to increase the productivity on their farm operations. These advisors provide this service under a competitive environment and are quite knowledgeable about crop genetics, soil types, and other productivity parameters. To integrate natural-resource management into the farmers' production-resource-management plans , these advisors must be able to assess the status of the natural resources and how the management activities of the farm operation impact the natural resources.

What was learned was that by using their existing access, knowledge, and skills that the advisors use to provide production advice to farmers, they were able to assess the farms' resources for environmental outcomes in a cost-efficient manner. Several of the advisors were able to assess a farm and six of its fields or common management units within a few hours. This was significantly less time than if a government staff or any professional would start an assessment from scratch, in that the farmer would need to gain the trust of the assessor and then provide them with the detailed information they would need to conduct the assessment. It could be estimated that an approach such as that would take on average, at least 40 hours, if not longer (Gieseke 2008).

Conservation Bridge for Agricultural Professionals

To further evaluate the agricultural advisors' role and to identify the farmers' interests and concerns, the Minnesota Pollution Control Agency's Environmental Assistance program funded the non-profit Minnesota Project effort "Conservation Bridge for Agricultural Professionals" (Gieseke 2009). In this project, agricultural professionals were paid a modest sum of $400 to conduct farm index-based resource assessments on up to six management units on the farm. A management unit could be considered a single field, or a combination of fields, that had similar soil types and cropping system. Up to seven indices could be used to assess the soil, water, and habitat resources of the farm operation. In surveying the agricultural professionals on the ease and ability of conducting these natural-resource assessments, a common comment was that the $400 was a reasonable payment if they were currently providing the farmer with production advice and services. But to conduct these resource assessments from scratch—that is to gather all the information on those management units and run the ecological models— would cost significantly more.

The farmers' perspective included five elements:

• Farmers understand the concept of using management indices to rate their farm operation.

• Farmers like the concept of measuring the management of their farm operation for themselves and others, but several were concerned about who would get the information, how it would be used, and other related concerns on privacy.

• The farmers often agreed with the "measurement" results, but many of the farmers who take part in these progressive efforts generally have worked on conserving their farm's resources.

• The farmers could see value in using this process as developing a related conservation plan document.

• The farmers felt that this type of resource-assessment process could be integrated with their production plans.

The resource assessors' perspective also included five elements:

• The resource assessors understood the concept of using management indices to rate farm operations.

• The resource assessors liked the concept and felt it could be very beneficial for many of the resource issues facing farmers from the local to national level.

• The resource assessors generally agreed with the "measurement" results but felt that some of the indices need to be further refined.

• The resource assessors stated that this process would be helpful for them to develop conservation plans and felt they would be more proficient after doing several of these.

• The resource assessors felt that this process could be incorporated into a farmer's production plans.

Farm-specific assessments in each of these examples provide a mechanism for farmers and their advisors to be engaged with resource-management outcomes at a level and scale not experienced since the early decades of the Soil Conservation Service. With tens of thousands of agricultural professionals each providing guidance and advice on tens of thousands of acres, it becomes feasible to envision a process in which a hundred million acres of farm and ranchland could be assessed.

Using the assessment definitions from Chapter 7, these advisor-generated assessments are described as a participatory approach using ecological models that can be incorporated into GIS. The benefit of this approach is that the site-specific data and local knowledge that is not available to the government or scientific community is applied to ecological index models that are accepted by government agencies and the scientific community. What is generated is a new data set that can be scaled from field to farm to watershed to nation and is developed from the perspective of those in political influence.

Providing a BMP Context

Best Management Practices (BMPs) are effective, practical, structural or nonstructural methods that prevent or reduce the movement of sediment, nutrients, pesticides, and other pollutants from the land to surface or ground water, or generate ecoservices. These practices are developed to achieve a balance between water-quality protection and the production of crops within natural and economic limitations. A thorough understanding of BMPs and the flexibility in their application are of vital importance in selecting BMPs that offer site-specific control of potential non-point-source pollution and the generation of ecoservices. With each situation encountered at various sites, there may be more than one correct BMP for reducing non-point-source pollution or to generate ecoservices. BMPs focus on management of inputs to provide for economic, environmental, and agronomic efficiency in production agriculture. Examples of BMPs include practices for the management of pests, nutrients, and waste; vegetative and tillage practices, such as contour farming, cropping sequence, and windbreaks; and structural practices, such as terraces, grade stabilization, and sediment control basins.

Despite the broad-based support for the use of BMPs, there still remains uncertainty as to what degree of improvement each and every one of the BMPs provide as BMPs fall prey to the same infeasibility issue of directly measuring outcomes. And even though research has been conducted throughout the 75-year history of the NRCS, through hundreds of academic exercises and through the renewed Conservation Effects Assessment Project (CEAP) efforts of the USDA, outcomes on the precise effects of BMPs in a particular field, within a particular watershed, cannot be determined by direct measurements or calculations.

But BMPs, like all agricultural practices, are not utilized independently but within the context of the characteristics and productivity of the field and within the production systems employed. In this framework, BMPs that are recommended can be applied within the context of the natural features, production plans, and with management indices. These BMPs can then be valued for their probable or potential outcomes rather than the cost of installation. Providing a long list of BMPs that a farmer can implement without the context of what the outcomes are desired, is parallel to providing a chef with a long list of ingredients without an understanding of what meal is desired. In each case, there are dozens of potential combinations that can be used to achieve a resource outcome or a meal. But if the outcome or meal is created outside the context of what is known or desired, the farmer's and chef's investment will not be recognized. Implementing BMPs are an important avenue to achieve resource outcomes, but they must be applied within a context that provides the capacity to recognize and value it.

For example, the 2009 Minnesota Pollution Control Agency's Watershed Achievements Report chronicles water-quality-improvement projects throughout the state (MPCA 2009). The report, organized by basin, summarizes water-pollution-reduction projects funded under the U .S. Environmental Protection Agency's Section 319 of the federal Clean Water Act and the MPCA's Clean Water Partnership Program. It reports that 235 watershed projects took place in Minnesota between 1997 and May 2009. It is estimated that during the same period, sedimentation was reduced by more than 81,000 tons/year. Phosphorus loading was estimated to have been reduced by more than 283,000 pounds/year. Implementing these BMPs and resource-management improvements on an individual-by-individual basis does improve water quality, but, since the practice implementation is not provided within any context of what is occurring beyond these 235 locales in the state, it is not possible to determine the state's relative progress in improving water quality or toward what level of improvement it is trying to achieve.

Unfortunately, the invisible hand can misguide government programs the same way it guides the rest of the economy, by a lack of vital information and the self-interests of the participants. When the cost of conservation practices and the need to spend program dollars is the outcome that provides the greatest reward, then government staff (and most anyone in that position) will fulfill that objective. It is not to say that the desires of the government staff are not to most efficiently apply state dollars to resource issues, but that people can only act as efficiently as the system allows while meeting their self-interests. The crux of a centrally planned economy based on a practice-based approach is that agents need to make decisions for others to keep the economy moving. The justification for this is that by spending funds to install BMPs, it will improve the water quality. And that is correct, except that this process and its participants cannot make a good determination on how to best allocate the financial resources to improve the natural resources. That information must emerge from a system that values outcomes within a context, not just individual practices. Management indices that can be applied to the practice within a field, within a farm, within a watershed, and at basin levels provide the context that the BMP is being applied. This scenario is not isolated to the state of Minnesota's efforts, but is generally the scenario for all local, state, and federal efforts.

Agricultural and Ecological Indices

Agricultural and ecological indices, like other indices, are developed to provide a type of simplified measurement for complex systems. One of the earliest pollution indices to appear in the literature was proposed by Green in 1966 and included the two air pollutant variables of sulfur dioxide and the Coefficient of Haze (Ott 1979). The use of ecological indices gained prominence in the 1970s with the advancement of air and water-quality indices. The use of many environmental indices, including the Oregon Water Quality Index discussed in this chapter, was discontinued in the 1980s because of excessive resources required for reporting index results (Cude 2001). Improvements in computer hardware and software availability and sophistication, coupled with a desire for accessible, easily understood water quality information, renewed interest in indices. The use of agro-ecosystem indices became more prominent in the 1990s with the use of the Environmental Benefit Index to evaluate potential resource outcomes of the Conservation Reserve Program and to rate the contract bids submitted to the USDA Farm Service Agency. In 1998, the NRCS made the decision to have new erosion-prediction technology in place in time for the 2002 Farm Bill and made improvements to the Revised Universal Soil Loss Equation v1 (RUSLE1). Those revisions created RUSLE2 that allows for estimations of soil loss, soil condition, tillage intensity, and energy use.

In 2004, the rules for the Conservation Security Program included the use of agricultural-management indices and ratings to determine program eligibility and potential program payments.

The use of indices in agricultural systems has been increasing, but refinements will continually be made. This section will list and describe some of the indices that have been developed to communicate these complex systems in a succinct manner. The intentions of this section are not to analyze the indices on their accuracy, but to provide examples of indices that can be used to assess resource condition, quantify changes due to resource-management strategies, and assess changes in resource condition due to external influences such as estimated climatic changes. If the core of a functioning ecoservice market is its ability to identify, assess, and quantify ecoservices, then the foundation of EcoCommerce will be a list of valid indices and similar indicators to allow the exchange of values to be made with confidence. These agro-ecological indices are organized by the these three uses: (1) to determine the condition or status of the resource, (2) to determine the impact of specific management activities, and (3) to estimate the effect that environmental changes have on the resource. These index or model categories are Resource Condition, Resource Management, and Resource Effect. Some of the indices can function in more than one manner, in that an index that describes a condition can also be used to demonstrate the relative change in the index by changing management activities. The indices listed in the Resource Condition section are indices used strictly for that purpose. The indices listed in the Resource Management section may be used for both resource condition and management objectives if applicable.

Resource-Condition Indices

The indices listed in this category provide a numerical rating of the condition or status of the resource such as the quality of the soil, water, and air. They can be used to identify the potential economic value of the resource, such as a crop-productivity index (CPI), or a water-quality index that is used to describe the quality of a water source in relation to its specific use. Resource-condition indices and resource-management indices (discussed in the next section) may be one of the same. For example, the soil-conditioning index (SCI) describes the status of the soil as the result of how the resource is managed. Due to its dual role of providing guidance on how a resource could be managed to improve its status, the SCI is included in the Resource-Management Index section. In contrast, the CPI does not include variables that can be influenced by the resource manager.

Water Quality Indices

Water quality indices improve the understanding of water-quality issues by integrating complex data and generating a score that describes water-quality status and evaluates water-quality trends. Although some information is lost when integrating multiple water-quality variables, this loss is outweighed by the gain in understanding of water-quality issues by the water users, public, and policy makers (Cude 2001). Water-quality indices can exist in a variety of forms depending on the type of the value that is being placed on the water resource. Five major supply categories of water use include public water, industrial, agriculture, aquatic life, and recreational (Ott 1979). Each one of these categories may place varying degrees of values on water-quality parameters. For example, a high dissolved-oxygen concentration is essential if good fishing is to be found in a body of water, but is only of marginal value in a drinking water supply, and it is highly undesirable for boiler-feed water. For this reason, some water-quality specialists do not accept the concept of a general water quality index and believe that an index should be developed for a specific water use. If an industry wants to communicate the type of water resource that it values for boiler-feed water, it would develop a specific index for boiler-feed water. If a prominent local water resource has a high public-recreational-value index, it is highly unlikely that the public would allow the water resource to become depleted with oxygen to appease the industry. But with a specific-use index, the industry can communicate to other users and dischargers of water of their needs. Specific-use water-quality indices allow the general commodity of water to become a specific and higher value commodity depending on its condition and how that is related to specific uses.

The Oregon Department of Environmental Quality developed the Oregon Water Quality Index to provide a simple and concise method for expressing the significance of data regularly generated from the department's Ambient River Water Quality Monitoring Network. The water-quality index aids in the assessment of water quality for general recreational uses (i.e. fishing and swimming). The water-quality index is determined by aggregating the six sub-indices of dissolved oxygen saturation, biochemical oxygen demand, pH, total solids, ammonia+nitrate nitrogen, and fecal coliform. These sub-indices were generated on scales of 0-100, which allowed for an aggregated scale of 0-100 and could be grouped in specific manners to express impairment categories. The five categories of oxygen depletion, eutrophication, physical characteristics, dissolved substances, and health hazards are generated by compiling sub-indices that impact that type of impairment. Eutrophication is measured by the ammonia+nitrate nitrogen and the total phosphorus sub-indices. Physical characteristics are measured by temperature and total solids (Cude 2001). The water-quality index applications allow for spatial comparison of water quality among river reaches or between watersheds, for long-term trend analysis, for showing the spatial distribution of ambient water quality on a river system. These applications can assist in the development and implementation of the EPA's Total Maximum Daily Load (TMDL) Plans for specific water bodies. Each TMDL has specific water-quality parameters and specific levels of pollutants that are needed to be achieved. Watershed-specific indices could be developed for each TMDL, so that resource managers, government agencies, industries, and non-profit organizations can communicate among themselves as it pertains to water-body goals. In Oregon, activities that degrade water quality in the Tualatin River and are regulated by TMDL allocations include logging operations, intensive agricultural and container nursery operation, confined animal-feedlot operation, industrial operations, municipal sewage-treatment plants, urban non-point-source pollution, and natural hydrological conditions. Using a watershed-specific water-quality index, each of these regulated industries could respond with the use of resource-management indices whose scores would be related to the desired TMDL index outcomes. The use of the water-quality-index scores also illustrates water-quality conditions on a spatial scale that allows for comparison of reaches in relation to resource activities that may degrade or improve water resources.

Soil Productivity Indices

The economic value of land, in relationship to its capacity to produce crops and other biomass, is directly related to its soil characteristics and the demand for specific crops. The Crop Productivity Index was created by the University of Minnesota (MGIO 2010) and is used by the Natural Resources Conservation Service to provide a relative ranking of soils based on their potential for intensive crop production. This index can be used to rate the potential yield of one soil against that of another over a period of time. Ratings range from 0 to 100. The higher numbers indicate higher production potential. These ratings do not take into account climatic factors, such as the differences in precipitation or growing degree days across a region. The ratings are based on physical and chemical properties of the soils and on such hazards as flooding or ponding. Available water capacity, pH, slope, soil moisture status, ion-exchange capacity, organic-matter content, salinity, and surface fragments are the major properties evaluated when these ratings are generated. The soil properties selected are those that are important for the production of corn in Minnesota. An individual map unit (for example, Canisteo clay loam, 0 to 2 percent slopes) will have the same index value wherever that map unit occurs throughout the state. Even though predicted average yields will change with time, the productivity indices are expected to remain relatively constant in relation to one another over time.

Air-Quality Index

As mentioned earlier in the chapter, the Air-Quality Index (AQI) is an index to describe how clean or polluted the air is and what associated health effects might be a concern. The AQI focuses on health effects one may experience within a few hours or days after breathing polluted air. The EPA calculates the AQI for five major air pollutants regulated by the Clean Air Act: ground-level ozone, particle pollution (also known as particulate matter), carbon monoxide, sulfur dioxide, and nitrogen dioxide. For each of these pollutants, the EPA has established national air-quality standards to protect public health. Ground-level ozone and airborne particles are the two pollutants that pose the greatest threat to human health in this country.

Other Resource Condition Indices

There are numerous other resource concerns beyond the examples of water, soil, and air indices described. The following section lists resource-management indices that can provide both a description of the condition of the resource as well as insight into how the land-management activities may affect the index rating. This dual application greatly expands the menu of resource-condition indices from which one may be chosen.

Resource Management Indices

Water-Quality Score

The Water Quality Score was developed by the USDA (2005) and is an approach adopted to account for multiple management activities that protect and enhance water quality on the farm. Each conservation measure contributes to a cumulative index score defined by the water-quality concerns (nutrient, sediment, pest, and salinity). There are many conservation measures, and they may contribute to each of the water-quality-concern index scores. For example, the conservation measure of cover crops contributes to every water-quality-index category. Thus measures that are more effective are weighted higher than measures that are focused on a single water-quality issue. The scoring system was used in determining eligibility for the federal Conservation Security Program.

Soil-and-Water-Eligibility Tool

The Soil-and-Water-Eligibility Tool (USDA 2008) measures the effect that conservation-practice implementation has on soil and water quality. It evaluates management practices based on their contribution to each soil function or water-quality concern. The soil properties that it scores include organic matter, nutrient cycling, soil habitat, physical stability, and moisture management. The water-quality properties it scores are sediment, salinity, and surface and groundwater pesticides, nitrogen, and phosphorus. It was developed by the USDA NRCS.

WIN-PST

The USDA-NRCS National Water and Climate Center developed and supports the Windows Pesticide Screening Tool (USDA 2009). It is a tool for screening environmental risk of pesticides that NRCS field office conservationists, Extension agents, crop consultants, pesticide dealers, and producers can use to evaluate the potential for pesticides to move with water and eroded soil/organic matter and to affect non-targeted organisms.

Phosphorus Index

The purpose of the Phosphorus Index (USDA NRCS 2004) is to provide field staffs, watershed planners, and land users with a tool to assess the various landforms and management practices for potential risk of phosphorus movement to water bodies. The ranking of Phosphorus Index identifies sites where the risk of phosphorus movement may be relatively higher than that of other sites. These identified parameters can be the basis for planning corrective soil-and-water-conservation practices and management techniques. Phosphorus indices were developed by the

USDA NRCS and university staff throughout the United States and utilize the RUSLE2 software.

MinnFARM Index

The Minnesota Feedlot Annualized Run-off Model (MinnFARM) was developed to calculate the annual pollutant loading from a feedlot in Minnesota (Schmidt 2008). It was developed by the University of Minnesota and the Agriculture Research Services for prioritizing feedlot pollution potential based on a single 24-hour rain event. With a limited number of inputs, MinnFARM estimates annual pollutant loadings for the pollutants of chemical and biological oxygen demand, phosphorus, nitrogen, and fecal coliform at a point defined as the end of a defined treatment area. In addition, the model predicts whether the feedlot is likely in compliance with Minnesota Pollution Control Agency water-quality standards.

Comet-VR

The Voluntary Reporting of Greenhouse Gases-Carbon Management Evaluation Tool (COMET-VR) is a decision-support tool for agricultural producers, land managers, soil scientists, and other agricultural interests. COMET-VR provides an interface to a database containing land use data and calculates in real time the annual carbon flux. It is a web-based decision-support calculation tool that allows users to estimate changes in soil carbon storage from agricultural-management history on cultivated lands for most regions and cropping systems prevalent in the United States (Paustian 2009).

CQESTR

CQESTR, pronounced *sequester*, is a carbon-balance model and process-based model that uses readily available field-scale data to assess long-term effects of cropping systems or crop-residue removal on soil organic carbon storage or loss in agricultural soils (Liang 2006). It computes the rate of biological decomposition of crop residue or organic amendments as they convert to soil organic matter (SOM). Input data for SOM calculation include crop rotation, above ground and below ground biomass additions, tillage, weather, and the nitrogen content of crop residues and any organic amendments. It is a Windows-based program that uses the USDA Revised Universal Soil Loss Equation (version 1) factors for crop rotation, yield (residue, root biomass), tillage information, and weather data.

RUSLE2

The Revised Universal Soil Loss Equation v 2 (RUSLE2) was developed primarily to guide conservation planning, to inventory erosion rates, and to estimate sediment delivery (USDA ARS 2008). Values computed by RUSLE2 are supported by accepted scientific knowledge and technical judgment, are consistent with sound principles of conservation planning, and result in good conservation plans. Daily calculations of time-varying factors include rainfall, runoff, slope length and steepness, soil erodability, crop management, and resource-management practices. It also includes location (climate) and soil type. RUSLE2 is applicable on cropland, grazing land, disturbed forestland, construction sites, mined land, reclaimed land, landfills, military land, and other areas where surface-overland flow occurs because rainfall exceeds infiltration.

Soil-Conditioning Index

The Soil-Conditioning Index (SCI) predicts the consequences of cropping systems and tillage practices on soil organic matter in a field (Cox 2008). Soil organic matter is a primary indicator of soil quality and carbon sequestration. The SCI is a tool used to predict the effect of soil management on the trend in soil organic carbon. A positive SCI indicates a cropping system that, if continued, is likely to result in increasing levels of soil organic matter. It has three main components including the amount of organic material returned to or removed from the soil, the effects of tillage and field operations on organic matter decomposition, and the effect of predicted soil erosion associated with the management system.

Soil-Tillage Intensity Rating

The Soil Tillage Intensity Rating (STIR) is a numerical value calculated using RUSLE2. It is based on factors determined by crop-management decisions being implemented for a particular field (USDA NRCS 2005). Lower numbers indicate less overall disturbance to the soil layer. By definition, no-till operations create a STIR value of 10 or less. Values may range from 0 to 200 and reflect the kind of soil disturbance from true no-till all the way to conventional plow systems, as well as the severity of the disturbance caused by tillage operations. Specific components of the STIR value include operational speed of tillage equipment, tillage type, depth of tillage operation, and percent of the soil surface area disturbed

Soil-Management-Assessment Framework

SMAF is a tool for assessing and monitoring soil quality following three basic steps: (1) indicator selection, (2) indicator interpretation, and (3) integration into an overall soil-quality-index value (Cox 2008). SMAF was designed as and is best used as a soil-assessment tool. It provides a comprehensive snapshot of current soil conditions that can be used to suggest opportunities for improving soil quality. The interpretations of multiple indicators in SMAF are accessible to nonscientists, are tied directly to the goals specified by the user, and enable the integration of productivity and environmental concerns. SMAF can be used to monitor changes in soil quality if repeated measurement and interpretation of the same selected indicators are made at the same location.

Pasture-Condition Scoring

The Pasture-Condition Scoring was developed by the USDA Natural Resources Conservation Service to be a monitoring and assessment tool for pastureland enrolled in conservation programs (USDA GLTI 2001). Ten indicators of vegetation and soil status are rated on a 1 to 5 scale and are summed to give an aggregate score, which is interpreted for management recommendations. If the pasture is located on the proper site and well managed, it will have a good to excellent overall pasture condition score.

Crop-Rotational-Intensity Rating and Crop-Diversity Index

The Rotational-Intensity Rating is an assessment tool that ranks the relative potential for soil water storage and crop water use. Cropping more frequently and including a larger proportion of high water-using crops in a rotation will increase intensity. The level of water use by the system should match the water available under "normal" conditions. If fields are consistently too wet, the current rotation lacks intensity. If fields are frequently dry, intensity is too high. Using rotations that have both high and low intensity segments or incorporating multiple rotations that vary in intensity helps to protect against variable weather conditions. The Crop Diversity Index provides a relative indication of the ability of a combination of crops to complement each other to prevent disease, weed and insect infestations, and maximize productivity, profitability, and soil quality. Having less diversity than needed can eventually lead to production and profitability problems. Adding more diversity than needed can reduce efficiency since it increases the number of crops that must be managed, handled, and marketed. It classifies crop plants into one of four morphological and growth habits: cool-season grass, warm-season grass, cool-season broadleaf, and warm-season broadleaf (NRCS 2001).

Forest-Soil-Quality Index

The Forest-Soil-Quality-Index was developed to integrate 19 measurable physical and chemical properties of soil into a single index number. The Forest SQI can be used to assess trends in forest-soil quality and establish baseline levels for different soil and forest types. The database can be stratified by eco-region, forest type, soil type, and other parameters (Amacher 2007).

Habitat-Suitability Index

The Habitat-Suitability Index (HSI) was developed by USDA NRCS to assist agricultural producers in determining their general habitat potential on their farm land (NRCS 1997). It rates habitat by land-use type (grassland, forest types, wetlands, cropland, and management) and the amount of areas devoted to each of these types. It is considered a habitat-planning tool for landowners and operators whose primary objective is agricultural production and secondary objective is habitat. The HSI has been modified to provide a species-specific-habitat index that includes invertebrates, fishes, amphibians, reptiles, waterfowl, upland game birds, raptors, songbirds, mammals, and animal-community models (FWS Report).

Environmental-Benefits Index

The Environmental-Benefits Index (EBI) is an index that has been used by the USDA Farm Service Agency since 1990 to rank farmers' requests to enroll land into the Conservation Reserve Program. It considers the environmental factors of wildlife, water quality, erosion, enduring benefits, air quality, and cost. The index continues to be updated for each CRP signup (USDA FSA 2006).

Resource Effect Indices

The resource-effect indices are used to understand the potential effect that specific environmental changes have on a resource. Resource-effect indices can be used as a planning and management tool, or used to consider the condition of a resource after changes have taken place.

Erosion-Productivity-Impact Calculator

The Erosion-Productivity-Impact Calculator is a generalized crop model that simulates daily crop growth on a hectare scale. Like most process-plant-growth models, it predicts plant biomass by simulating carbon fixation by photosynthesis, maintenance respiration, and growth respiration. Several different crops may be grown in rotation within one model execution. It uses the concept of light-use efficiency as a function of photosynthetically available radiation to predict biomass. It has been modified to simulate the direct effects of atmospheric carbon dioxide on plant growth and water use (Easterling 1992).

Agricultural-Production-Systems sIMulator (APSIM)

The Agricultural-Production-Systems simulator (APSIM) is a tool for analyzing whole-farm systems, including crop and pasture sequences and rotations, and for considering strategic and tactical planning. APSIM allows users to improve understanding of the impact of climate, soil types, and management on crop and pasture production. It is a powerful tool for exploring agronomic adaptations such as changes in planting dates, cultivar types, fertilizer/irrigation management, etc. It is site-specific but can be extrapolated to national and regional levels using geographical information systems (APSIM 2010).

Spatial Tools for River basins and Environment and Analysis of Management options

The Spatial Tools for River basins and Environment and Analysis of Management (STREAM) instrument is an instrument for river-basin studies with emphasis on management aspects. STREAM uses a spatial distributed water balance model for simulating the water balance in large river basins. This model enables the analysis of the impacts of climate change and land-use changes on the fresh-water hydrology of a river basin. The instrument uses remotely sensed data for determining land use. STREAM has been applied for several river basins around the world including the Rhine, the Ganges/Brahmaputra, the Amudarya, and the Yangtze. An important issue related to river-basin-management studies for these regions is how to maintain the natural resources in the basin in order to satisfy the needs for food and water for the population. Water use and withdrawals, such as the spatial distribution of agriculture and urbanization use and the storage of water in the open flood plain and groundwater aquifers can be simulated. The STREAM can be applied to entire river basins with different sizes for which it considers the full-year hydrological cycle (Aerts 1999).

CENTURY

The CENTURY agro-ecosystem model is a soil organic model that simulates carbon and nutrient dynamics through an annual cycle over time scales of centuries and millennia. The producer sub-model may be a grassland/crop, forest, or savanna system, with the flexibility of specifying potential primary production curves representing the site-specific plant community. CENTURY was especially developed to deal with a wide range of cropping-system rotations and tillage practices for system analysis of the effects of management and global change on productivity and sustainability of agro-ecosystems (NREL 2006).

Indices for EcoCommerce 101

In review of the list of indices in this chapter, it may be apparent that the indices were not developed with the objectives to standardize the units or create a correlation between condition and management indices. These indices were developed in an independent fashion with specific interests in mind. In an efficient EcoCommerce structure, resource-condition indices would be related to resource-management indices that when incorporated, could generate the estimated resource effects. These indices would use standardized scales and units so that the objectives and goals for stakeholders can be aligned, communicated, and valued with relative ease. To develop an EcoCommerce model for the hypothetical Kimball farm operation, several index examples from this chapter will be chosen and then modified to illustrate how EcoCommerce would coordinate the use of various indices. The indices that are chosen should not be assumed to be the indices that an EcoCommerce structure would adopt. The exact process to choose the types of indices and the exact indices to use does not belong in this book, but should occur within the realm of stakeholders' interests and intentions. The intentions of the short list of real and theoretical indices described below are to illustrate the interrelations that ecological indices could have as well as to have correlated indices to apply EcoCommerce.

Resource-Condition Indices

Resource-condition indices describe the state of the resource, such as the air quality in a city at a particular moment, or the water quality in a river during a certain period or moment. EcoCommerce will utilize these indices to describe both the current state and the desired state of quality that is desired. For example, a resource-condition index can describe the water quality of the Valley River, as included in the Kimball Farm operation in Chapter 3. This could function in much the same manner as the Oregon Ambient Water Quality index, in that it will use specific sub-indices and measurements to develop the index. A Valley River water-quality index could be developed using the specific water-quality parameters. It would describe the desired water quality on the scale of 0 – 100. This index could also be related to the Valley River Total Maximum Daily Load (TMDL) plan. These plans are developed to determine pollution source and to allocate load allowances. If a TMDL index for the Valley River (TMDLi-VR) was developed and correlated to agro-ecological and forest-related indices, then specific resource-management-index scores could provide assurance that particular land units and land-operator strategies are meeting the load-allocation intentions of the TMDL plan.

Resource-Management Indices and Ratings

Resource-management indices describe how management strategies may affect on-site or off-site resources. They may also have the characteristic of a resource-condition index. The following indices will be used in this book's example of EcoCommerce as it pertains to the Kimball farm operation. They are either directly adopted from the list of indices or are created specifically to illustrate EcoCommerce possibilities. The lower case "i" denotes that these indices are created for the purpose of this book only and are not to be confused with the USDA indices noted earlier with a capital "I." No equations will be applied to these "i" indices, but a narrative will be included to state their purposes. The "i" indices also reside on a scale of 0-100 scale with 100 representing an optimum-resource condition or management strategy.

SCi – soil-condition index – addresses the soil parameters addressed by the NRCS SCI. The SCi is influenced by land characteristics, management strategies, location, and weather.

fSQi – forest-soil-quality index –addresses soil parameters and functions in forested area.

WQi – water quality index – addresses non-point-source pollution such as sediment, nutrient, fertilizers, and chemicals that occur during run-off events. The WQi is influenced by land characteristics, management strategies, location, and weather.

CQRi – carbon-sequestration index – addresses carbon sequestration in a similar manner as the CQSTER model.

BTUi – British thermal unit index – addresses energy used for the production of a crop and the energy stored within the crop following harvest and storage. The BTUi is used to refine energy-balance calculations of the production of biofuels from grain and cellulosic biomass.

HSi – habitat-suitability index – addresses habitat in a similar manner as the NRCS habitat-suitability index. It considers habitat potential on a land unit in which the primary land use is for production agriculture.

FLi –feedlot index – is an index based on the similar functions and capacities as the MinnFARM index.

plHSi – pollinator HSi – is an index based on the HSI, in that it uses a farm-management plan as the primary objective of the land use and habitat for pollination species as secondary objective. In the EcoCommerce structure it provides an example of a regulating ecoservice index that can be correlated to the general HSI.

phHSi – pheasant HSi – is an index based on the HSI, in that it uses a farm-management plan as the primary objective of the land use and habitat for pheasants species as a secondary objective. In the EcoCommerce structure it provides the example of a species-specific index that can be correlated to the general HSI.

In Section III, these nine resource-management indices will be applied toward the EcoCommerce examples including the Kimball farm operation and will be examined as to how economic values are derived from them.

Preliminary Classification Scheme

To describe these examples of EcoCommerce indices, a simple classification scheme will be illustrated. The capital letters represent the type of index such as the SCi is the soil condition. A lowercase letter at the end could represent if it is an index ("i") or a rating ("r") or a score ("s"). Lowercase letters in the front of the capital letters represent a sub-index to the primary index. For example, the plHSi, is an index based on the habitat-suitability index with a focus on pollinator habitat ('pl").

CHAPTER 9

Creating Landscape Intelligence

A Failure to Communicate

The need for a more effective method to communicate how farming strategies lead to agro-ecological outcomes is realized by any farmer attempting to describe those outcomes on their specific farm operation. Often, the first impulse is to request that measurements should be taken for each parameter on each farm. Of course, it was discussed in Chapter 2 that non-point-source pollution and most land-management-related ecoservices are difficult or impossible to measure. One could provide an aerial photo that shows how the land use is patterned across the farm. This photo interpretation would vary by season as perennial and annual vegetation tracks will reveal differences. This photo could be enhanced by overlaying various land data such as streams, topography, and wetlands. The farmer could complement the aerial photo with a list of BMPs that were installed on the farm, but a list of BMPs does not provide a quantification of resource-management outcomes. Finally, the farmer could offer a tour of the farm operation and show firsthand how the conservation practices are installed or used on the land. If it were raining, the observers or inspectors for farmers to provide this production-resource intelligence. This incentive is contained in the federal Farm Bill policy, and this model for gathering production-resource-management intelligence would also function for gathering natural-resource intelligence.

"Certified" Production-Landscape Intelligence

The 2008 Food, Energy and Conservation Bill and its predecessors (generically called the Farm Bills) are written approximately every five years. An intention is to provide a financial and risk-based safety net for farmers so that the nation will have a controllable level of food-supply security. This has been accomplished by providing various types of subsidies, services, and products to farmers who produce the 20 or so commodities specified in the Farm Bill.

Subsidies have varied throughout the 70-year history of the Farm Bill, but in essence, it has provided a base-price flooring, subsidized crop insurance, crop-disaster payments, reduced-interest loans, counter-cyclical and direct payments, and, most recently, revenue-based payments. Many of these payments are directly related to provisional ecoservices, the type of crops, number of acres, and the number of bushels per acre that are harvested. To enroll in a Farm Bill, the farmers agree to farm their land in a manner that meets the USDA requirements for Highly Erodable Lands and so-called Swampbuster that states that wetlands on the farm cannot be drained, nor have been drained, after the signing of the 1985 Farm Bill. These requirements are called "conservation compliance" and address two ecological-sensitive areas on the farm. The remaining lands "in between" these two ecologically sensitive areas on the farm can be farmed in any manner that the farmer sees fit and still receive support payments. In addition to agreeing to fulfill "conservation compliance," the farmers also agree to certify their acres each year with the USDA Farm Service Agency. Certifying acres is a process by which the farmer provides the local USDA Farm Service Agency office with information on what types of crops were planted, the planting date, which tracts were planted, and how many acres were planted on their entire operation. Usually by June 30th of each year, the USDA has collected this "landscape data" for all farmers enrolled in the Farm Bill. These "certified acres" provide the base information to understand the potential supply of the nation's and world's grain market. This allows the market's invisible hand to digest critical information related to the existing and potential supply and demand, and, therefore, to determine the potential value of a bushel of wheat or a pound of chicken.

The USDA and numerous private firms take this data and begin to incorporate more data, the number of growing degree days (GDD), the amount of precipitation, historical production data, and numerous other information and strategies for analyzing this data for the purpose of determining how many bushels of grain, bales of cotton, or whatever production information they desire. Periodically, government-generated production reports are issued to update the market on the state of the crop. Private firms contribute their perspective and interpretation of the acres planted, weather impacts, and their variations of calculations. Since this data is numerical, generated at the field and tract level, and have other databases (weather, etc .) applied to it, it can be an additive process and can be scaled up to generate information from county, to state, to region, to nation, and globally. As the growing season progresses, information about the growing food, feed, bio-fuel, and fiber supply is fed to the invisible hand. These production-related calculations have been developed and are respected to the level that warrants the risk of speculation and developing insurance costs. This landscape data, along with other databases, indices, and calculations provide estimates of yield per acre to the tenth of a bushel. Subsequent reports that may adjust the national average corn yield from 155.8 bushels/acre to 156.5 bushels/acre may impact the market prices prior to even a bushel being harvested or weighed.

When harvest begins and actual production data is created, this "harder" data is also fed into the system, and the invisible hand continues to assess and react. Without this continuous supply of data during the growing season, the invisible hand would have very little information about the production plans, intentions, and outcomes of the farmers' production until the harvest was collected and stored. And even then this information would not be available to the market unless farmers would provide it to some organizational entity or put the grain up for sale in the market.

It would be difficult to overstate the value that this land-management data and the resulting intelligence has in relation to a functioning food-supply market. Without this data, numerous "unknowns" would cause miscommunication and assumptions that result in unnecessary marketing swings and subsequently, poor planting decisions by farmers, and poor buying decisions by processors. A market that cannot locate or assimilate data reliably will generate market failures to some degree. The more knowledgeable the market is, the more "right" it will be in reflecting the real need and price for a product or service.

Lacking Ecoservice-Landscape Intelligence

It may seem unfortunate that after 75 years of a centrally planned conservation economy that a similar landscape-intelligence database does not exist for ecosystems and ecoservices. To be fair, there are numerous inventories; the NRCS Natural Resource Inventory (USDA NRI 2009) is

Without landscape intelligence that is derived from the level of landscape management, proposed direction and policies that have the intentions of creating an effectual ecoservice demand fall short of reaching the producers of ecoservices in a manner that allows them to adjust their management practices to achieve outcomes. This was a message from the Millennium Environmental Assessment; if the assessment is completed at a scale that does not engage resource managers, the value of the assessment is significantly reduced.

Without knowledge of what is being produced on the landscape, an efficient ecoservice market cannot emerge. Since as soon as the market wants producers to sequester a certain number of "tons of carbon equivalents," the most logical question is how many "tons of carbon equivalents" are being sequestered now and how many tons do we need to sequester. If that number was obtained with an accepted level of uncertainty, the next question may be "What is the landscape's potential to emit a certain amount of 'tons of carbon equivalents?'" If the overall intentions of generating carbon-credit markets are to sequester enough carbon to alter the atmospheric composition, it behooves the market to attempt to understand the landscape-management intelligence at the level on which the carbon-sequestration trades are being conducted. In the Chicago Climate Exchange, the carbon units are generated at a field-and-farm level by tracking land-management activities related to tillage and cropping systems. If trades are being made at that level and landscape intelligence is being generated at levels greater than that, it is highly probable that market inefficiencies will be generated that will lead to some level of market failure (whether that failure is acknowledged or not). A unique characteristic of ecoservice markets is that the outcomes are public goods, and, therefore, the self-interests of both buyers and sellers are the same thing. They both want a menu of inexpensive land-management practices that are identified as sequestering large quantities of GHGs. By forcing both buyers and sellers to operate within a context of land-management outcomes, not just individual projects, the market may be forced to accomplish the overall national and global goals and not just generate more ecoservices continually through many, many isolated transactions.

Acquiring Landscape Intelligence

To envision a process that collected enough data so that a farmer, watershed manager, a state, and a nation could make natural-resource policy judgments based on a stackable and scalable database may seem insurmountable. Obstacles to acquiring this data may be numerous, but four primary concerns emerge quickly. First is the cost of gathering the information. Second is how to manage and update the data. The third and fourth concerns are who gets to use the data and for what purposes. These are technical, scientific, financial, and political issues. From a technical perspective, acquiring this data would be relatively straightforward, reasonably valid, and financially feasible. As stated, the USDA FSA routinely gathers spatially oriented landscape intelligence as it pertains to crop-production data. In fact, a few years ago, during my crop "certification" process, I was also asked to include landscape data other than just croplands. On completion of the exercise, the FSA had wooded, pasture, prairie, wetland, and cropland areas identified on every square foot of the farm. In essence, I "certified" the landscape-management plan on the entire operation. This was conducted using the same maps, the same personnel providing the data (farmer), and the same personnel entering the data (FSA employee) into the same computers used for certifying production acres. Perhaps the only difference is that more computer data storage is needed and additional time in gathering, providing, and inputting the data would be necessary. With these efficiencies readily at hand, it would be presumed that the marginal cost of creating this landscape intelligence would be much lower than the potential marginal value. How this data is viewed and how much confidence the scientific community has in it will be a function related to their involvement in developing and ownership of the system. Confidence in the landscape-intelligence data should be earned through the use of resource-management indices that are developed by scientific communities within the USDA, universities, and other institutions. This data can also be applied spatially within a geographical information system with the support of remote sensing and similar field checks as used for production data. Once gathered, the management of the data could be as straightforward as managing the certified acres data. It could be sorted and queried depending on the government needs and intentions and how the ecoservice markets value this data.

Value-added Landscape Intelligence

Of course, even with a technically and financially feasible means to gather and manage a landscape intelligence, the larger obstacles are often related to the political and financial aspects of providing that data. These are the third and fourth concerns listed: who gets to use the data and for what purpose. The political stance can either be that the data is valuable and that farmers should be compensated for gathering and providing it as a means toward identifying ecological assets, or that this information will create an environmental liability for farmers. A scenario that illustrated this occurred in the fall of 2009 (Ortiz 2009). A Nebraska natural-resource district sued the USDA and its Farm Service Agency, alleging that it had farmers would be more inclined to enter that market framework. If these values were apparent, the decisions about land use would be made prior to planting. A farmer would decide on which land-use options would provide the best return-on-investment, possibly by receiving multiple incentives for water quality, habitat, and carbon sequestration for a single resource-management activity. Since the farmer is paid for outcomes, not the cost of a practice, the farmer is economically rewarded for targeting the ecoservice-generating practices to the land units that best accomplish the symbiotic goals of the stakeholders.

Upon completion of the cropping year, outcomes could be reported to the Farm Service Agency in the form of various resource indices when crop-production-outcome data is provided by the farmer. The result is food-production data, water-quality-production data, habitat, all of which are highly valued resources that will be produced when an effectual demand is applied toward them. In a mature EcoCommerce system, the market will begin to understand which farming systems produce the most profitable combination of provisional and regulating ecoservices.

Integrating Government Decision Framework

The USDA Office of Ecosystem Services and Markets was created by The Food, Conservation, and Energy Act of 2008 H .R. 2419, Section 2709: Environmental Services Markets, the intentions of which are to assist in the development of new technical guidelines and science-based methods to assess environmental service benefits, which will in turn promote markets for ecosystem services. These guidelines are designed to facilitate the participation of farmers, ranchers, and forest landowners in emerging environmental services markets and include three elements:

- A procedure to measure environmental services benefits

- A protocol to report environmental services benefits

- A registry to collect, record, and maintain the benefits measured

To implement Section 2709 of the Farm Bill, a federal Conservation and Land Management Environmental Services Board was established on December 5, 2008 to assist the Secretary of Agriculture in adopting the technical guidelines that the federal government will use to assess ecosystem services provided by conservation and land management activities. The Board's guidelines will focus on scientifically rigorous and economically sound methods for quantifying carbon, air and water quality, wetlands, and endangered species benefits in an effort to facilitate the participation of farmers, ranchers, and forest landowners in emerging ecosystem markets.

Environmental Services Board members include the Secretaries of the Interior, Energy, Commerce, Transportation; the Assistant Secretary of the Army, Civil Works; the Chairman of the Council of Economic Advisors; the Director of the Office of Science and Technology Policy; the Administrator of the Environmental Protection Agency; and the Assistant Deputy Under-Secretary of Defense for Environment, Safety and Occupational Health. The Secretary of Agriculture chairs the board; the Chairman of Council on Environmental Quality, and the Administrator of the Office of Information and Regulatory Affairs, Office of Management and Budget, are vice-chairs. The membership and mission of the Environmental Service Board is significant relative to the state of the ecoservice markets today. The extent of the membership will also create a bureaucratic challenge to move these federal agencies toward an integrated landscape-intelligence system that can implement the guidelines objectives mentioned (USDA OESM 2008).

One of the duties associated with the Board includes recommending to the Secretary of Agriculture current federal department and agency programs that quantify or monetize environmental services benefits or otherwise utilize market-based environmental approaches. Accomplishing this duty will provide a significant list of potential ecoservice market demands and perhaps initiate a comprehensive landscape-intelligence effort as described in the *Value-added Landscape Intelligence* section.

CHAPTER 10

Building EcoCommerce Portfolios

Portfolio Organization

As with any collection of valuables, a portfolio is used as a means to assemble and organize one's assets. A collection of ecoservices can be organized by basically two perspectives: that of natural capital resources and that of production-management units.

Natural-Resource Perspective

Organizing an EcoCommerce portfolio by the resource of concern could be structured using the USDA Natural Resources Conservation Service categories of Soil, Water, Air, Plants, Animals and Energy (SWAPA & E) or a similar list using the natural resources. The resource perspective is often used by government agencies and advocacy groups whose interest and focus is on environmental issues. This is a valid perspective as the ecoservice markets provide value based on the generation of ecoservices produced by ecosystems. It is also the organizational structure toward which Congress often allocates natural-resource funds. Due to this, funding flows down this path to implement particular practices to effect particular resources. The most challenging aspect of this approach is that farms and the agro-ecosystem in which they reside are not managed from the natural-resource perspective, but rather a management-unit perspective. And farms and the agro-economy are not structured from an activity or practice perspective, but from an outcome perspective of bushels harvested and pounds of livestock derived from land-management units and activities.

Management-Unit Perspective

Organizing an EcoCommerce portfolio using land-management units could be structured using farm, farmstead, feedlots or livestock facilities, forests, field, pasture, and range. Using a management-unit perspective, specific management strategies can be applied to each unit to produce the desired outcomes. The SWAPA & E components are addressed within each of these management units rather than trying to assess water quality across several areas that do not have management commonalities. This is often more palatable for land managers as the production-management practices of each unit directly impacts both production and natural resources. This is aligned with how the agro-ecosystem and agro-economy function, in that practices within the management units produce both economic and ecological outcomes. If value is placed on grain and water quality, then a resource stakeholder has an opportunity to influence the management through creating an effectual demand for either commodity. The other significant advantage to organizing an EcoCommerce portfolio by management units rather than by specific resources is that the intentions of EcoCommerce is to influence land-management activities at the farm level. Management units can also organize multiple geographical configurations to describe outcomes for specific resource parameters at the scale or scope desired. Geographical configurations could include farm, watershed, cellulosic shed, river basin, or other polygons.

Management-Unit Portfolio

Using the seven management units that have the capacity to generate the SWAPA & E ecoservices, a simplified ecoservice portfolio template, called the EcoCommerce Portfolio, can be designed (Table 10.1). This simplified template identifies the seven types of management units on the left column. Each type of management unit could be subdivided if necessary. For example, if the farm contained two feedlots, three forests, 10 pastures, and 20 fields, they all could be represented by subdividing the management unit further down the portfolio spreadsheet. Likewise, if other components of the resources of concern are identified, they, too, could be extended further across the spreadsheet. Queries could be conducted to sort out the management units or ecoservices as desired.

Table 10.1	EcoCommerce Portfolio					
Management Unit	Ecoservice Parameters					
	S	W	A	P	A	E
Farm ID						
Farmstead						
Feedlot						
Forest						
Field						
Pasture						
Range						

Standardizing the Index Scale

As mentioned in Chapter 8, the list of management indices available today were developed independently of each other with the result that their numerical scales are not aligned. The USDA Soil Conditioning Index has a zero point to describe a neutral score with positive numbers representing good soil-management practices and negative numbers representing the opposite. A range of -2.0 to 2.0 would describe significantly different soil-management strategies. The Water Quality Score ranged from 0 to over 100, and the Habitat Suitability Index ranged from 0 to 100. The resource-management indices in use today have as much diversity in how they are expressed as Ott discovered in the 1970s. For convenience of speaking a standardized resource-management language and for communicating the value of an ecoservice portfolio, it would be advantageous for all the indices and scores to use the same scale to illustrate the relative values of the calculations. It is not the intentions of this section to determine the exact process to follow for recalibrating each index or scoring, much as it is not the intention of this book to recommend the specific indices and scoring systems to use. The intentions of this section are to illustrate the advantages of choosing indices and aligning their scoring methods on a scale of 0 to 100 to create a greater ease in discussing resource outcomes. On the scale of 0 – 100, 0 represents resource degradation, 50 represents maintaining the resource condition, and 50-100 represents a graduated scale toward increasing resource-condition improvement. This standardization will allow both the professional and lay person to understand the general management outcome or potential ecoservice value. A common scale is critical to illustrate outcomes graphically and statistically and to create an ecoservice unit that can be traded with greater ease.

EcoCommerce Portfolio #1

To create an EcoCommerce portfolio, specific management units and specific outcomes must be applied. Table 10.2 lists the management units and any subunits, along with the acreage. Management indices representing ecoservice parameters are listed on the top, and applicable index scores are listed on the grid. It should be noted that these are fictional management indices that are developed based on actual indices listed in Chapter 8, or created to illustrate a potentially valuable ecoservice. These included the soil-condition index (SCi), forest-soil-quality index (fSQi), the water-quality index (WQi), carbon-sequestration index (CQRi), British thermal-unit index (BTUi), habitat-suitability index (HSi), feedlot index (FLi), pollinator HSi (plHSi) and a pheasant HSi (phHSi). Each index operates on a scale of 0-100.

Table 10.2		EcoCommerce Portfolio #1								
Management Unit	Acres	EcoCommerce Parameters								
		FLi	SCi	fSQi	WQi	CQRi	BTUi	HSi	plHSi	phHSi
Farm	500							75	82	80
Farmstead										
Feedlot		96								
Forest										
#5001	50			75		88		82		
Fields										
#1001	100		75		87	92	82			
#1002	100		72		75	88	88			
#1003	100		67		72	81	72			
#1004	150		62		78	77	75			
Total	450									
Ac-Wgt Average			68.2		78.0	83.6	78.8			
Pasture										
Range										

For an agro-ecological professional, the EcoCommerce Portfolio #1 can illustrate how the landscape resources are being managed without even knowing the details of the farm's natural characteristics or management strategy. Other information that is critical to the resource manager, but not the resource stakeholder, is absent from the template and includes the soil types, the field's topography, or cropping systems. An EcoCommerce-trained resource professional could review the template briefly and determine if the resources are prone to degradation or if significant conservation measurements and activities are being applied relative to these fields. In this portfolio, farmstead, pasture, and range management units are not included due to the situation that the operation does not contain them or that no management value is applied toward them.

In this example, all the units assessed are being managed in a manner that is greater than 50, meaning that the resources are not prone to degradation. An acre-weight average can also describe how the fields are being managed overall. Some fields may provide greater resource benefits than others in a more economical manner than others. In these cases, an acre-weighted attribute will allow farmers to meet resource goals in the most efficient manner. It should be noted that in some cases, especially soil erosion, mitigation attempts in one field cannot "correct" or mitigate erosion in another. Mitigation within the farm operation could address such issues as carbon, water quality, and wildlife.

A Singular EcoCommerce Portfolio

A significant challenge with today's ecoservice markets is their creation of multiple avenues and processes in which land managers can engage. While numerous options seem ideal in a market economy, numerous types of units and processes for exchanging value become a burden, increasing the costs of entering a market. Multiple market pathways may initially create an attractive gross margin, only to have the market stakeholders dilute the value by requiring the land managers to follow several unique administrative avenues to acquire the value. Currently, these disparities not only exist among the stakeholders, but also among programs and processes within an entity. These disparities were created through the natural evolutionary process of the early ecoservice markets when most were unfamiliar with what was exactly needed to create a functioning market. As each individual group of entrepreneurs sought out processes and procedures to fit their markets, they naturally diverged and converged depending on the circumstances. Regardless of the reason, the resulting independence of each market not only creates a level of frustration for potential ecoservice providers but raises the transaction costs of each exchange and has the potential to dilute the value for resource-management activities that are creating multiple ecoservices. In contrast, having a singular portfolio and process is especially beneficial with the unique market of ecoservices, in that a singular conservation practice applied can generate multiple values to multiple stakeholders. A single resource assessment process and template will allow communication from the land owner to the stakeholders to describe the resource-management outcomes that are of interest to them. Since this information can be generated by agricultural professionals in a fairly efficient manner, transaction costs are reduced, and market-entry costs can remain low.

EcoCommerce Portfolio #2 (Table 10.3) acts as a singular resource portfolio that organizes ecoservices that are generated by agriculture and land-management units, and categorizes ecoservices by Resource-

regulations, federal grant programs, and to customize their plants' energy-balance calculation. To accomplish this, their portfolio would contain the farms, the corn, and the biomass that is supplied and the types and categories of ecoservices are generated. The portfolio below lists six farms that total 6,000 acres. The ecoservices that the farms produce are related to carbon sequestration, soil quality, corn production, energy balance, and habitat. Etank Ethanol is interested in ecoservice units that can be used to establish both a sustainable resource-management level and ecoservice units that can be used to generate and calculate resource credits. To meet these needs, Etank Ethanol uses carbon sequestration, BTU, soil condition, and habitat-suitability indices.

Etank Ethanol anticipates that their self-interests associated with these ecoservices will include (1) preparing themselves for any energy and climate-change legislation that either incentivizes or taxes carbon-related energy use, (2) preparing themselves for enrollment in the USDA Biomass Crop Assistance Program or similar government programs that promote biomass utilization, (3) promoting their industry by improving energy-balance calculations, (4) supporting their farmer suppliers in managing their soil for long-term productivity capacity, and (5) establishing the bio-refinery industry as an industry that is accountable to environmental issues.

To meet these objectives, Etank Ethanol has established criteria and policy related to the resource-management levels and how credits will be established. Etank Ethanol has established the minimum index levels to accept corn and biomass for the following indices; CQTRi level of 70, SCi level of 51, BTUi level of 80, and the HSi level of 78. Any amount above those levels may generate a credit, and any level below requires the farmer to purchase credits. For example, Farm# 5205 exceeded the CQTRi requirements by 18 units per acre on 750 acres for a total of 13,500 credit units. All credits can be traded among the farmers except the SCi. The rationale for this is that, unlike the other resource parameters, soil productivity is innate to specific field and increasing a SCi in another location does not produce overall and long-term capacity of the region's soil to generate corn, biomass, or other provisional ecoservices. Habitat, energy balances, and carbon-sequestration losses can be adequately offset by their production in other areas that may be more suited to economically generate these values. According to Etank Ethanol's portfolio (Table 10.4), their farmer suppliers generated an excess of 31,700 CQTR acre-credits that can be traded among the Etank Ethanol suppliers or, perhaps converted to CO_2e units and traded with the CCX or other carbon market. The farmers also generated an excess of 2,350 BTU acre-credits that could be included in Etank Ethanol energy balance. The producers fell short of their habitat objectives with -50,450 HSi acre-credits. In this scenario, Farm#5189 accounted for 41,400 of those negative HSi acre-credits. All farmers met the SCi threshold. While this is a fictional scenario, these types of management outcomes are real and occurring on farms across the world. How these credits are eventually calculated, valued, and traded is the workings of the market and the policies of industry, government, and consumers.

Table 10.4		Etank Ethanol - EcoCommerce Portfolio						
		Resource Management Levels				Resource Credits		
Farm ID	Acres	CQTR [70]	Sci [51]	BTUi [80]	HSi [78]	CQTR	BTU	HSi
5205	750	88	65	88	86	13,500	6,000	6,000
5206	550	65	75	78	94	-2,750	-1,100	8,800
5100	1200	77	54	92	65	8,400	14,400	-15,600
5188	850	95	66	68	72	21,250	-10,200	-5,100
5189	2300	65	98	76	60	-11,500	-9,200	-41,400
5233	350	78	78	87	69	2,800	2,450	-3,150
Total	6000							
Average		78	73	82	74			
Acre-Wght		75	77	80	70			
Totals						31,700	2,350	-50,450

Retail-based EcoCommerce Portfolio

If Walmart and other retail sectors are going to establish a method to determine a level of "sustainability" embedded in their products, they will need succinct measuring tools from a variety of industries. Their portfolio will be based on the ability to describe what products were produced in a definable, sustainable manner. It is not as likely that they would want to track resource credits that are generated above and beyond this level of sustainability, although that all depends on how they envision EcoCommerce and if EcoCommerce itself provides monetary gain beyond value-added products. If it is assumed that the goals of the retailers are to provide consumers with information that the production practices used to create the product were sustainable, then their portfolio would only include resource-management-level indices that can describe a "sustainability level" and not generate a resource-credit calculation. With these intentions, it would not be necessary to identify how each resource parameter is being managed with the use of many singular indices. For this process to be manageable, a compound index that represents the culmination of multiple resource parameters would be useful.

In this case, two EcoCommerce Portfolios or a combination portfolio would be necessary. One portfolio (Table 10.5) would be generated by the supplier (in this case Butter Land Company) to communicate and transfer information to the retail outlet. Butter Land Company would compile producer portfolios (similar to Table 10.3) to determine if their producers meet the "Sustainability Index" criteria to maintain market access to the Retail Outlet. Butter Land Company may need to identify the Sustainability Index for each product they supply and how many units are supplied. Since Butter Land Company receives the producer's portfolio on a yearly basis, the data management burden is limited.

Table 10.5		Butter Land Company #23A EcoCommerce Portfolio					
Product UPC	Units	Ecoservice Indices					
		CQTRi	SCi	WQi	BTUi	HSi	Sustain Index
1000100995	50,000	85	88	84	76	75	81.6
100774995	15,000	65	87	45	65	76	67.6
1004380995	12,000	78	65	68	45	54	62.0
1891100995	45,000	87	98	72	48	89	78.8
1000165395	875	51	65	91	98	83	77.6
9537200995	1260	98	77	53	76	81	77.0
1749739995	35,000	64	54	87	65	80	70.0
	Average	75	76	71	68	77	73.5

Depending on the demands of the retailer, the supplier may identify how each product they manufacture was produced using the five indices listed or just using the compound index value of the Sustainability Index. In the example, the product represented by UPC # 1000100995 has a sustainability index of 81.6. In the suppliers' agreement, it could be stated that all products supplied must have a sustainability index of at least 70. The retail outlet would also need to account for their sustainability claims and would need a sustainability portfolio of some sort. The retail outlet would have an EcoCommerce Portfolio (Table 10.6) to combine the information from all the suppliers.

The example lists the sustainability index for a particular product supplied by seven vendors. The retail outlets compile these indices and can describe the composite sustainability index for the product. All suppliers met the index threshold of 70. As EcoCommerce matures and retail outlets and suppliers become integrated on their efforts, value can be applied toward suppliers that supply products that are rated more sustainable.

Table 10.6	Retail Outlet EcoCommerce Portfolio		
Product UPC 1000100006			
Sustainability Index - Composite (unit-weighted) Score			76.8
Supplier ID#	Quantity (units)	Sustainability Index	SI units
23A	50,000	81.6	4,080,000
33B	35,000	72.3	2,530,500
43A	42,000	75.8	3,183,600
54A	12,000	85.3	1,023,600
23C	6,000	77.6	465,600
55D	67,000	77.0	5,159,000
34E	23,000	70.0	1,610,000
Total Units	235,000		18,052,300
Average	58,750	77.1	2,578,900

Government-based EcoCommerce Portfolio

Due to the several levels of government and numerous objectives, there are numerous activities they must conduct as it pertains to natural-resource management. These include providing technical and financial assistance, regulating activities, monitoring, training and data management, and, most likely, several more. Since many government offices and intentions were developed over time and based on constituency and congressional demands, not all government efforts are coordinated toward a common goal. This is a reasonable outcome, since congressional members represent different sectors of society and each sector has its own self-interests to promote. What is less reasonable is that government agencies do not have a succinct and transparent manner to describe and value the land-management activities they desire to achieve. A reasonable solution to this conundrum is for each government agency to develop an EcoCommerce Portfolio to describe its land-management demands.

There are several types of government entities that have the responsibility to develop and administer watershed plans. The motivation to develop these plans can be initiated by citizenry groups or industries, that have opportunities to receive state and federal funds or the requirement to establish a waste-load allocation for point-source and non-point-source pollution discharges such as occurs with the EPA Total Maximum Daily Load requirements. In any case, each plan should have similar characteristics: a watershed and water-body assessment, water-quality goals, and a strategy and plan to achieve the goals. This same framework could be applied to groundwater supplies, habitat, or other ecosystems and components.

An EcoCommerce watershed portfolio for the Valley Creek Watershed (Table 10.7) lists the three subwatersheds, divided into urban and rural, and the water-quality index score goal that the Valley Creek Watershed

District has determined will be necessary to achieve the desired water quality in each of Valley Creek's subwatersheds. If it is the legislated duty of the District to provide information, guidance, and support to the watershed inhabitants to meet the water-quality index goals, then the Valley Creek could best serve those inhabitants by determining what level of management is needed on the land, what percentage of land area has been assessed, what percentage of those assessed acres meet the goal, and the remaining acres that need to be assessed. In the portfolio example provided, 34 percent of the watershed acres have been assessed with 56 percent of those acres meeting the water-quality index goal. A watershed portfolio developed in this manner illustrates both the assets and liabilities and provides a means to determine the spatial extent of the water-quality issues. The source of this data would be individual farm and urban portfolios that could be associated with geographical information systems. While the ultimate intentions of the District's activities is to improve the water quality of Valley Creek, it may be in their self-interests to compensate land managers for providing the data that generates this level of landscape intelligence rather than spending money on implementing conservation practices prior to knowing where in the watershed that improvements need to be made. This is not to imply that land-management scenarios that have obvious and negative impacts on water quality should not be addressed. But if a government unit is to be successful in improving water quality throughout the watershed along a continuum of time and activities, then a system to account for land-management activities that affect water quality must be incorporated and valued.

Table 10.7		Valley Creek Watershed EcoCommerce Portfolio						
Subwatersheds	Acres	WQ index (goal)	Acres Assessed	Percent Assessed	Acres Meeting Goal	% Ass'd Acres meeting goal	Acres Remaining to be Assessed	Percent Remaining to be Assessed
Upstream#1-Rural	15,000	88.0	6,500	43.3%	5,500	85%	8,500.0	57%
Upstream#1-Urban	1,200	88.0	1,200	100.0%	100	8%	0	0%
Upstream #2-Rural	65,000	75.0	22,000	33.8%	15,000	68%	43,000	66%
Upstream #2-Urban	2,800	75.0	1,400	50.0%	150	11%	1,400	50%
Lower Reach-Rural	250,000	78.0	67,000	26.8%	45,000	67%	183,000	73%
Lower Reach-Urban	55,000	78.0	35,000	63.6%	8,500	24%	20,000	36%
Total Rural	330,000		95,500	29%	65,500	69%	234,500	71%
Total Urban	59,000		37,600	64%	8,750	23%	21,400	36%
Total	389000	80.3	133,100	34.2%	74,250	56%	255,900	66%

Commoditizing Ecoservices

The use of agricultural management indices (like all indices) generates a numerical outcome that describes the status, trend, or movement of a particular system relative to some temporal, spatial, physical, chemical, or biological reference point. That index-derived number can have a value placed on it just like any other unit of measurement.

As illustrated in the various portfolios, ecoservices can be packaged and transferred to provide other entities the utility to meet their objectives. This value can also be applied to products to represent that the materials are produced and processed within a given sustainability criteria. The EcoCommerce "commodities" are the ecoservice units that describe how the management of the natural capital benefits the ecosystem to allow the regenerative processes of the bio-economy to remain intact or improved upon. The services provided to the economy are the soil and habitat management that creates the clean water and allows wildlife to reproduce. If an entity desires a stream of clean water to provide a city with a supply of drinking water, and it is determined that a watershed that has a certain acre-weighted water-quality index value would provide that stream of clean water, then every acre that is managed for that water-quality index or greater has a certain value in relation to clean water. The *value of use* of clean water is understood by all of us who depend on it. The *value in exchange* or the commoditized value of that clean water can be determined by micro-economic supply-and-demand forces. The value of the capacity to supply or the value of the natural capital that produces that clean water can be determined by micro-EcoCommerce supply-and-demand forces. The burden on EcoCommerce is for its ability to define the value of the capacity to supply ecoservices. In today's economic system, the capacity of physical capital (factories, etc) to produce is readily incorporated into the cost of the product and the company's portfolio. The EcoCommerce portfolio brings the value of production capacity into the economic system.

A gallon of clean water does, initially, seem like a more reasonable and realistic commodity to trade, rather than a resource-management strategy that is determined through the application of an index to shed relatively clean water. But if there were a method to directly measure the quality and quantity of gallons of clean water that were shed from a farm field, then a system for regulating the quantity or quality of water or an incentive program for the production of a certain amount and quality of water would probably have been developed within the Clean Water Act policy framework at the time that regulations for point-source pollution were enacted.

Many of today's ecoservice markets have avoided the strategy to commoditize ecoservices and instead attempt to develop contracts to generate and *deliver* a certain resource such as clean water and wildlife. This does not appear to be a streamlined solution. Developing a contract to provide a payment for a certain quality and quantity of clean water would have to consider all the vagaries of weather and the dynamics of agriculture. By the time all the exceptions and omissions were included into the contract, it would be expected that the intention of the contract would be similar to the intention of a management index, yet void of any transparency and simplicity.

Consider just the quality and quantity issues of an extended drought or a flash flood. Any farmer with an ecoservices contract that was required to provide a certain volume of clean water would have to be held harmless on their inability to deliver. A farm operation that resided in a drought area would deliver little or no clean water under a low or nonexistent flow. The farm operation in a flash-flood area would also deliver little or no clean water but within a large voluminous flow. A contract for the direct delivery of a certain amount of clean water would only be valid under average weather conditions.

Using agricultural-management indices as the means to commoditize resource-management strategies allows buyers a succinct and transparent means to describe the resource outcomes they desire and to be able to provide an exact monetary value that they are willing to invest in that potential outcome. The ability to generate an ecoservice portfolio and transfer those values to other entities in a transparent and efficient manner will be perceived to be a commodity resource by the invisible hand, and value will be created and exchanged.

Natural-Resource Accounts Foundation

The creation of a natural-resource accounting process within the System of National Accounts, as described in Chapter 1, could be supplied with data from singular or multiple EcoCommerce portfolios created for a particular level of EcoCommerce activity (farm, processor, and retailer) and for specific ecoservice units and values. A water-quality index for the Upper Mississippi River Basin could be compiled through a state-sponsored watershed portfolio or through the myriad of portfolios that processors generate through direct commerce with the land managers. Institutions, such as an EcoCommerce Registry, could provide the data-processing, oversight, and housing of the data. Analysis and reporting of the resource-management outcomes could be officially announced on a yearly basis, as it would seem only practical for land managers to report on their outcomes after the year is over. Or it could be reported more frequently such as the crop-production analysis and report. Even though official production numbers are usually not available until January after the production year is complete, the government and industry is constantly applying production-calculation techniques to the "certified" acres data generated in June. One could assume that if farmers "certify" their management strategy in June of each year, EcoCommerce professionals would be able to use the production data along with rainfall, temperature, and other climate-related variables to provide a similar estimate of the natural-resource-production data. Analyzing and reporting this data to the extent of production data does not seem economical at this point, but some level of interest and value will need to be applied toward it to generate data that is sufficient for including natural-resource accounts in the System of National Accounts.

SECTION 3
APPLIED ECOCOMMERCE

OVERVIEW

Applying EcoCommerce is a process that provides incentives via markets to resource managers for producing ecoservices. The unique challenge with EcoCommerce is how incentives for ecoservices can be formalized within the economic system. This challenge is met by addressing the perspective given by Dr. Bob A. Stewart, West Texas A&M University Professor of Soil Science at an University of Minnesota, April 2008, lecture on emerging issues in soil and water. He was asked if either policy reforms or the market will provide farmers the support to reduce resource degradation. Dr. Stewart replied by stating that many farmers in his region are "burning up the soil" and using ground water at a rate that is greater than the rate of recharge. He added, "But these farmers are making rational economic decisions. If they did not make these decisions and in turn were no longer competitive in the marketplace and lost their ability to economically sustain themselves, they would be making irrational decisions." He concluded by saying that whether it is by the hand of policy or the hand of the market place that provides the support for farmers to make rational decisions that improve resources, is not an answer that could be provided by him but must be answered by society (Stewart 2008).

For society to answer these questions, the society must be able to engage within the decision-making framework. The EcoCommerce framework allows the value of ecoservice to be formalized within traditional economic activities and processes. The economic participants are given the responsibility to define a level of sustainability, rather than allocating that role to a government agency. This is accomplished by posting resource indices, ecoservice units, prices, and transactions in a manner that is transparent and assessable, similar to commodity price units and postings. Unlike traditional economic components, ecoservices are public goods whose benefits can be used by many. This attribute that has been a hindrance to the development of ecoservice markets is actually an advantage to EcoCommerce. With the use of indices to measure resource-management levels, a so-called Sustainability 1.0 level can be achieved through a shared responsibility of many industries, governments, non-profit organizations, retail outlets, and consumers. As public goods, ecoservices can be managed using both exclusive and non-exclusive transactions. Non-exclusivity allows many stakeholders to procure products from one producer as long as that producer is meeting an acceptable resource-management level. This process of sharing costs and values becomes the flip side of the "tragedy of the commons" coin and generating ecoservices becomes the "opportunity of the commons." Exclusive transactions are also a component of EcoCommerce in a similar fashion as today's ecoservice markets function, in that, a measurable or calculated unit and credit is established. The primary difference is that EcoCommerce allows the economy to define a sustainability baseline using non-exclusive ecoservices prior to requiring stakeholders to purchase additional ecoservice credits to achieve a so-called Sustainability 1.5 level. For participants to engage in EcoCommerce does not require a complete understanding of EcoCommerce any more than engaging in an economic system requires complete knowledge of economics. The vast majority of EcoCommerce participants will be able to engage in EcoCommerce by only understanding how their self-interests can be met. As long as the cost of obtaining market knowledge and the cost of market entry are less than the ecoservice benefits, participants will enter the market and trades will ensue. Section III illustrates how this process creates motivation to produce ecoservices and then how the transaction process unfolds to account for and compensate ecoservices. The EcoCommerce participants included in this chapter are fictional, although the intention is to provide realistic scenarios, and therefore, real businesses and existing circumstances are included in the fictional representation.

CHAPTER 11

The Emergence of EcoCommerce

Seeds of EcoCommerce

The seeds of EcoCommerce have been residing in legislation, organizations, and agribusiness, and on the farms for several years, perhaps decades. There has been a sense and a tension that something needs to be done or some policy needs to be written to cause these efforts to sprout. As a soil and water conservation technician in the 1990s, I worked with dozens of farmers to implement conservation practices that would improve the soil and water resources and saw firsthand how these practices functioned. But I would comment that the work we were completing was relatively "token" work to keep us going until the "real program" came along. My sense was that as a government agent, there was no feasible way that we could address all the clients' issues. Ecoservice markets provided some hope as they emerged, but then many withered quickly. Some grew and

According to Mike Duke, President and Chief Executive Officer, Walmart Stores, Inc ., "The index will bring about a more transparent supply chain, drive product innovation and ultimately, provide consumers the information they need to assess the sustainability of products. If we work together, we can create a new retail standard for the 21st century".

Walmart's reach, as gathered from their Sustainability Product Index Fact Sheet, is to compel their primary suppliers to then influence those secondary suppliers and down the supply chain. Walmart did not decide to bring their control down to the producers themselves. They could not do this any more efficiently than centrally control the production of all the products they sell. What they do efficiently is to set the parameters for their products and to allow the invisible hand of the economy to operate. When they set the parameters via a sustainability index, they are, in essence, providing more information for the invisible hand in its millions of calculations. When individuals and entities act on this information in their own interest, then theoretically the most efficient sustainability outcomes are achieved. As the world's largest retailer, Walmart has the capacity to initiate and influence the direction toward a more sustainable production system. And if consumers gravitate toward products identified as sustainable, all retail outlets will be inclined to seek out a level of product sustainability as well.

The market relationship that a producer would have with Walmart could be defined as a "participatory benefit," or more simply "market access." That is, if the supply chain can adequately prove that the production of the retail item is done so in a sustainable manner, then that supplier will be allowed to participate within that retail outlet or allowed to carry a seal of approval. If the "sustainability" seal does generate demand and provide a significant, additional profit, the retail outlet may be motivated to pass those profits down the production chain to encourage additional supply. To initiate EcoCommerce, Walmart's suppliers could require agricultural-productions systems to be managed to a level of sustainability as defined by management indices. This then creates value for a level of resource management, and, in some instances, if a producer would not be able to meet those sustainable levels, then those operations could purchase sustainability credits, however they are defined.

Bio-Economy-Induced EcoCommerce

For all intents and purposes, a bio-economy has existed since the first trade took place involving agriculture products thousands of years ago. But in the recent "discovery" of a bio-economy, it is often in relation to biomass that is converted to fuels, energy, and products rather than having those fuel and products produced from petroleum-based resources. These biomass resources can be any vegetation, herbaceous or woody, annual or perennial and can be derived from any component of those plants. A primary source for the liquid fuel of ethanol is the corn kernel, but various processes and uses for all types of biomass has been used, demonstrated, or researched to determine its feasibility and cost-effectiveness.

Cellulosic materials are being researched as the fuel source of the future, as cellulose is a common organic material on the planet. As progress continues to be made on reducing the costs of converting cellulosic material to fuel, a double-edged sword is created. If and when a cost-effective process is developed to convert common cellulose to a liquid fuel, the invisible hand will compel growers and owners of cellulose to bring this material into the market stream. This will provide consumers with plentiful, and, therefore, relatively inexpensive liquid fuel supply, which, in turn, encourages the conversion of this energy source into contemporary higher valued products.

The question posed to the bio-industry, which includes farmers, transporters, processors, and consumers, is whether the industry can utilize this carbon-based fuel source and not degrade the natural capital on which it depends. If the bio-industry does develop a cost-effective conversion, but does not value the management of the natural capital that generates the cellulose, the invisible hand would encourage management that degrades the natural capital. The challenges to the bio-industry are two-fold: it must provide a mechanism to demonstrate that the industry can convert biomass in a manner that is energy positive and do so in manner that does not significantly degrade the capacity of the production and natural resources.

The most probable EcoCommerce value types associated with bio-industry are that of a "participatory," "incentives," and "resource credit trading" values. If the bio-industry is compelled to develop production and natural-resource management standards, then these standards will be used as a screening tool to allow the producers to sell their biomass stocks to the processor. An example would be for the biomass processor to require that all fields that supply corn kernel and corn stover must maintain a soil-conditioning index at a defined sustainable level. Meeting this standard would allow the producer to "participate" in the market. This participatory requirement, like that of the retail sector, puts the cost of meeting these standards on the producer but gives them access to a market outlet.

If the producer meets those production standards, the next value stream would be the carbon balance of the production system. For example, if a producer is able to produce a bushel of corn that has an energy content of 400,000 BTUs and the production of that bushel of corn consumed 150,000 BTUs (not including sunlight energy), then there would be a positive balance of 250,000 BTU/bushel. This positive energy balance could be purchased by the bio-industrial processor to be included in their overall energy balance of their operation. If other corn producers are not able to provide a positive energy balance, these corn producers may purchase the BTU credits from producers that have excess. The bio-processor may also raise the value of the higher energy balance to encourage the adjustment of production systems to meet these demands.

These energy balances are related to the overall carbon emissions and potential offsets that may exist in a carbon-credit-trading market, but they are different. An energy balance describes if the entire process provides more, less, or the same amount of energy than if the process did not exist, whereas, the carbon calculation determines whether the overall process will have a positive, negative, or neutral carbon footprint. Other bio-refineries such as soy diesel, an electrical utility plant, or a specific factory that uses biomass as an energy source would be market participants. To initiate EcoCommerce, a bio-refinery could request that all corn and cellulose that is brought into the plant need to meet a certain resource-management standard and have a BTU index that is favorable to the energy life cycle and carbon markets.

Agricultural-Producer-Induced EcoCommerce

EcoCommerce could arise from an individual farmer. Farmers are on the frontlines of resource management as their occupations are dependent on the agro-ecosystem. Agriculture is a diverse industry and participants in the field fall on the continuum of excellent land stewards to those who have less regard for the natural capital that they and their industry depend on. There may be two motivational avenues to initiate EcoCommerce. One is that numerous local, state, and federal agencies have a myriad of methods, processes, and paperwork to evaluate, assess, and regulate resource management on farms. To consolidate these requirements, a farmer may attempt to use the succinct and transparent EcoCommerce portfolio to communicate to these agencies and the ecoservice markets. Another avenue that may be taken is to "even the playing field" on resource management in the countryside. A land operator that has a short-term lease has less interest in maintaining the integrity of the natural capital than a farmer with a longer vision and economic interest. An EcoCommerce framework would not necessarily force land stewardship on all farmers but it would provide additional value to those who practice it. For instance, Walmart's suppliers that have a sustainable threshold would not allow market access to those that do not meet that threshold. If the EPA's TMDL regulatory process advances and begins to require watersheds and their inhabitants to make water-quality improvements, a farmer may engage in the EcoCommerce process to seek a practical and efficient "regulatory assurance." Those land managers who do not meet an identifiable resource management would lack an assurance process and access to certain markets.

Agricultural-Organization-Induced EcoCommerce

The numerous attempts by government, non-profit, and the private sector to generate ecoservice markets have not gone unnoticed by agricultural political organizations. In the climate-change legislation, agricultural policy groups fought hard along with the support of House Ag Committee Chairman Collin Peterson (D-MN) to ensure that the House Bill stated that the USDA, not the EPA, would control how carbon credits may be generated for agriculture. Farmers are already quite committed to processes, procedures, and paperwork of the USDA by their enrollment in commodity and conservation programs and developing another track with another federal agency with which they are not familiar or comfortable may not sound appealing.

If the agricultural industry recognizes that this proliferation of individual ecoservice markets will continue, then it may be in their best long-term interest to induce an EcoCommerce-type economy under the premise that they will be able to guide the process toward a more manageable procedure. An agricultural-induced EcoCommerce could emerge on two fronts, one of a defensive move to head off attempts from other government agencies that would impose their version of environmental management to generate and value ecoservice and/or an offensive move to develop a system to capture ecoservice values from the management of their production and natural resources.

If the top of the ecoservices food chain demands ecoservices (as in the case of retail stores, bio-fuels industry, non-profit, and government organizations), then the burden of these numerous opportunities will fall on the primary producers of the ecoservices, mainly farmers, ranchers, and foresters. Within this opportunity will also be the definition of the type of values that the producer may pursue, whether that is an increase in value of the product, gaining regulatory assurance, participatory benefits, or resource-credit trading. In time, if the transactions are efficiently conducted and the trades represent a fair exchange of services, the invisible hand will sort out which value types make the most sense. But, in the early stages of EcoCommerce, there can be positions by certain suppliers and consumers that will develop a direction or trend that may influence how EcoCommerce evolves.

These evolutionary components will be directed from the top, through consumers and stakeholder purchases, but the ecoservices must be produced from the on-the-ground level. Depending how this unfolds, a significant portion of the value could reside with those producers as in an

EcoCommerce ventures.

Federal Government-Induced EcoCommerce

Government agencies at the federal, state, and local levels provide significant technical, administrative, regulatory, and financial support toward reducing non-point-source pollution as discussed previously. Any of these funds could be directed toward a succinct and transparent index-based process and could initiate EcoCommerce at some level and provide motivation for others to contribute toward desired outcomes.

The USDA could also be an active participant in EcoCommerce as it pertains to the biomass industry. The passage of the Biomass Crop Assistance Program (BCAP) subsidizes the production of biomass for fuel and energy by providing a payment up to $45/ton for tonnage delivered to a processing plant. One stipulation is that the growing and harvesting of this biomass must not degrade the natural and production resources of the farm operation. This new program requires the farmer enrolled in the BCAP to meet the Farm Bill's conservation compliance requirements. These requirements are associated with Highly Erodable Lands (HEL) and Swampbuster, a provision to prevent drainage of wetlands. While these are important, they are minimal standards and do nothing to quantify the energy balance or the carbon footprint that are presumably important aspects of the BCAP. If the BCAP adopted the EcoCommerce format and used existing indices or develop new indices, the ratings could be readily incorporated into the farm operational plan, a carbon-credit trade, water-quality trade, and it could also refine the energy and carbon lifecycle calculations for individual farms, bio-processors, and bio-refineries. A more positive energy balance would provide political support for the industry and an internal incentive as a cost savings.

State Government-Induced EcoCommerce

State governments are coming under greater scrutiny regarding natural resource goals. EcoCommerce and the use of management indices could be a method for conservation agencies to develop "measurable outcomes." Measurable outcomes are being demanded by legislators as fewer dollars are often available for financial assistance. Since ecoservices and non-point pollution are directly immeasurable, EcoCommerce management indices would provide a cost-effective means to measure outcomes at the desired scale (practice implementation, farm, watershed, and basin). State agencies are also under scrutiny to use better methods to target limited conservation funds. Management indices can provide a means to locate areas most prone to resource degradation and also evaluate what percentage of the problem the conservation dollars will address on that particular field, farm, watershed, or basin. Under an EcoCommerce structure, each layer and unit of government would utilize an index-based system to address all or part of its responsibility. The EcoCommerce Portfolio could be used to set their standards, assess the resource management condition, evaluate and compile results, and report to their respective legislative body on the status the resources of their concern. If a state department has a responsibility to protect the groundwater recharge area of a community well, then a method could be employed to describe the areas that are most vulnerable to contamination and also how the management of those vulnerable areas affects recharge waters. Any information less than that illustrates a lack of resource-management intelligence, and additional technical and financial support that is often requested cannot be applied with efficiency. In this case, the value of the management intelligence is primarily to determine the management needs. The management of wellhead areas could be described as succinctly as the economic indicators are used to describe economic conditions.

Legislative-Induced EcoCommerce

State and federal legislators continually ask for progress reports as they pertain to natural resource management, with little response in the way of a comprehensive land-use assessment. An EcoCommerce Portfolio (such as Table 10.7) would provide a broad-based landscape intelligence that could describe resource management in a fairly clear, succinct, and spatially oriented manner. At minimum, it would be far more clear and understandable than reports on how much sediment was delivered or presumably saved that cannot be related to how much is being lost. The information in Table 10.7 is only possible using an EcoCommerce framework as that is integrated within the production management plans of the farm operations. Since the plans are integrated, agricultural professionals can provide annual confirmation and updates cost-effectively.

Local Government-Induced EcoCommerce

Local governments such as counties, conservation districts, watershed districts, and townships must often deal with environmental and natural resource issues similar to state and federal agencies, but often with far fewer resources. Local governments could adopt the EcoCommerce framework and portfolio to provide a succinct, transparent, and cost-effective means to set requirements as they pertain to natural resource issues. By establishing management guidelines based on land-use indices, the burden of the work would be borne by the land owner with the results readily communicated to county commissioners and planning boards. The watershed district could declare that certain soil and water management levels practiced across the watershed would improve the water quality in the basin by a certain percentage. The conservation districts within that area could provide technical and financial assistance to farmers to determine if they meet those levels as well as assistance to reach those levels.

Conclusion

Whichever industry or individual starts down the path toward the adoption of an EcoCommerce process, it will do so prior to the establishment of all the policies, institutions, and knowledge that will create a mature EcoCommerce. In fact, the pioneers that adopt EcoCommerce processes and components will be the creators, or at minimum, the participants who influence the development of Macro- and Micro-EcoCommerce components.

CHAPTER 12

Macro-EcoCommerce

Macro-EcoCommerce

Essentially, Macro-EcoCommerce is defined using the same concepts as Macroeconomics. Those include (1) the study of the economy as a whole and the variables that control the macro-economy; (2) the study of government policies meant to control and stabilize the economy over time; that is, to reduce fluctuations in the economy; and (3) the study of monetary policy, fiscal policy, and supply-side economics. Macroeconomics has three primary differences that separate it from microeconomics. First, microeconomics studies individual components, whereas macroeconomics studies the economy as a whole. Microeconomics treats the economy as so many separate components, whereas macroeconomics treats the components of the economy as one unit, as one aggregate; that is, it looks for relationships between the various components. Second, government involvement in microeconomics is relatively small, and relegated to public goods, regulation, and welfare, whereas government involvement in macroeconomics is nearly total. Only government makes and enforces monetary and fiscal policy. Finally, whereas microeconomics has been around since the mid-18th century, macroeconomics began only as a reaction to the Great Depression of the 1930s.

With this economic perspective, Macro-EcoCommerce is (1) the study of a particular region, watershed, or ecosystem as a whole and how various resource-management activities affect the productive capacity of those areas and ecosystem; (2) the study of government policies meant to maintain or improve ecosystem function and capacity over time; and (3) the study of ecoservice units, valuation, and the economic advantages of producing ecoservices. Macro-EcoCommerce is concerned with aggregates such as ecological condition, resource management activities, capacity of natural capital, and the various policies and values placed on these components. Macro-EcoCommerce has its roots in the New Deal and growth in society's environmental awareness beginning in the 1970s and the subsequent passage of the Clean Air Act and Clean Water Act. In subsequent decades, it became apparent that environmental regulations improved the natural resources but that the individual actions were not coordinated with the overall ecological strategy. Much like the failure of simple classical economical models to explain the prolonged existence of high unemployment during the Great Depression provided the impetus for the development of macroeconomics (Case 2002), so did the process of applying individual conservation practices fail to address the prolonged existence of non-point-source pollution and resource degradation.

Government involvement in the macroeconomy includes fiscal, monetary, and growth policies. Fiscal policy refers to government policies concerning taxes and expenditures. Monetary policy consists of tools used by the Federal Reserve to control the money supply. Growth policies are government policies that focus on stimulating aggregate supply instead of aggregate demand. Government involvement in Macro-EcoCommerce could include fiscal and growth policies. Fiscal and growth policies would be used in a similar fashion in Macro-EcoCommerce, but with regard to natural capital output and capacity rather than physical capital output. The three macroeconomic market arenas of goods and services, labor, and money would also function within Macro-EcoCommerce, albeit these markets would have a narrower focus on natural capital. In a mature state, Macro-EcoCommerce and macro agro-economic policies and functions may be similar in nature.

Macro-EcoCommerce Policy Factors

Four classes of factors affect policy choices: ideology, policymaking institutions, politics, and accepted [economic] knowledge (Cukierman 2009). Although EcoCommerce, as described in this book, is not yet in existence, existing ecoservice markets and climate change policy discussions shed light on some of society's ideologies, politics, and knowledge of this topic. With these glimpses, a potential EcoCommerce system and some of the components of these policy factors will be identified.

Ideologies

Ideology determines the broad, long-term objectives to which policymakers of a nation aspire. While those objectives are seldom fully achieved, they constitute important input into attempts at forecasting policy responses. For example, the belief in democracy and the allocative efficiency of private enterprise is a core characteristic of Western ideology, while the current belief in free enterprise subject to tight control by ruling elites characterizes China (Cukierman 2009). In this broad view, ideologies needed for a successful EcoCommerce system must have common roots in a nation's economic ideologies.

Shared Responsibility

One such ideology that will emerge is that managing the natural resources becomes a shared responsibility, not just the responsibility of the federal government and landowners. This will require new relationships and new occupations, but the transformation of the centrally planned conservation economy into an EcoCommerce-based system does not consist of overhauling organizations, retraining professionals, or rewriting conservation-practice manuals. Both the commodity economy and the government conservation delivery system over the last century have developed an extensive understanding of both vocations and have created professionals and organizations in both fields.

The most significant change is that those who engage in EcoCommerce will have to conduct their work with an outcome-based perspective rather than a practice-based perspective. This will cause a shift in activities, but these shifts will generally be made by individuals under the guidance of the invisible hand of self-interests and the processes of microeconomics and Micro-EcoCommerce. Any change under these circumstances is usually made under a high level of control of the individual, and, therefore, change is often accepted at a much higher level. There will be new occupations related to a shared approach. By sharing the responsibility of achieving resource-management goals, the cost for the government and other stakeholders will decrease, transaction costs will be lower, and the objectives can be identified and met.

Opportunity of the Commons

The ideology of "opportunity of the commons" addresses the uniqueness of these public goods called ecoservices. The challenges of rewarding land stewardship or reducing non-point-source pollution are related to the attributes of the "tragedy of commons" and other economic

EcoCommerce Clearinghouses

EcoCommerce Clearinghouses would be created to support trades among producers and buyer of ecoservices. These could be created on several boundaries including geographical, political, and parameter-specific. These clearinghouses may have roles to play specific to industries, such as biomass processing or wildlife corridors. The evolution of the exchange and clearinghouse will be guided by the values and participants in the ecoservice markets.

Accepted EcoCommerce Knowledge

Policies are developed using an accepted knowledge base of the particular topic. The knowledge base for ecoservices is growing rapidly, but it still is relatively small and not uniformly accepted. In Collin's NASF presentation, she stated that there are five themes:

- It is more than carbon.
- We need unified standards.
- Stakeholders must be involved.
- We can learn from experience.
- Cross-government coordination is key.

These recurring themes are related to industry knowledge and communication. For EcoCommerce to be adopted, consumers, land managers, governments, and corporations must understand how EcoCommerce affects their self-interests. An acceptable knowledge base would address these themes and demonstrate how they are interrelated.

Resource-Centric Market

EcoCommerce is a resource-valued economy rather than a practice-based economy. Placing value on ecoservices (resource-management outcomes) provides the weight to tip the scales back to a resource-driven process. Over the last seven decades the centrally planned conservation economy drifted from an on-farm resource-driven process to a Congressionally allocated, program-driven process. In that transformation, the processes, paperwork, and contracts that permitted the application of a conservation practice became the center of value. Due to that, the conservation system tracks individual conservation practices, and not the ecoservice outcomes associated with that conservation practice.

For example, a field may have a grassed waterway installed, a buffer strip planted at the field edge, and a change in the tillage system. Each of these practices can be analyzed for its potential to reduce non-point-source pollution or to create ecoservices, but they are not valued in that manner.

A resource-centric economy, such as EcoCommerce, recognizes the SCi, WQi, HSi, BTU index, and other outcome measures and allows participants to value these resource outcomes. Of course, the costs of installing and implementing these practices are relevant, just as the various input costs of producing corn are relevant. But the grain commodity market does not reward the farmer who spends more money to produce corn, only how much corn is produced. Whether it's corn or clean water, a resource-valued economy rewards those who produce more of it and the producer gets to decide if the marginal costs to produce one more unit of the resource are in their self-interests. EcoCommerce is a resource-centric market using ecoservice units such as management indices, rather than a practice-based market.

Connecting Ecoservices to the Landscape

The next step in applying an efficient EcoCommerce structure is connecting the ecoservice units to the landscape so that an ecoservice inventory can be established. Without this knowledge, institutions and policies cannot provide the basis for the market marvel of establishing a market-clearing price. This landscape intelligence was introduced and described in Chapter 9 and is based on the USDA certification process for land management related to the production of provisional ecoservices (crop commodities). These land-management activities include crop type, crop rotation, acres, planting dates, and quantified yields for commodities and production systems related to corn, soybeans, cotton, rice, alfalfa, pasture, etc. Since few ecoservices can be directly measured, ecoservice yields are determined by management indices (described in Chapter 8). By applying indices to the landscape with the same intentions as in the development of cropping system intelligence, the ecoservice market participants would begin to understand to what extent they need to apply incentives to achieve a desired outcome.

Connecting the Land Management to Resource Productivity Benefits

The value of land-management activities is ultimately tied to the improvement in the capacity of the natural capital. Rivers with the capacity to assimilate a quantity of pollution discharged into them provide clean water to urban centers, recreation, fish, and wildlife. Habitats with the capacity to produce pollinators, birds, mammals, carbon sequestration, soil quality, clean water, and fresh air contribute toward an increase in natural capacity and those economic values.

These economic values could be described using a numerical rating such as in a Natural Resource Accounts based on resource condition indices described in Chapter 8. Resource condition indices describe the status of a resource such as using the EPA's Air Quality Index to describe air quality. This could also be applied to an impaired water body that is required to have an EPA TMDL Plan developed for it. For example, if a river has a water quality score of 65 on a scale of 0-100 and remains listed on the impaired waters list until its score is above 75 for two years, then higher management index scores from indices such as the SCi and the WQi could be incentivized.

This relationship could also exist for wildlife in a particular region. If larger-scale Natural Resource Accounts are related to smaller-scale resource management activities, some correlating system (linear or otherwise) must be devised to provide individual resource managers, or better yet, self-directed groups of resource managers, a means to converge and deliver the ecological and economic benefits of a desirable index score for the region. The development of Natural Resource Accounts at regional levels would be the basis for national ecological indices and Natural Resource Accounts at the national level.

Managing "Economies of Configuration"

These ecoservice units and how they are connected must become the knowledge base to provide EcoCommerce participants with a means to address one of the most daunting tasks of any economy: determining the most efficient allocation of human, physical, social, financial, intellectual, and natural capital to create wealth and profit and to reduce or eliminate negative externalities. This is addressed by the invisible hand and it is capable of meeting those goals in many situations. To illustrate the difficulties of this daunting task within an agro-economical and agroecological situation, a Big Creek watershed modeling project was conducted in Illinois (Ruhl 2007). Lant, *et al.* (2005) attempted to sort out how the interplay between economy and ecology affects the farmers' decisions. The variables included agricultural and environmental policies, farmers' choice of land use, and the package of ecosystem goods and services that the farmers and the Big Creek watershed could produce. In the model used, the State of Illinois's "T by 2000" (a program to induce farmers to incrementally reduce soil erosion to the "tolerance" level T that soils can withstand without losing long-term productivity), the CRP and the farmers' profit are decision drivers.

One finding of this modeling exercise was that overall farmer income could be maintained with the proper application of these options. The results included a significant conversion of corn and soybeans fields into alfalfa, hay, CRP, and no-till. This precise outcome may not be applicable in the agro-economy at-large, but it did reveal a need to integrate production and natural-resource-management decisions.

Perhaps an even a more dramatic finding was the potential for different variations in the landscape that were evaluated to find optimum combinations to provide both economic and ecological outcomes. A production possibilities frontier (PPF) graph (as described in Chapter 1) was used to illustrate the tradeoffs between gross marginal return (farm profits excluding land costs) and increasing the CRP Environmental Benefits Index scores. In review, a PPF is used to demonstrate that economic efficiency lies on an arc-shaped line, and that land-management decisions (in this case) either lead to more grain production or more ecoservices. The arc represents total efficiency and where it lands on the line represents the balance of what was produced. Figure 12.1 illustrates three points on the line that represent various quantities of gross marginal return and environmental benefit index points. Point A, in the upper left, represents the highest gross return and Point C, bottom right, the highest environmental benefits. As land use changed from row crop to more hay, pasture, and CRP (from point A to point B to point C), it caused a gross return decrease and environmental benefits increased. (As shown in Figure 12.1 that was developed with data provided by Ruhl (2007) with references to Lant (2005)).

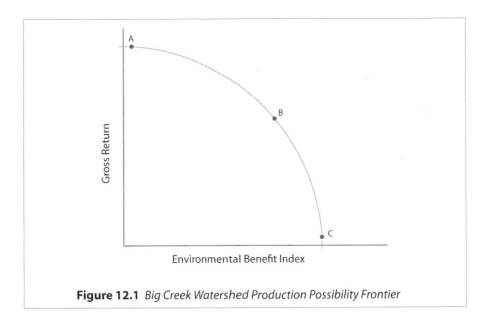

Figure 12.1 *Big Creek Watershed Production Possibility Frontier*

This movement was modeled by running dozens of generations of land-use change options in the pursuit of determining optimum integrated outcomes. The exercise demonstrated how difficult it can be to assign specific land uses to specific fields to achieve these goals. These difficulties can be further appreciated by examining the number of possibilities that exist for a relatively small watershed. Due to the number of permutations, there can be an extremely high number of possible land-use patterns. This is calculated by using the number of land use patterns in a watershed, *raised to the power* of the number of possible uses. If there are 1,000 fields and 10 possible land uses for each field, there are 10^{30} possible land uses. If there were four possible land uses, it would equate to 10^{12}.

What was concluded by this advanced modeling exercise was that first, individual land-use choices and the land-use patterns that these create at larger spatial scales are the driving factor in creating ecosystem services. Second, there is a limit to the package of ecosystem services and goods a watershed-scale landscape is capable of producing. Third, there can be tradeoffs between ecosystem goods and ecoservices, and society must choose what it wants from a set of possibilities. Fourth, current land-use patterns may be suboptimal, so we may be able to improve multiple goals simultaneously by closely examining the patterns. Considering these large "economies of configuration," it reveals the tremendous challenges posed to a centrally planned conservation economy as it pertains to identifying how to most efficiently allocate limited financial resources to improve the natural resource base. Ruhl concluded that there is a narrow set of social circumstances under which owners of natural capital will forgo current personal profit in order to improve long-term public assets by investing in natural capital or to shift current production to increase ecosystem services at the expense of ecoservice goods for which they currently receive market rewards. He added, "Finding that set of social circumstances is our challenge, and it is a difficult one" (Ruhl 2007).

From this perspective, EcoCommerce will be successful if participants are knowledgeable in the extensive decision-making processes and possibilities as it pertains to producing provisional and regulating ecoservices. In addition, of course, it is the intention of EcoCommerce to create a process so that land managers need not forgo personal profit to generate ecoservices, but that they will conclude that it may in their self-interest to supply ecoservices.

Hierarchy of Ecoservice Values

From an institutional and market perspective, ecoservices can be valued in a tiered or hierarchical fashion. This value is not imbedded in an ecological foundation, but from the perspective of the stakeholders and how the ecoservices are accounted for. The hierarchical order would begin with valuations that can be applied broadly and based on a level of resource management, rather than a quantified unit or credit. A

Resource Management Level value can be applied to market valuation types (Participatory/Market Access, Regulatory Compliance, Liability Protection, and Resource Incentive Payments) and are all based on how the land is managed. Annual confirmation, reporting, and auditing could be conducted in a specified time period each year such as during March, after harvest records have been organized, and prior to the next crop season. Reporting could be provided on a field, management unit, or farm-level scale and compiled as averages or ranges. Using this process, the resource management market provides incentives for management outcomes, rather than resource management practices and activities.

The Resource Credit market would trade measurable or calculated units of ecoservices, rather than basing ecoservice value on a certified level of resource management for a specific area. For immeasurable ecoservices, some model or index or similar method will be used to calculate and quantify the ecoservice credits. Directly measured units such as methane capture, water discharge from a controlled storage pond, or BTUs need no models or indices and are often the exception to accounting for ecoservices.

Using this hierarchy, the two category types of ecoservices can be utilized separately or in a complementary fashion, where the resource credit market can utilize the resource management structure for three purposes: (1) to use management indices to identify the existing inventory and/or capacity of natural capital to generate ecoservices, (2) to use management indices to establish an acceptable level of management for entry into the resource credit market, and (3) to use the management indices as a basis for calculating credits.

Defining Sustainability

The ecoservice hierarchy can also be also be used to define two levels of sustainability that would be funded in different manners. Walmart, the Forest Stewardship Council, and Oceans of Abundance are entities that are applying pressure to their markets to motivate the invisible hand to define a level of sustainability it can provide for consumer goods, forestry products, and fish, respectively. Suppliers to these markets will be motivated to meet these sustainable criteria to continue to enjoy market access. In many cases, there will not be a direct increase in economic value to the suppliers. Since it is in the consumers' self-interest to pay no more for products that are produced in a sustainable manner, the retailer will not pay more for sustainable products unless it becomes necessary. The point that the market defines this level could be called, Sustainability 1.0, and could represent the socially defined ecological equilibrium. In traditional supply-and-demand graphs, it would represent the market-clearing price.

Sustainability 1 .0

This level of sustainability, so-called Sustainability 1.0, will be defined primarily through participatory benefits such as market access, liability protection, and regulatory assurance and compliance, rather than direct payments for ecoservices. Sustainability 1.0 can also be supported by resource incentive payments from local, state, and federal governments, non-profits, and other ecoservice transactions that specify a particular level of resource management for specific needs. Sustainability 1.0 will be a level that both micro- and macro-economic forces determine can be reasonably provided as it pertains to resource management strategy changes. Defining Sustainability 1.0 involves a complex interplay of social, political, scientific, and economic principles using relatively simple indices.

Sustainability 1 .5

Making progress toward higher levels of sustainability will require both the market economy and the centrally planned conservation economy to compensate resource managers. This higher level, a so-called Sustainability 1.5, will include the resource credit markets such as carbon and GHG trades, water-quality trading, and resource incentive payments. The two sustainability levels create a push-and-pull effort to move sustainability measures forward. They push the bio-economy toward a higher level of resource management by providing market access and other benefits to meet Sustainability 1.0, and they pull the progressive resource managers with monetary incentives to meet Sustainability 1.5 levels. The Figure 12.2 describes this by overlaying these sustainability levels to illustrate their relationship. In theory, two equilibriums exist. D_0 is the line that represents the demand generated by retailers, government regulators, incentive programs, insurance companies, and other industries that will require a level of resource management to achieve benefits. Sustainability 1.0 equilibrium is represented by E_1 with a value of $P_{1.0}$. D_1 is the line that represents the demand generated by cap-and-trade, water quality trading, government incentive programs, and other measures that quantify and pay for specific quantities of ecoservices. Sustainability 1.5 equilibrium is represented by E_2 with a value of $P_{1.5}$. Figure 12.2 is similar to a Positive Externality Graph (Figure 1.13) and is the result of EcoCommerce incorporating positive externalities into the economy in a stepwise manner. The supply curve represents the ecological capacity-to-supply, in the same way that economic graphs represent capacity-to-supply. At $P_{1.0}$, certain land management strategies are employed to provide a quantity of Q_5. Q_5 is the socio-economically defined level of sustainability that one must achieve to participate in the markets such as Walmart, Farm Bill benefits, biofuel processing, and the range of agro-economic opportunities. At $P_{1.5}$, additional land management strategies are employed to generate credits for specific ecoservice markets. The additional value applied toward ecoservice credits compels some land managers to increase their output of ecoservices to meet the related, but separate, D_1 line. This implies that some markets will have a willingness-to-pay above the socioeconomically defined sustainability level.

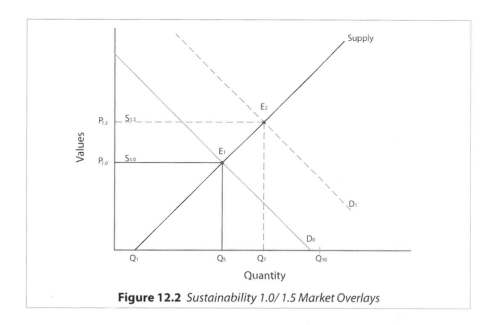

Figure 12.2 *Sustainability 1.0/ 1.5 Market Overlays*

This S1.0 – S1.5 structure adds a necessary plateau in the effort toward achieving sustainability. From this perspective, today's ecoservice markets leaped over Sustainability 1 .0 and ventured toward Sustainability 1.5. It is perhaps this long stride that has gotten those markets off on such poor footing. In essence, the immature markets of carbon and water quality have been attempting to compensate resource managers for a much larger share of the ecoservice value than the economy and its individual ecoservice markets are capable of supporting, and in some cases the markets would be paying for ecoservices with no regard to a baseline management level. And they attempted to do so without the advantage of landscape intelligence - the data that provides markets with the information needed to create the market marvel, the market clearing price and, perhaps, sustainable criteria that guide buyers and sellers of goods and services.

Politics

Policies are also greatly influenced by politics and are a result of the political system, the flip side of the coin that allocates limited resources. The other side of the coin, of course, is an economic system that allocates limited resources. Although ideologies, institutions, and accepted knowledge bases are not static enterprises, they can be described in a manner that can be generally accurate. Politics, on the other hand, are more prone to subjectivity and fluctuations and this section will not attempt to thoroughly define the politics of EcoCommerce. Perhaps a prudent approach lies in analyzing the political perspectives and potential self-interests of the various stakeholders discussed in Chapter 11 that described the motivating factors related to the emergence of EcoCommerce. Since both economic and political systems operate within the context of self-interests, the stance of any particular stakeholder can be determined by a thorough understanding of how he can achieve those self interests.

Since EcoCommerce would presumably have the greatest impact on the agricultural community, it could be assumed that those in that community would have strong political stances. There is always a faction that does not want change and their stance is self-evident. There are many in agriculture today who recognize changes related to environmental issues are inevitable, but they are unsure how those changes should be defined. In this group, the politics of EcoCommerce will be related to how to control the system once it emerges - the classic Pandora's Box. If the EcoCommerce language of management indices is efficient for communicating ecological assets and a matrix-type portfolio is an efficient method to transfer this information and values, it could be presumed that this same system could also function as a regulatory tool. If the agricultural community moves forward with EcoCommerce, it may feel that there is a risk in hurting themselves through further environmental scrutiny rather than reaping the benefits of their ecological assets.

This scenario was made clear to me during an EcoCommerce-type discussion I had a few years ago with a lobbyist employed by an agricultural political organization. I stated that no one really had a viable, potential solution for agro-environmental issues and that the "football [potential solution] was just lying on the ground." He replied with the question and answer. "Do you know what we do at the Capitol when there is a football lying on the ground? We kick it as far as we can." It was made clear to me that it is in the lobbyist's self-interest to never "carry the ball" ahead of their constituency group, especially when control of the issue is not ironclad.

Of course, there is also a risk that someone will eventually pick it up if the agricultural community continually "kicks the ball." Agriculture has traditionally relied on and has been successful with a defensive strategy, but as fewer political players remain on agriculture's team and more players come into the environmental camp, an EcoCommerce offensive strategy may be warranted.

CHAPTER 13

Demand Side Micro-EcoCommerce

Micro-EcoCommerce

Essentially, Micro-EcoCommerce is defined using microeconomics, a branch of economics that studies how households and firms make decisions to allocate limited resources in markets where goods or services are bought and sold. Microeconomics examines how these decisions and behaviors affect the supply and demand for goods and services (which determine prices), and how prices, in turn, determine the supply and demand of goods and services. Therefore, Micro-EcoCommerce studies how resource managers (farmers, ranchers, foresters) and firms make economic decisions related to maintaining and improving natural resources and the prices associated with ecoservices. Micro-EcoCommerce studies how ecoservice units and their valuation guide decisions and alter behavior related to the capacity of natural capital.

EcoCommerce Value Types

In Chapter 3, the Kimball farm scenario illustrated the difficulty that resource managers (potential ecoservice suppliers) may encounter in determining the quantities and value of ecoservices generated. The ecoservice value types were described in Chapter 6 as market access/ participatory benefits, liability protection, regulatory compliance, resource incentive payments, and resource credits.

Describing Ecoservice Demands

A function of Micro-EcoCommerce is to identify and define sustainability values and to express ecoservice demands. The stakeholders provide incentives for ecoservices for three primarily motivations. First: procure products that were produced within the context of a certain level of sustainability due to consumer demand. Second: purchase ecoservices within a certain geographical area such as field, farm, watershed, cellulosic shed, or GHG market driven by government, industry, or other regulatory or incentive programs. And third, purchase resource credits due to mitigation requirements. To accomplish this efficiently, these firms must understand and develop their perspectives of sustainability. They also need to know what types of production systems are sustainable and if bio-economy participants (farmers, ranchers, foresters) have sufficient resources to provide products within these sustainable production levels.

Much like the macroeconomic factors that affect policy choices (ideology, policymaking institutions, politics, and accepted knowledge), similar factors will affect the definition of sustainability and microeconomic choices. A person's or entity's ideology, their community organizations and businesses, their political biases, and their knowledge base will all contribute toward their definition of sustainability and the value applied to it. To reach consensus on what a sustainable production system is and what outcomes are necessary, each entity must determine the types of ecoservices they are demanding and how to describe those demands.

The first step in this process is to identify the factors that are providing motivation to achieve their EcoCommerce objectives and to generally describe their primary valuation type and the ecoservices of interest. Several stakeholders of Kimball's operation who were listed in Chapter 3 are listed under each EcoCommerce valuation type. Ecoservice values may be applied to one or more valuation types as they do not need to be exclusive. In other words, one land-management strategy may meet one stakeholder's market access criteria and another stakeholder's criteria for resource incentive payments or another's liability protection. The following pages describe how businesses, industries, and government entities will begin the process to determine how they will value ecoservices. The following descriptions may or may not be based on actual industry or government benefits and should be considered fictional, but possible, scenarios in an EcoCommerce economy. Some of the programs have been amended to illustrate how they could provide a basis for ecoservice demands.

Market Access and Participatory Benefits

Butter Land Company and a Sustainable Dairy Supply

Butter Land Company makes butter and sells it to national and international retail outlets under product and store brand names. They have been receiving requests from buyers to provide a "Product Sustainability Plan" that describes how the product is produced, processed, and delivered in relation to the products' ecological cost. One of its customers is Walmart. To initiate the process, Walmart sent questionnaires to its suppliers to ask about energy and climate, material efficiency, natural resources, and people & community. These questions relate to how the suppliers operate and if they have established sustainability purchasing guidelines that address such issues as environmental compliance. Butter Land Company has conducted energy and environmental audits for its operation but did not have sustainability purchasing guidelines for procuring milk. The company purchases its milk supply from about 1,000 dairy producers of sizes ranging from 50 cows to 5,000 cows. Butter Land Company has discussed sustainability issues, but is unaware of a process that is efficient, widely accepted, or industry approved. What they are aware of is the diversity of farm operations as they pertain to location, management, and environmental issues and the difficulty in corralling the proper environmental issues within a manageable process. Walmart and the other retailers are not providing specific sustainability guidelines for each industry, and therefore, each industry or business is responsible for identifying a process that meets the needs of its suppliers and their customers.

To make the proposition more challenging, several of dairy producers informed Butter Land Company that they provide other commodities to other processors that are also pursuing sustainability guidelines. Butter Land Company's interest in ecoservices includes their customers' interest in addressing greenhouse gas emissions, energy, and natural resources.

Etank Ethanol and a Sustainable Ethanol Supply

Etank Ethanol makes ethanol and sells it on the open market. The corn ethanol industry has been under scrutiny regarding its environmental impact as it receives government support indirectly through Farm Bill policies related to corn production and directly through a per-gallon blending subsidy. Etank Ethanol believes the best method to address these concerns is to become a more efficient industry in terms of energy balance and environmental impact. Numerous studies have been published on corn ethanol energy balances, but Etank Ethanol's specific circumstances were not reflected in these more general studies. Etank Ethanol would like studies to reflect its in-house efficiencies as well as the production efficiencies of the farms that produce the corn. Etank Ethanol's interests in ecoservices include those related to energy and carbon balances, water, and soil. It requires land managers to meet a minimum management threshold prior to supplying them corn and wants to develop an in-house resource credit market.

Round Wood Company and Wildlife Sustainable Wood Products

The Round Wood Company is in a similar situation as the Butter Land Company, in that its customer is requesting that lumber suppliers procure product produced in a sustainable manner. In the case of the Round Wood Company, the customer is demanding that lumber be harvested in a manner that maintains or improves wildlife habitat, and it is interested in promoting a level of sustainability. It is not interesting in resource credit trading.

Valley Creek WWTP for Watershed Management

Valley Creek Waste Water Treatment Plant processes sewage and other waste water streams to reduce nutrients, chemical/biological oxygen demand, and turbidity from the town of Valley Creek. The US EPA is demanding that it reduce its effluent limits due to its phosphorus discharge and the resulting oxygen levels. To meet these demands, the treatment facility is examining the possibility that land managers in the watershed could trade water quality credits with the Valley Creek WWTP. For land managers to be eligible, Valley Creek WWTP is requiring that land managers meet a minimum management threshold described by a water quality index.

Electric GenCo/BCAP and a Sustainable Biomass Supply

Electric GenCo generates electricity using coal as its primary energy source and is adding capacity by including a boiler for biomass that it is procuring from farmers and foresters. Electric GenCo has not had good public relations since it added coal-burning capacity five years ago. To improve its public image and reduce its carbon footprint, its current expansion will use locally produced biomass. This has raised concern that the area's agricultural and natural resources and remaining isolated groves and forested areas may be subject to extensive biomass harvesting. Electric GenCo is demanding that all biomass harvested for delivery meet soil, water, and habitat sustainability standards, and it is interested in promoting a level of sustainability and the potential to trade resource credits.

Chicago Climate Exchange for Carbon Sequestration Credits

The Chicago Climate Exchange (CCX) provides the trading platform for carbon and GHG credits. It requires land managers to meet a minimum management threshold prior to engaging in the resource credit market.

USDA FSA Biomass Crop Assistance Program

The FSA provides a subsidy for the production of biomass that is sold to USDA-approved conversion facilities. To be eligible for the program, land managers must meet minimum management thresholds for soil, water, habitat, and carbon. The federal biomass program requires farmers to meet existing Farm Bill conservation compliance requirements, which are for highly erodable lands (HEL) and draining wetlands.

2012 USDA Farm Bill

The USDA crop and revenue insurance is evolving toward a comprehensive focus on whole-farm revenue, ensuring robust disaster aid and insurance coverage but some trimming of subsidies on field crops. To reduce the risk of crop failures, more sustainable soil management practices on the whole farm may be a prerequisite for enrollment.

Liability Protection

Farmland Insurance Company and Resource Management Assurance

Farmland Insurance Company provides liability coverage, including environmental damage caused by farming activities. The company recognizes that a comprehensive management plan that includes natural resources reduces that probability that a farmer will experience an event that causes environmental harm. The Farmland Insurance Company is interested in ecoservices that include soil, manure, nutrient, and water management. It is interested in promoting a level of sustainability rather than trading resource credits.

U .S. Department of Agriculture's Risk Management Agency and Cropping Systems

The RMA represents the 16 carriers that provide crop insurance to an estimated 270 million acres of all crops grown in the U .S ., an estimated 78 percent of all tillable land. The group also helps develop policies, claims procedures, research on new plants, and new genetic-seed processing for the agriculture industry. It also recognizes that soil quality provides risk protection for soil erosion, drought, and nutrient sequestration. These attributes reduce the risk that the crop will not produce to the insured level. RMA will provide a 4 percent premium reduction to farmers who maintain or improve the condition of their soil. It is interested in promoting a level of soil productivity (sustainability) rather than trading resource credits.

Resource Incentive Payment

USDA Natural Resource Conservation Service for Resource Management

The USDA NRCS administers the Conservation Stewardship Program III that provides payment to farmers, ranchers, and foresters who provide ecoservices for soil, water, air, plants, animals, and energy. It is interested in promoting a level of sustainability rather than trading resource credits.

Game Bird Habitat Unlimited for Habitat Management

The non-profit, Game Bird Habitat Unlimited seeks to increase the numbers of game birds by increasing the quality of their habitat. Its ecoservice demands include targeting habitat components where it can leverage the greatest overall habitat gains. It is interested in promoting a level of sustainability rather than trading resource credits.

USDA Farm Service Agency for Conservation Reserve Program

The USDA FSA administers the Conservation Reserve Program and determines eligibility through the Environmental Benefits Index. In this (fictional) scenario, the EBI compound index is calculated by a formula that includes the indices of SCi, WQi, HSi, and pIHSi.

Regulatory Assurance/Compliance Protection

Big River County Planning and Zoning for feedlot permit

Valley County Planning and Zoning are responsible for issuing and enforcing feedlot permits and ensuring the county water plan is implemented. Feedlot expansions have consumed a great deal of time due to concerns of citizens who are not confident that increased livestock numbers will not degrade water quality. The P&Z is interested in requiring feedlot operators to meet land-management standards related to water quality.

State TMDL Plan for Water Quality Management

The Valley County Planning & Zoning is also challenged to reduce non-point-source pollution identified in the Valley Creek TMDL plan. It is interested in promoting levels of sustainability rather than trading resource credits.

Resource Credit Trading

Valley Creek WWTP for Water Quality Credits

Valley Creek Waste Water Treatment Plant processes sewage and other waste water streams to reduce nutrients, chemical/biological oxygen demand, and turbidity from the town of Valley Creek. The US EPA is demanding that it reduce its effluent limits due to its phosphorus discharge and the resulting low oxygen levels. To meet these demands the treatment facility is exploring the idea of land managers trading water-quality credits with the Valley Creek WWTP. Valley Creek WWTP's demand in ecoservices includes those related to nutrients, oxygen demand, and turbidity, and it is interested in promoting levels of sustainability and the potential to trade resource credits.

Valley Creek Watershed District for Water Quality Credits

The District seeks to improve water quality and reduce fluctuations in the quantity of water flowing in Valley Creek. Its ecoservice demands relate to reducing storm run-off and increasing landscape water storage capacity, and it is interested in promoting levels of sustainability and the potential to trade resource credits.

Chicago Climate Exchange for Carbon Credits

The Chicago Climate Exchange (CCX) provides the trading platform for carbon and GHG emitters to purchase carbon credits from land managers. The CCX makes the connection between those with demand carbon credits and those who have the capacity to supply them.

Defining Sustainability Demands

As each entity concludes what its objectives are for particular ecoservice demands, its next step is to further define the desired level of sustainability. This is the point in the process when the EcoCommerce structure must be adopted to provide a unified and comprehensive ecoservice market. If entities move forward and define ecoservices and sustainability without a unified approach, ecoservice markets can only progress to the point that they are at today, where value and organization are relatively low. The EcoCommerce structure allows for ecoservice units to act as recognizable "coins" or units of value whose origin, context, and values are accepted by the economy at large. Using the EcoCommerce common denominators (such as indices or related measurement outcomes) allows for multiple pathways and processes to be used to determine a level of sustainability, while ending up with a commonly used result that can align interests.

Processes to Define Sustainability

The processes used to reach a common denominator will most likely be a function of how extensive and broad-based the groups of stakeholders are. Examples of the processes may include directly adopting USDA national standards for resource management indices. A second, more extensive process that can be used is a highly involved disparate stakeholder process that leads to the development of a policy possibility frontier outcome as discussed in Chapter 8. A third process to define sustainability among stakeholders uses a consultant and brokerage approach in which ecoservice unit types and levels of management are negotiated based on the producer's ability to generate ecoservices and the ability of the stakeholder to generate sufficient demand. This approach may be appealing because there is currently a limited amount of broad-based knowledge about the EcoCommerce structure, and the negotiation process will provide much of the knowledge support. Therefore, many initial attempts at defining sustainability include processes related to education, communication, collaboration, and discussion of sustainability measurement tools and overall progress toward a direction that gives confidence and assurance to those involved that they understand how human activities affect ecosystems.

A turnkey service to provide vertically integrated solutions would identify concerns, define plan objectives and sub-objectives, conceptualize quantifiable benchmarks and indices, define and assemble the means, describe the plan (including objectives, indices, and means), assess the achievement, translate the achievement into perceivable EcoCommerce values, link such value to the end user, and finally, evaluate, update, renew, and revise the plan on a ongoing basis. Each of these processes can be tailored to specific needs.

Describing Sustainability Levels

Due to the many variables and thought processes involved in reaching a decision on what a sustainable level is, it is highly likely that each independent effort will reach a different conclusion. And that is perfectly acceptable and inevitable. The list of stakeholders involved with Kimball's operation contains private sector food, fuel, and fiber processors, government regulators, electrical utilities, non-profit wildlife organizations, local and federal government incentive programs, and an ecoservice exchange board. The success of EcoCommerce lies in its ability to allow individuals and entities to describe the level of sustainability they feel is optimal considering all the economies of configuration that exist within their economic opportunities, constraints, and region. Using standardized management indices, individual entities, following their unique process, can quantify a level of sustainability that meets their needs and can be correlated with other entities' unique processes and outcomes. Walmart's sustainability efforts, for example, include a global process to engage many stakeholders on multiple efforts. It would be reasonable to expect that such a comprehensive process would include the three mentioned processes to define sustainability levels as well as other novel approaches. As long as the processes use common ecoservice units to describe sustainability levels, the final EcoCommerce products can be co-mingled with any other industry results. Assuming that ecoservice stakeholders employed a reasonable process to describe ecoservice demand and by using standardized units to describe sustainability levels, a table can be developed to illustrate the demand.

The EcoCommerce Trading Table

Using standardized ecoservice units and specific values applied to these units, sustainability criteria can then be displayed in a similar manner to how the Chicago Board of Trade (CBOT) displays the price of provisional ecoservices of corn, soybeans, cotton, and other commodities Table 13.1 describes the sustainability level that was defined on a scale of 0-100 by each entity and the corresponding ecoservice market signals (prices and units) that are provided to Kimball and other resource managers with ecoservices capacity. Due to the potentially large number of individual stakeholders who could participate in EcoCommerce, tables listing these prices and units may be customized to meet individual and specific entities needs. A table could be developed for Kimball, as shown below, or for all land managers in a watershed or cellulosic shed.

Table 13.1	EcoCommerce Trading Table										
Valuation Type / Stakeholder	Resource Management Level								Resource Credits		
	SCi	WQi	CQRi	BTUi	HSi	FLi	plHSi	phHSi	BTU /millon	CO2e tons	WQQ ac-ft
Partic. Benefits/Market Access											
Butter Land Company	65	65	65		65	95	65				
Etank Ethanol	65	65	65	50	60				$0.50		
Round Wood Company					75						
Valley Creek WWTP		75									$10.00
Electric GenCo	65	65	65		65			65		$3.50	
USDA FSA CC	51	51	51		51						
CCX			60							$0.15	
Landlord											
USDA FSA BCAP	60	55	60		55		55				
Liability Protection											
USDA RMA	65										
Farmland Insurance	70	70				99					
Regulatory Compliance											
Valley River TMDL (EPA)	60	75									
VC Watershed District		75									
County Feedlot Permit	60	60			60	95					
Resource Incentive Payment											
County Tax Rebate		75									
Game Bird Habitat Unl								85			
USDA FSA CRP	75	75	75		75		75				
USDA CSP III	50	70			75		80				

The EcoCommerce Trading Table shows the Valuation Type, Stakeholder (or buyer), and the units of ecoservices in either the Resource Management Level category or the Resource Credit category. It includes eight management indices (on a scale of 0-100):

- SCi – soil condition index
- WQi – water quality index
- CQRi – carbon sequestration index
- BTUi – British Thermal Unit index
- HSi – Habitat Suitability index (general)
- FLi – Feedlot Index
- plHSi – pollinator HSi
- phHSi – pheasant HSi

Hierarchy of Ecoservice Categories

Ecoservices are divided into the two major categories: Resource Management Level and Resource Credit. The Resource Management Level category contains ecoservices that are based on resource management with unitless measurements. They are all based on a level of farm resource management that can be identified through the use of management indices or similar rankings. The valuation types of Market Access/Participatory Benefits, Regulatory Compliance, and Liability Protection are based on an operation meeting its overall RMLs. The size of the operation needn't necessarily be included in this type of reporting system. The valuation type of Resource Incentive Payment is based on a quantity of ecoservice delivered on a per-acre basis and therefore, acreage amounts of specific management units would be part of the reporting system. Reporting could be provided on a field-management unit or farm-level scale and compiled as averages or ranges. Using this process, the Resource Management Level market provides incentives for management outcomes, rather than relying on singular conservation practices and activities.

Using this hierarchy, the two categories of ecoservices can be utilized separately or to complement each other. In a complementary fashion, as noted previously, the resource credit market uses the Resource Management Level structure for three purposes: (1) to establish an acceptable level of management for entry into the resource credit market, (2) to use the management indices as a basis for calculating credits, and (3) to use management indices to identify the existing inventory and/or the capacity of the natural capital to generate ecoservices.

A resource credit market would trade measurable or calculated units of ecoservices, rather than basing ecoservice value on a certified level of resource management for a specific area. For immeasurable non-point-source pollution and ecoservices, some model or index or similar method will be used to quantify ecoservice credits. Directly measured units such as methane capture, water discharge from a controlled storage pond, or BTUs would need no models or indices. Directly measured ecoservices are often the exception to accounting for ecoservices.

Alignment of EcoCommerce Opportunities

For individual resource managers (farmers, ranchers, and foresters) the list of stakeholders and potential ecoservice values become the starting point for determining if it will be advantageous to provide ecoservices. The list of stakeholders can be sorted from a few perspectives. Four of the entities *(Butter Land Company, Etank Ethanol, Round Wood Company, Electric GenCo)* purchase traditional commodities. Managing his farm to their desired level of sustainability provides Kimball with market access. Since a significant portion of Kimball's income comes from selling provisional ecoservices such as corn, milk, and lumber, it is in Kimball's self-interest to meet those sustainable goals. The remaining firms are sorted again by those that demand a level of sustainability and those that demand resource credits. Five of the entities *(Farmland Insurance Company, U .S. Department of Agriculture's Risk Management Agency, USDA Natural Resource Conservation Service, Game Bird Habitat Unlimited and Valley County Planning and Zoning)* provide monetary incentives either in payment or reduction in taxes and premiums for meeting a level of sustainability. Since Kimball must meet a certain level of sustainability to gain market access for four of the entities, the marginal cost of meeting and reporting additional sustainability requirements may be less than the marginal benefit.

The final three entities (*Valley Creek WWTP, Chicago Climate Exchange,* and *Valley Creek Watershed District)* are interested in resource credits that are generated above and beyond a baseline level of sustainability. Kimball will evaluate the production of these ecoservices in much the same manner that he evaluates the production of provisional ecoservices. Resource credits are exclusive in their sale and require a higher level of accounting, tracking, and reporting.

Aligning these ecoservices has benefits for resource managers as the costs of producing the ecoservices can be simultaneously applied to meet the demands of several entities. These cost savings will not be lost on ecoservices buyers either. To capture these efficiencies, symbiotic relationships, partnerships, and informal and formal agreements among private, public, and non-profit sectors would naturally emerge as a coordinated effort to meet their self-interests.

From Effectual Demand to Aggregate Demand

There has always been some level of demand on the ecosystems and the ecoservices generated by them. This universal demand can be defined as an "absolute demand" described by Adam Smith (1952) in that it is the sum of all demand regardless if a price is paid for a "unit" of a good or service. With an EcoCommerce framework and process, individuals and entities can strive to create an effectual demand for specific ecoservices that traditionally have been excluded from economic transactions. An effectual demand is defined as a price or value that motivates producers to generate a specific good or service. In analyzing the EcoCommerce trading table (Table 13.1), it is apparent that several entities have placed value on ecoservices related to soil, water, carbon, and habitat. By using standardized ecoservice units, individual entities can create an effectual demand. Then, these entities can jointly create an aggregate demand that should lead to price or value discovery. Depending on the cost of providing these ecoservices, individual stakeholders may have difficulty generating an effectual (sufficient) demand to encourage the production of those ecoservices. With multiple stakeholders placing value on specific ecoservices, the aggregation of demand for specific ecoservices would have a greater ability to entice the production of ecoservices. This aggregation of demand can occur incrementally.

For example, a farmer with a WQi of 55 may determine that the marginal cost to achieve a WQi score of 70 is too great in relation of the marginal benefit of a reduced insurance premium. But if benefits are received for achieving WQi score of 60, and then 65 for other stakeholders, then the marginal cost of the next increment may be less than the benefit of the reduced insurance premium.

CHAPTER 14

Supply Side Micro-EcoCommerce

Identifying an Ecoservice Supply

Unlike traditional economic goods and services, a supply of ecoservices is generated at some level within all ecosystems whether an economic value is applied to it or not. These are valuable ecoservices and exist as a *value of use*, rather than a *value in exchange*. Returning to the Kimball farm operation and the Bio-Economy's Conundrum described in Chapter 3, Kimball predominantly received market signals for provisional ecoservices related to traditional commodities. Due to this scenario, Kimball produces known quantities of valued provisional ecoservices as well as a certain unknown quantity of regulating ecoservices. Without a known quantity of known parameters, ecoservice economic values cannot be ascertained with efficiency. This great unknown, in fact, is the opposite scenario as the market marvel in that the market clearing price efficiently allocates resources to entice a supply. Through the EcoCommerce trading table (Table 13.1), Kimball can identify the type and quantity of ecoservices units that the market and government desires. In addition, Kimball can determine his capacity to generate the type and quantity of ecoservices and their potential value in relation to the ecoservice units. According to Kimball's EcoCommerce portfolio (Table 14.1), he has identified the capacity to generate regulating ecoservice types related to water quality, soil quality, carbon sequestration, pollination, energy, and habitats (both general and species-specific). Kimball is producing these regulating ecoservices within the context of producing provisional ecoservices. The regulating ecoservices are being supplied in an integrated manner with corn, soybeans, timber, and other crop and livestock production on his farming operation.

Box 14.1 Why Pay For What We Are Already Getting For Free?
It is a fact that many land managers operate their lands in a manner that provides clean water, sequesters carbon, and employs other ecoservices without any compensation from government or the market. As a result, many opponents of ecoservice markets feel it is a waste of government funds or a burden on the market to start paying for these ecoservices. In other words, they feel that these positive externalities of the economy should remain as externalities. But "free" positive externalities are usually generated through unintended consequences of the current economic scenarios. When the current economic scenario changes, these "free" externalities may no longer be produced. If a reasonable value were placed on the ecoservices regardless of the reason they are being produced, then the marginal benefit of potentially changing the economic scenario and then losing the ecoservice value may not be sufficient. In other words, if the value of ecoservices is only included when an economic activity does not provide them, then the economic activities that do provide ecoservices are at an ecoservice market disadvantage. If the ecoservice value is always applied, then entrepreneurs will strive to obtain value from all potential economic streams.

Kimball's EcoCommerce Portfolio

EcoCommerce uses a *matrix portfolio* approach that organizes simple and compound indices and allows for specific weighting, comparison, averages, ranges, or other mathematical functions to represent the ecoservice values. The EcoCommerce Portfolio accounts for ecoservices produced by the management activities within a specific land-use area.

It is structured so that the farm management units are represented in a vertical column. These units may consist of farm, farmstead, feedlots, fields, pastures, and forests. They are the management units of the farm. Ecoservices units are placed within the management unit that best represents the origin of the ecoservice. A Habitat Suitability Index (HSi) and other wildlife habitats are probably best determined by using all of the natural and production resources on the farm operation, and therefore, the management unit is the farm. Individual fields may be combined into a larger management unit as long as the both the natural resources and production strategies are similar. Fields with the same cropping systems but different soils, topography, or other features should be considered different management units.

The rationale for not compiling land units with different soils and topography is that different resource outcomes will be generated under the same management strategy. The horizontal heading row lists the ecoservice units that are either measured by RML or by resource credits. The horizontal headings are similar to the horizontal heading in the EcoCommerce Trading Board table. In Kimball's EcoCommerce portfolio, he has only accounted for the ecoservice units that are listed on the trading table, as those are the only ecoservices that have an effectual demand applied toward them. Also, he only lists ecoservices as they pertain to a RML that has not included resource credits at this time. The rationale for this is that in EcoCommerce, resource management thresholds are the primary ecoservice market that must be appeased prior to generating resource credits. These ecoservice plateaus allow the economic participants to define levels of sustainability and determine what additional ecoservice credits are needed. In theory, there could be an infinite number of ecoservices that could be valued, as unique ecoservice units may be defined by individual stakeholders that desire a specific ecological outcome. As long as the indices and scales used in both the trading table and Kimball's portfolio are the same, transactions can be conducted with a higher level of coordination and lower costs.

Table 14.1		EcoCommerce Portfolio #2						
		Ecoservices						
Management Unit	Acres	Resource Management Level				Resoure Credits		
Farm		HSi	plHSi	phHSi		mBTU	CO2e (tons)	WQQ (Acft)
	500	75	82	80				
Feedlot		FLi						
Fd#1	5	96						
Forest		fSQi	CQRi	HSi				
#5001	50	75	88	82				
Fields		SCi	WQi	CQRi	BTUi			
#1001	100	75	87	92	82			
#1002	100	72	75	88	88			
#1003	100	67	72	81	72			
#1004	150	62	78	77	75			
Total	450							
Ac-Wt Ave		68	78	84	79			
Pasture								
Range								

Basket Bundled Ecoservices

The matrix portfolio can also begin the process of ecoservice bundling. Either basket or merged bundling can provide economic benefits to both the supply and demand aspects of ecoservices. The basket bundle is a more sophisticated approach that permits the sale of individual or combinations of ecoservices to different purchasers. The result is likely to be a more efficient allocation of resources and higher returns to sellers (Landell-Mills 2002). If a merged-bundle approach is desired, Kimball will have the option to calculate outcomes using the index provided by the purchaser, such as the Environmental Benefits Index (EBI) used by the USDA FSA to determine CRP eligibility. If the EBI merged-bundle approach contained soil, water, and habitat parameters, only one score would be given.

It may be more efficient for an entity to manage its ecoservices in that manner, but individual ecoservice parameters get masked in the merged bundled process. Similarly, a Walmart Sustainability Index may only need to contain one score representing the sustainability level of food that is grown for a processor. The challenge of beginning with many merged bundle approaches, rather than individual basket-bundle approaches, is that, as EcoCommerce evolves on all fronts, it would be much more cumbersome for land managers to adjust multiple merged-bundle ecoservice packages rather than adjust individual ecoservice parameters that other entities use to create their unique merged-bundle package. Ideally, a merged-bundle approach would use an equation that allowed individual indices to become the factors and weighting criteria for specific resources that would be included within the equation. Beginning with a platform that allows individual, basket, and/or merged sets of ecoservices to be created allows the market players to gain sophistication in generating and trading ecoservices. Tables 14.2-14.5 represent basket bundles of ecoservices by valuation types. The top of the table lists Kimball's Resource Management Level (RML) scores, the stakeholders, and the self-determined sustainability levels they demand. A strike-through number means that Kimball RML does not meet the minimum threshold required by the EcoCommerce stakeholder. Blank columns represent ecoservices that are not included in that particular basket. Essentially, each valuation type basket contains individual bundles that Kimball created for each stakeholder.

Table 14.2	Market Access/Participatory Benefit Basket							
Kimball's RML	SCi	WQi	CQRi	BTUi	HSi	plHSi	phHSi	FLi
	68	78	84	79	75	82	80	96
Stakeholders								
Butter Land Co	65	65	65		65	65		
Etank Ethanol	65	65	65	50	60			
Electric GenCo	65	65	65		65			
BCAP	55	55			55	55		
Round Wood Co					85			
Valley Crk WWTP		75						
2012 Farm Bill	51	51	51		51			

Kimball's EcoCommerce opportunities related to market access and participatory benefits include the seven stakeholders listed in Table 14.2. The ecoservices include soil, water, carbon, energy, and habitat and the stakeholders include three processors: a utility, a municipality, and access to two government programs.

Table 14.3	Liability Protection Basket							
Kimball's RML	SCi	WQi	CQRi	BTUi	HSi	plHSi	phHSi	FLi
	68	78	84	79	75	82	80	96
Stakeholders								
Farmland Insurance	70	70						99
USDA RMA	65							

Kimball's EcoCommerce opportunities related to liability protection include two stakeholders listed in Table 14.3. The ecoservices include soil and water and the stakeholders include a private sector insurance company and a government-subsidized crop insurance entity.

Table 14.4	Regulatory Compliance Basket							
Kimball's RML	SCi	WQi	CQRi	BTUi	HSi	pIHSi	phHSi	FLi
	68	78	84	79	75	82	80	96
Stakeholders								
Valley River TMDL	60	75						
Valley Creek WD		75						
Cty Feedlot Permit	60	60						95

Kimball's EcoCommerce opportunities related to regulatory compliance include three government entities listed in Table 14.4. The ecoservices include soil, water, and feedlot management and the stakeholders include a state Total Maximum Daily Load program for water quality, a local watershed district, and a county-level permitting process.

Table 14.5	Resource Incentive Payment Basket							
Kimball's RML	SCi	WQi	CQRi	BTU	HSi	pIHSi	phHSi	FLi
	68	78	84	79	75	82	80	96
Stakeholders								
County Tax Rebate		75						95
Game Bird Hab Unl							85	
USDA CSP III	50	70			75	80		
USDA FSA CRP	70	70			70	70		

Kimball's EcoCommerce opportunities related to resource incentive payments include three government entities and a non-profit organization listed in Table 14.5. The ecoservices include soil, water, and general and specific habitats and the stakeholders include a county water planner, the local habitat group, and two federal government programs: the Conservation Stewardship Program III and the Conservation Reserve Program.

In summary, Kimball met the criteria for all stakeholders in the Market Access/Participatory Benefits basket except for the Round Wood Company, as Kimball's HSi was less than 85. With this management level, Kimball has access to markets that purchase his milk and corn to produce butter and ethanol. He is eligible to participate in the USDA BCAP program to receive financial incentives. He can also participate in the water-quality-trading market for the WWTP if he is able to produce water quality credits above the RML specified. This also allows Kimball to consider entering the resource credit market for greenhouse gases and BTUs as listed in the trading table. In the Liability Protection Basket, he met the USDA RMA criteria, but not the Farmland Insurance criteria for the premium reduction. In the Regulatory Compliance basket, he met the standards for Valley River TMDL, Valley Creek WD, and the County Feedlot Permit. For the Resource Incentive Payments basket, Kimball met the County Tax Rebate, the Game Bird Habitat Unlimited, and the USDA CSP III standards.

Box 14.2 EcoCommerce and Duplicity, Additionality, and Permanency

Duplicity is considered when one land management activity is conducted that provides an ecoservice such as carbon sequestration as well as the ecoservice of water quality. Additionality is considered if the producer is currently sequestering carbon; they should only be rewarded if they supply more. Permanency is, of course, something that lasts forever or a defined amount of time. Since ecosystems function in a cyclical manner, very few ecoservice outcomes remain in the same state permanently. Permanency in ecosystems results in such carbon-based outcomes as limestone, coal, and oil. In addition to their cyclical nature, ecosystems also function in a manner that is often symbiotic, resulting in many benefits usually greater than the sum of the components and functions. Developing an ecoservice market opposed to these traits that are by nature quite economically and ecologically efficient is debilitating to the ecoservice markets at the onset. Ecoservice markets should be allowed to function on a relatively level playing field as commodity (provisional ecoservice) markets as it applies to permanency, duplicity, and additionality. For example, Kimball's farm has generated the provisional ecoservice of corn for more than a century, beginning when Kimball's grandfather started farming. The three Kimball generations have basically been providing a permanent supply of corn one year at a time. In fact, that is the only way that a permanent supply of corn or any other ecoservice can be supplied. The Kimball farmers have decided to grow corn each year based on the market signals and government policies. The market price that has been paid to the Kimballs for their corn has not been based on whether they had provided corn in the past, or whether they planned to provide corn in the future. The market price of corn is not affected by Kimball's activity of harvesting corn stover for bedding his animals or for supplying an electric utility. None of these permanency, additionality, or duplicity stipulations was applied to Kimball's corn production. The fact that Kimball's production of clean water can be used by many potential buyers and his corn crop by only one buyer at a time should be reflected in the value that can be exchanged. Since ecoservices do provide benefit to the commons, an economic system that allows value to flow from the users of the commons, and onward to the stewards of the commons, will allow the invisible hand to guide both participants toward a level of sustainability.

Sustainability 1.0

As described in Chapter 12 in Macro-EcoCommerce, a Sustainability 1.0 level will be achieved by land managers meeting a level of resource management that becomes expected by those stakeholders who purchase their products. These levels will be defined by individual stakeholders using processes defined internally. The only qualification that must be met is that common management indices or compatible scoring processes are used to allow a matrix portfolio to be constructed that allows scores to be used individually, or combined through a basket and merged-bundle approach. In this manner, Sustainability 1.0 can be defined collectively and independently by private industries, retail outlets, non-profits, and local, state, and federal programs.

Sustainability 1.0 is not a static level. It will fluctuate depending on the willingness of consumers to collectively pay to support it. With an EcoCommerce structure and process, the economy would have a means to express Sustainability 1.0. One may conclude that Kimball does not meet a Sustainability 1.0 level as he does not meet the wildlife criteria for the Round Wood Company or the insurance premium reduction criteria for Farmland Insurance. This conclusion may be a moot point, as Sustainability 1.0 cannot be set or owned by any single entity, including the government. Certain entities such as a government agency or Walmart can generate significant influence by setting the sustainability bar much higher. But much like economic supply and demand forces that guide consumers, EcoCommerce supply and demand forces allow for feedback and adjustment in the process to define sustainability. This partially occurs today as the economy also expresses a level of sustainability to the best of its ability such as through "green" markets. The significant obstacle to overcome for consumers and the economy to advance their efforts is that there is no adequate method to express the level of sustainability they desire. The result is that many costs and benefits associated with "green" markets remain as economic externalities. EcoCommerce incorporates these economic externalities within various types of transactions and allows their values to be expressed.

Hierarchy of Ecoservices

The hierarchy of ecoservices described in the previous chapter applies equally to both demand and supply. In Kimball's portfolio, he has listed the RML index ratings and correlated them to the stakeholders' sustainability criteria to determine if his operation has met the levels to allow him to participate in the resource credit market. As stated in the last chapter, using this hierarchy, the two category types of ecoservices can be utilized separately or to complement each other. With this hierarchical structure, it is in the interests of some buyers (market access, liability, direct payment) to require a higher level of resource management from the farmers and in the interest of other buyers (resource credit) to require a lower level of resource management.

The advantage of a lower Sustainability 1.0 level is that it would be less expensive for farmers to generate additional resource credits. These opposing advantages may provide the dynamic tension that is currently lacking in ecoservice credit markets in that both the buyer and seller of the ecoservices benefit from having ecoservices easily and inexpensively generated. But that is only an assumption, as the dynamics and interactions of an economy and the invisible hand are often far too complex to accurately predict.

Supplying Sustainability 1.5

Sustainability 1.5 can be described as a higher level of resource management whose outcomes are additional ecoservice units above the Sustainability 1.0 RML. To generate this value for ecoservice units, policies that create markets are needed. These could include a carbon cap-and-trade policy, or a bio-refinery policy that states a certain positive energy balance level must be maintained. In these cases, tons of sequestered carbon are valued, and, in the case of the bio-refinery, excess sequestered BTUs are valued. Since Sustainability 1.5 requires units of ecoservices to be accounted for, these trades are exclusive among producers and users. This is in contrast to the Sustainability 1.0 process in which a unitless RML can be applied toward multiple stakeholder demands. Ideally, Sustainability 1.5 transactions would include only ecoservices that are provided above the Sustainability 1.0 level. This may seem an obvious goal, but without a system to account for the ecoservices provided by a Sustainability 1.0 level, ecoservice units purchased for resource credits may or may not be in addition to 1.0. Accounting for the ecoservices generated in Sustainability 1.0 will require a type of landscape intelligence that was described in Chapter 9.

Generating Resource Credits

Resource Credit categories are for directly measured ecoservices such as the quantity of methane collected from a contained manure digestion unit, or the quantity and quality of water that is discharged from a storage pond or wetland with a controlled outlet. Resource credits can also be calculated using management indices or similar methods. These ecoservices can have a value or price applied per unit of production such as tons, cubic feet, and acre-feet. Using this EcoCommerce system, the trading table (Table 13.1) is a compilation of ecoservice demands from many sectors, locations, and perspectives. Due to nearly unlimited combinations of ecoservice postings, the trading tables can be customized for individuals, watersheds, or other specific geographical regions. Posting units and prices of ecoservices that reflect the supply and demand using these categories will create market transparency and allow the market to establish a market-clearing price. According to Table 13.1, there are three resource credit opportunities available to Kimball:

1. WQQ – a water quantity and quality payment of $10/acre-foot, paid by the waste water treatment plant to mitigate its discharges

2. CO_2e – a GHG sequestration payment of $0.15/ton paid by an industrial emitter and exchanged through the CCX or a payment of $3.50/ton paid by Electric GenCo

3. BTU – a energy lifecycle payment of $0.25/bu/net million BTUs paid by Etank Ethanol to generate a greater net-positive energy cycle

Table 14.6 lists the resource credits that have been generated by Kimball's management strategies.

Water Quantity and Quality Credits
Kimball could engage in the WQQ credit by reestablishing a wetland. It is estimated that the basin could hold 150 acre-feet and reduce the concentration of nitrates to the 7 parts per million that was specified by the Valley River WWTP. The basin is 9 acres in size and has a crop productivity index of 76, representing a relatively low production capacity on Kimball's farm. Kimball is able to harvest an average of 120 bushels of corn/acre and 30 bushels of soybeans/acre.

Carbon Dioxide Equivalents
Kimball could construct an anaerobic manure digester to generate about 800,000 cubic feet of methane per year from his 100-cow dairy herd. At 0.062 pound/cubic feet, Kimball generates 49,600 pounds or about 25 tons (Fulhage 1993). Kimball can then combust the methane for heat and/or electrical production and gain GHG-reduction credits through the process of methane destruction that converts methane to the less potent GHG of carbon dioxide. One GHG methane unit is equivalent to 20 carbon dioxide units. Kimball's capture and destruction of 25 tons of methane is equivalent to 500 tons of carbon dioxide.

British Thermal Units Energy Cycle

Kimball is also considering how he may increase net BTUs from the production of his corn bushels. Kimball currently averages 160 bushels of corn per acre. His energy inputs are calculated at 8.3 million BTUs/acre/year. His average yield generates a gross BTU output per acre of 62.8 million and a net BTU output of 54.4 million BTU/acre, or 340,106 BTUs per bushel (Lorenz 1995).

Table 14.6		Kimball EcoCommerce Portfolio						
Management	Acres	Ecoservices						
Unit		Resource Management				Resouce Credits		
Farm		*HSi*	*plHSi*	*phHSi*		mBTU	CO2e (tons)	WQQ (Acft)
	500	75	82	80				
Feedlot		*FLi*	*CO2e*					
	5	96	500				500	
Forest		*fSQi*	*CQRi*	*HSi*				
	50	75	88	82				
Fields		*SCi*	*WQi*	*CQRi*	*BTUi*			
#1001	100	75	87	92	82	5442		150
#1002	100	72	75	88	88	5513		
#1003	100	67	72	81	72	5513		
#1004	150	62	78	77	75	8162		
Total	450					24630		
Ac-Wt Ave		68	78	84	79	54.4		
Pasture								
Range								

Applied Landscape Intelligence

Resource Management Intelligence

One of the more valuable databases for any market to function efficiently is the information that describes the inventory and the ability of the physical capital to generate a particular quantity of a good or service. As mentioned in Chapter 5, the immature ecoservice markets are functioning rather blindly regarding the natural capital's capacity to generate ecoservices as it pertains to land management activities. Without a database that reveals the amount of carbon that is being sequestered or the quantity and quality of water that a farm or landscape has the ability to shed, the value of additional carbon and water-quality units becomes disconnected and somewhat arbitrary. The grain commodity markets would be as nearly paralyzed or highly inefficient without knowing the planted acres of particular crops, the growing degree days that that crop is receiving, the soil moisture profile, the sales of fertilizer, and other crop growth inputs. This landscape and production intelligence allows the market (and government) to determine the potential supply, the need, the location, and market price of an ecoservice commodity. Prior to acquiring this intelligence at the landscape scales of watersheds and basins, farm scale levels of intelligence will allow EcoCommerce to move forward in a progressive manner.

Resource Condition Intelligence

With the use of geographical information systems, landscape intelligence can be generated for particular ecoservices, markets, processors, natural features, or locations. Using an index-based system, a resource condition index could be generated for a TMDL water body and correlated to resource management indices of the landscape. A cellulosic bio-refinery could require that the landscape on which it depends must have a minimum soil condition index score and all fields must be managed above a minimum threshold. These strategies will provide a quantification of the capacity of the landscape to meet management levels or generate ecoservices. A landscape with a high soil condition index has a higher capacity to sequester carbon, nutrients, and water.

Acquiring Landscape Intelligence

This intelligence will be viewed as a highly sensitive database that many land managers may not want revealed. But since its importance to a functioning ecoservice market is no less important than crop production intelligence is to the commodity markets, an effectual demand must be generated to bring this intelligence to the marketplace. Unlike a more tangible commodity that naturally generates measurable units and prices and creates the market marvel, ecoservices need an EcoCommerce-type structure to bring units, prices, and a market marvel. As stated in Chapter 9, farmers willingly provide crop production data to the USDA Farm Service Agency as one of the criteria to maintain enrollment into the federal Farm Bill. The value of providing this proprietary information to the USDA is reflected by the support policies of the commodity title. The value of providing ecoservice landscape information could be obtained in a similar manner as Farm Bill eligibility requirements, or as an ecoservice market entry requirement described earlier as well. A third method to obtain landscape intelligence would be through value obtained from local and state government entities whose role is to understand how the land is being managed in relation to non-point pollution and ecoservices. If a state agency is responsible for a drinking-water supply and that supply is generated by a landscape catchment area, it would be in the interest of that state agency to obtain the landscape intelligence that describes how land is being managed in relationship to water contamination and purification processes.

A fourth method would be to obtain landscape intelligence as a secondary interest of a private sector that is acquiring the ecoservices through a market access process. This data would contain some level of information for a landscape intelligence database. How this information is used will be determined by ecoservice supply contract agreements. While the government entities, particularly the USDA, would have the means to begin generating and valuing landscape intelligence, an ambitious and trustworthy agricultural organization may be able to provide that service. A fifth method to acquire this landscape intelligence is through enrollment in the federal and state cost-share programs. If a farmer is considering a conservation practice, it only seems logical that both the farmer and the government entity investing in this operation would want to determine the RML of the farm, how the conservation practice would affect it, and to what extent the conservation practice would improve the farm's resources as an overall percentage.

Applying Landscape Intelligence to EcoCommerce

The demand for resource management intelligence beyond the farm did not emerge until environmental organizations and government programs began to focus on off-farm impacts. From a programmatic perspective, this occurred in the mid-1990s when the singular practice program of the USDA NRCS, the Agricultural Conservation Program, was replaced by the Environmental Quality Incentive Program that initially required a whole farm plan prior to implementation of singular practices. These changes were, in part, supported by the need to address issues at the watershed scale such as hypoxic conditions in the Gulf of Mexico. Using resource management intelligence, such as that generated by an EcoCommerce portfolio, one could scale the resource management outcomes from a farm's "back 40" up to the nation's "lower 48." In other words, the impact of soil erosion from individual fields can be compiled to the impact on individual watersheds that can be compiled to the impact on the Gulf of Mexico. As EcoCommerce and other ecoservice markets grow, it is imperative that some level of inventory be estimated and a level of capacity to produce the ecoservice is understood.

Watershed Markets and Landscape Intelligence

A municipal waste water treatment plant (WWTP) that is required to improve its treatment process or purchase water quality credits to offset its discharges can most efficiently make that decision if it is knowledgeable about the watershed landscape management and its relationship to the stream's water quality. The WWTP and other water quality stakeholders could obtain that landscape intelligence by applying a water quality index (WQi) to the landscape. If it is learned that the overall management of the watershed has an average index of 55, (a relatively low level), then the WWTP could choose the most cost-effective approach to obtain its mitigation credits. One approach could be that if the WWTP determined that a watershed average WQi of 70 would provide sufficient improvement, it could provide incentives to land managers to achieve that watershed average on a yearly basis. In this case it would be assigned a certain number of mitigation credits for each increment in the WQi that was achieved.

A second approach may require the farmer (or all farmers in the watershed) to meet a specific WQi on the entire farm operation (or entire watershed) to become eligible to engage in a trading program. In this approach, a farmer might have to meet a RML of a WQi score of, say, 65 and then he would be eligible to participate in a water quality credit market. When he meets the WQi standard of 65, he can receive Resource Incentive Payments for water quality credits such as a specified quantity and quality of water from a storage pond or wetland, or credits determined by the use of the WQi. As noted in Chapter 5, most water-quality-trading markets today are not functioning, particularly those attempting to meet water-quality improvements for public waters related to the TMDLs. In part, this lack of success is due to the high transaction costs and the low level of confidence that traders have in the program's ability to meet the desired water quality standards. It is the opinion of the author that successful water-quality trading programs between point-source discharges and non-point-source pollution generators will require a hierarchical approach that requires a certain level of resource management to occur on the landscape prior to trading credits. Once that is achieved, the land manager may enroll in the next hierarchy or tier of water-quality credit trades that will be based on water-quality storage practices such as wetlands and ponds that provide a measurable or near measurable system to account for the quality and quantity of water that enters the TMDL-restricted water body. The rationale for this approach is that point-source pollution has its greatest negative impact on the water body during low-flow conditions, and most non-point-source improvement practices have their greatest positive impact during high-flow conditions. The most logical approach to address low-flow conditions is to provide upland storage and treatment during high-flow conditions and allow the gradual release to compensate low-flow conditions. (Symbiotically, the storage of water during high flows reduces in-channel erosion and sedimentation.) These offsetting credits, along with a known level of watershed resource management could provide the level of confidence needed to allow the fledgling and failing water-quality-trading markets to progress.

The water-quality-trading markets of today have experimented with moving forward without the apparent necessity of obtaining sufficient data. That method has much lower start-up costs, but the result is limited transactions and a limited ability to understand what progress is being made.

Leveraging Resources with Landscape Intelligence

In addition to landscape intelligence to better allocate resources toward improvements, farm and watershed intelligence can leverage additional resources to achieve an ecological objective. For example, from the inception of the NRCS, its goal has been to maintain and improve the soil resources of farms and nation. With this objective, the USDA could develop an incentive-based policy declaring that achieving a certain soil conditioning index score is valued at $10/acre. The EPA does recognize the soil conditioning index as a viable tool to determine soil loss and recommends its use in water-quality trading programs (Abdalla 2008).

The EPA could approve a state's TMDL plan stating that water or soil index scores of greater than 50 provide "reasonable assurance" that the sedimentation/turbidity goal of that plan is reached. If the farmer submits the information to receive the "TMDL Assurance," the EPA would have the ability to confirm that with the USDA. A biomass processing facility that needed to reduce its carbon footprint for the bio-refinement of fuels could state that it will accept any type of vegetative cellulosic materials from fields that maintain a soil index of 75. A state natural resource agency, seeking to improve water quality in designated trout streams, could provide an incentive of $5/acre for all lands managed to a soil index score of 80. This information would be presented by Farm# and Tract#, just as crop information is currently provided to the Farm Service Agency by the farmer.

Under this simplified and unified outcome-based policy strategy, the farmers and stakeholders can best leverage their activities and their funds to achieve their resource management outcomes. In the case of the designated trout stream, a farmer may not be motivated by a $5/acre incentive. And if he were, the transaction costs of compiling, recording, and reporting this data may be too excessive to make the transaction attractive. But he may be motivated to reach that resource management outcome of 80 if he were able to acquire $10 from the USDA (perhaps through resource incentive programs), receive assurance that he meets TMDL objectives, and provide the bio-refinery with five tons of cellulose per acre at $45/ton. The biomass incentive program then matches the amount that is paid for each ton of biomass, so in this case they would receive $45/ton in BCAP funds.

In managing these "economies of configuration," the farmer first analyzed the costs of achieving a soil index of greater than 50 and then for each subsequent increase in ecoservices, he determined the marginal costs to provide that ecoservice. The government and bio-refineries may or may not be aware of all the values associated with the farmer's increasing the soil index, but it would be in their best interest to become acquainted with all the stakeholders that are attempting to bring an effectual demand toward soil resource improvement management. As the farmer analyzes the costs, he begins to aggregate the benefits, and each additional incentive that is applied by a stakeholder allows the stakeholders to lower their future prices to obtain the same level of resource management.

When the farmer addresses his self-interests, he determines that producing five tons of biomass/acre under a management regime that produced a soil index of 80 would provide him with $465/acre and he would receive assurance that he meets the TMDL Plan (Table 14.7).

Table 14.7	Leveraging Resource Management Outcomes		
Soil Index	Stakeholder	Direct Value	Indirect Value
50	USDA NRCS	$10/acre	
50	US EPA	TMDL Assurance	
75	Biomass	Market Access	$45/ton ($225)
75	USDA BCAP	$45/ton ($225)	
80	State Agency	$5/acre	
Total $/acre		$240.00	$225.00

In addressing objectives of the federal government, the USDA and the EPA meet their biomass, soil, and water-quality goals and received "landscape intelligence" that describes how that farm is managed in the context of the watershed, basin, and gulf. The bio-refinery received its raw materials at less cost and minimal transaction costs related to determining if the biomass met BCAP sustainability requirements. All this information began as- and remains - the property of the farmer unless agreements allocate the use or ownership of the "landscape intelligence" to the USDA, EPA, state, or the biomass refinery. In each case, the value of the ecoservice and the landscape intelligence are significant and complementary.

Landscape intelligence can also be created for the ecoservice demands being placed on a landscape. By using an EcoCommerce trading table that is customized for a particular watershed, milk shed, cellulosic shed, or a wildlife habitat, an aggregate demand overlay could be generated for specific ecoservice parameters. These overlays illustrate where supply and demand intersect. This landscape intelligence, particularly for the supply side, is a highly valuable component for a functioning EcoCommerce or any ecoservice market.

CHAPTER 15

Integrating EcoCommerce

Integrating Commodity and EcoCommerce Objectives

One of the major challenges facing today's ecoservice markets is that many operate outside the context of the agro-economic conditions of the farm operation. The result often is that although there are costs and values associated with ecoservices, they cannot be easily integrated or correlated with the ecological and economic operating plans of the farm. As stated previously, the provisional ecoservices provided by farms, ranches, and forests (food, fiber, and fuel) will remain the higher-valued commodities relative to regulating ecoservices. Therefore, the relatively less tangible and less valuable regulating ecoservices will have a better chance at acquiring market share if their market is integrated within the established commodity markets and farm-management strategies. This situation, perhaps, becomes more balanced when a RML criteria is required to gain access to particular commodity market. In that case, providing ecoservices is essential to selling the higher valued commodities. Table 15.1 describes the Kimball farm's commodity and ecoservice production objectives. His objectives include the production of milk, corn, wheat, soybeans, and lumber. To qualify to market these commodities to the stakeholders listed, he must meet the RML criteria as described by management indices. Kimball anticipates meeting all the production standards except for the Round Wood Co.'s habitat requirements. If he exceeds these production standards, he may also be eligible for resource credits that act as a value-added component to the commodities. In addition to access to these markets and generating resource credits, Kimball may also meet resource management criteria to obtain value through participatory benefits, liability protection, and regulatory compliance. By meeting the Valley River water-quality criteria (TMDL), he is eligible to generate resource credits through the Valley Creek WWTP trading program.

Table 15.1	Integrated Commodity and EcoCommerce Production Objective Sheet																		
EcoCommerce Incentives	Resource Management Level									Market	Commodities						Resource Credits		
	SCi	WQi	CQRi	BTUi	HSi	FLi	phHSi	pIHSi	EBI	Access	Milk	Corn	Wheat	Soyb	Biomass	Lumber	BTU	CO2e	WQQ
Monetary Benefits											cwt	bu	bu	bu	ton	bd ft	million	ton	ac-ft
Butter Land Co.	65	65	65		65	95		65		x	22000								
Etank Ethanol	65	65	65	50	60			65		x		5600			200		1905		
Round Wood Co.					75														
Electric GenCo	65	65	65		65		65			x					150			500	
Commodity Market										N/A		6400	1500	6750		150k			
County Tax Rebate		75								x						45			
USDA FSA CRP	75	75	75		75			75	95	x									
USDA FSA BCAP	60	55	60		55			55		x					350				
USDA NRCS CSP III	50	70			75			80		x									
Participatory Benefits																			
USDA FSA CC	51	51	51		51					x									
Valley Creek WWTP		75								x									
Liability Protection																			
USDA RMA	65									x									
Farmland Insurance	70	70				99													
Regulatory Compliance																			
Valley River TMDL	60	75								x									
VC Watershd District		75																	150
County Feedlot Permit	60	60			60	95													

In more detail, Table 15.1 lists the entities that provide a market signal for both provisional and regulating ecoservices. Under the RML section, the ecoservice signal target is given a score of 0-100. The following column, Market Access, denotes if Kimball has met the ecoservice target. In the two types of markets he is pursuing, Commodities and Resource Credits, the numerical listing denotes what he was able to sell. This included the commodities of milk, corn, wheat, soybeans, biomass, and lumber, and the resource credits of carbon, energy, and water quality.

For Kimball to meet these RMLs on each field, he would employ multiple strategies. This is similar to meeting production objectives, as the fields' natural characteristics and capacity dictate the type of management strategies that Kimball may use to achieve yield goals.

EcoCommerce allows the land manager to integrate natural resource objectives into the same dynamic process used to achieve production resource objectives. This integration of both objectives places ecoservices within the same market realm as traditional commodities. In a similar manner where land managers have supplied traditional commodities to the marketplace, they will find themselves as suppliers of ecoservices in the EcoCommerce economy. This is in contrast to their current roles as the "customer" of the traditional centrally planned conservation programs that has their origins in the USDA.

Resource Management Level Values

As illustrated in Table 15.1, Kimball has secured access values associated with meeting a certain RML on the farm operation as denoted by the "x" in the rows associated with industries, governments, and programs. In addition to access, the following monetary values are also associated with achieving a RML.

Liability Insurance Premium Reduction

Kimball is managing his crop fields for a soil conditioning index that meet the requirements for the Risk Management Agency crop insurance of a 4 percent premium reduction. Kimball currently pays $30/acre on 450 acres for a total of $13,500. The premium reduction is $540.

County Tax Rebate

Kimball's land management meets the WQi requirement of the County Water Plan and therefore receives $1.50/acre tax rebate on the 400 acres of land he owns for a total of $600. In return, the county receives Kimball's "landscape intelligence" data.

Federal Resource Management and Landscape Data Incentive

Kimball also qualified for the USDA CSP III program that rewards land managers for managing their natural and production resources in a manner that meets the NRCS standards and for providing "landscape intelligence" data on the land that he manages. The CSP III pays $18/acre on his 500 acres for an amount of $9,000.

Resource Credit Values
Water Quantity and Quality Credits

Kimball reestablished a wetland. The basin holds 150 acre-feet and reduces the concentration of nitrates below the level that was specified by the Valley River WWTP. The basin is 9 acres in size. If the basin is able to discharge water at or below the concentration limits, then Kimball would gross $10/acre-foot and $1,500/year or $166/acre/year.

Carbon Dioxide Equivalents

Kimball constructed an anaerobic manure digester that will generate about 800,000 cubic feet of methane per year from his 100-cow dairy herd. At 0.062 pound/cubic feet, Kimball generates 49,600 pounds or about 25 tons (Fulhage 1993). Kimball can then combust the methane for heat and/or electrical production and gain GHG-reduction credits through the process of methane destruction that converts methane to the less potent GHG of carbon dioxide. One GHG methane unit is equivalent to 20 carbon dioxide units. Kimball's capture and destruction of 25 tons of methane is equivalent to 500 tons of carbon dioxide. According to the trading table, those credits would be worth between $75 and $1,750/year depending on whether Kimball sold those through the CCX or directly to Electric GenCo.

British Thermal Units Energy Cycle

Kimball evaluated his energy balance for corn production and is averaging 160 bushels an acre of corn. His energy inputs are calculated at 8.3 million BTUs/acre/year. A yield of 160 bushels/acre generates a gross BTU output per acre of 62.8 million and a net BTU output of 54.4 million BTU/acre, or 340,106 BTUs per bushel (Lorenz 1995). Etank Ethanol is paying $0.25 for every million net BTUs that are generated. Selling his corn to Etank Ethanol with the BTU credits attached to the bushel nets Kimball an additional $0.085 per bushel. With an average yield of 160 bushels, Kimball gains $13.60/acre/year on those 5,600 bushels sold to Etank Ethanol.

EcoCommerce Values

EcoCommerce values are generated through the application of resource management strategies and accounting for them using RML and resource credit processes. Table 3.2 lists the primary and secondary commodities that Kimball produced in response to market signals. Table 15.2 includes only the direct monetary values associated with ecoservices and does not include other indirect or non-monetary values included in Table 15.1.

Note that Table 15.2 was not developed with extensive economic analysis, but is provided to give a general sense of how primary and secondary commodity production objectives may compare to ecoservice market objectives. In this case, Kimball's gross income was increased by $13,866 or 2.7 percent and his net income rose $9,685 or 13.0 percent. The net values associated with the ecoservices are crude estimates and some rely on the assumption that many of the costs of producing the ecoservices were associated with the crop production costs. In summary, EcoCommerce values could produce significant marginal benefits, as long as the market entry and transaction costs associated with generating, identifying, recording, and reporting were minimal. In the case of market access, those benefits are quite significant to the operation.

Table 15.2			Kimball's Integrated Commodity and Ecoservice Sales					
Commodities Primary	Acres	Qty	Primary Processor	Product	Qty	Gross Return	Net Return	Secondary Processor
Corn-grain (bu)	75	12,000	Kimball Cows	Milk (cwt)	6600	$99,000	$11,550	Butter Land Co.
Corn-silage (tons)	75	600	Kimball Cows	Milk (cwt)	8800	$132,000	$15,400	Butter Land Co.
Alfalfa (tons)	40	320	Kimball Cows	Milk (cwt)	6600	$99,000	$11,550	Butter Land Co.
Wheat (bu)	30	1,500	Open Market	Unknown	N/A	$8,250	$1,050	N/A
Corn-grain (bu)	35	5,600	Etank Ethanol	Ethanol	N/A	$22,400	$1,925	N/A
Soybeans (bu)	150	6,750	Open Market	Unknown	N/A	$67,500	$6,750	N/A
Corn-grain (bu)	40	6,400	Open Market	Unknown	N/A	$25,600	$2,200	N/A
Lumber (bd-ft)	50	150,000	Round Wood Co.	Furniture	N/A	$7,500	$3,500	N/A
CRP (EBI)	5		USDA	Habitat		$750	$125	
Sub-Totals	500					$462,000	$54,050	
Secondary								
Biomass-stover (tons)	[75]	150	Electric GenCo	Electricity	N/A	$6,750	$2,250	
Biomass-wood (tons)	[50]	200	Etank Ethanol	Energy	N/A	$9,000	$3,000	
Biomass-BCAP		350	USDA BCAP	Electricity	N/A	$15,750	$5,250	
Wheat Straw (tons)	[30]	50	Kimball Cows	Manure	1500			
Sub-Totals						$31,500	$10,500	
Ecoservices	Units	$/Unit	Stakeholder					
BTU (million)	1905	0.25	Etank Ethanol			$476	$400	
CO2e (tons)	500	3.50	Electric GenCo			$1,750	$0	
WQQ (ac-ft)	150	10.00	Valley Creek			$1,500	$35	
Soil Condition	450	1.20	RMA			$540	$500	
WQi	400	1.50	County			$600	$550	
CSP III	500	18.00	USDA NRCS			$9,000	$8,200	
Sub-Totals						$13,866	$9,685	
						2.7%	13.0%	
Grand Total						$507,366	$74,235	

Role Reversal Effects

Within an EcoCommerce economy that values ecoservice outcomes, the farmers' roles are reversed from a conservation customer to that of a conservation supplier. The government's role reverses, in part, from conservation supplier to conservation customer along with other ecoservice stakeholders. When the valuation process shifts from practices and activities to ecoservice outcomes, the role of the farmer also changes. Since the farmers would provide the ecoservices, much like they provide corn, they naturally become the supplier under the guidance of the invisible hand. In quick review, within a centrally planned system that is focused on practices, the farmer is the customer. If he signs up for a conservation program, the process involves the following:

• Government staff runs applicants through a winnowing process.

• Government staff identifies a practice that meets the farm's resource concern.

• Farmer applies for financial assistance.

• Farmer receives financial and technical assistance.

• Farmer hires contractor or consultant services.

• Farmer receives conservation service, installs/implements conservation practices.

• Conservation agency signs off on project.

As a customer, the farmer is obligated only to ensure the activities meet the contract requirements. In many cases, the NRCS or government partner staff conduct the work and complete the paperwork except for the landowner's signature. This process seems to meet farmers' expectations as the American Customer Satisfaction Index (ACSI) shows that farmers and ranchers are happy with the conservation technical assistance they get from the NRCS and conservation districts. The assistance provided received a satisfaction index of 81 out of a possible 100, which is 10 points higher than Americans rate private sector services and 12 points higher than the index for Federal government services (USDA NRCS 2001). This process, which includes both financial and technical assistance, does improve the production and natural resources on many farms in the nation, but this practice-based system cannot identify and meet the all-encompassing resource management needs of an adequate number of the farms in the nation.

Under a market-oriented system that focuses on ecoservice outcomes, the farmer becomes the supplier. In EcoCommerce, the farmer's role consists of several functions:

• Assessing the farm's production and natural resources

• Identifying market demands and values

• Developing an integrated resource management plan to supply ecoservices

• Marketing potential and existing ecoservice outcomes to government, industry, people, and private entities

• Providing assurance documentation for ecoservices for the period the transaction occurs

As a supplier, the farmer is obligated to achieve and maintain ecoservices and is motivated to acquire assistance and provide these ecoservices in the most efficient manner possible. Under this system, EcoCommerce objectives and processes are more aligned with the farmer's objectives and processes because the farmer can integrate both his production management and his natural resource management activities with greater ease. As an ecoservice supplier, the farmer can review the market calls and determine if he can acquire the capacity to generate these values and if they can be produced on his farm in an efficient manner. And, much like the production outcomes and costs of production resources, the strategy that the farmer applies may or may not produce the outcomes. All production plans carry the risk of being unable to produce desired outcomes, and these, too, are included in the decisions within the "economies of configurations." Applying value to what is desired reverses the primary economic roles of both farmer and government. That is not to say that the current centrally planned conservation economy becomes obsolete, but that in the long term, the greater value will be placed on what society wants, not on the actions taken to produce the outcomes.

Agricultural Professionals become Natural Resource Professionals

As value is applied to ecoservices, the invisible hand will compel farmers to seek out advice on how to best secure this value at a lower cost. Farmers may ask, "How can we most effectively allocate our resources to achieve the valued outcomes?" The supply of natural resource management professionals in the last few decades has generally come from government agencies, universities, and non-profit organizations whose mission it is to expand and improve the natural resource base (Gieseke 2008). The supply of agricultural-production resource management professionals has largely been produced from industry, agriculture, universities, and organizations dedicated to supplying commodities and raw materials from agriculture, forest, and rangelands. Since an ample supply of both natural and production resources has historically been available, both professional groups have had the luxury of working independently of each other and were not necessarily required to understand the important role each of them plays in the ecological and economic field. With an increase in citizen and consumer demand, it is becoming apparent that both of these resources must be delivered in sufficient quantities. To meet this demand, attempts to incorporate the skill bases from the natural resource management and production resource management will converge. In an EcoCommerce system that demands outcomes and minimal transactions costs, it appears that the production resource managers are in a better position to adopt and utilize the skill bases of the natural resource manager and guide the integrated resource processes.

There are four main reasons for this shift:

1. Most natural resource professionals are NRCS employees and local government staff (mainly soil and water conservation district employees). The NRCS agency employs about 13,000, 10,000 of whom are considered mission-critical staff to deploy conservation and 80 percent of whom are eligible for retirement by 2011. Similar trends are happening at state and federal levels. A severe shortage of experienced staff at the federal level will occur.

2. To properly manage resources, an on-the-ground presence is required. It has become very expensive to put people on the ground, and agriculture professionals currently have that capacity.

3. Managing natural resources within a farm operation requires a thorough understanding of operational goals, needs, and limitations. This information is often embedded within the agricultural professional and acquiring it from scratch takes significant time.

4. Influencing the management of the farm operation requires a trusted relationship with the farm operator and agricultural professionals with financial and business relationships with farmers are in an ideal situation.

The government conservation professional wouldn't become obsolete, but would probably provide natural-resource management advice to agricultural professionals and landowners whose natural resource management needs are more complex or at a higher level. For example, a habitat suitability index describes the general habitat conditions of a farm operation whose primary goals are agriculture production. Achieving a high HSI score is probably within the range of farmers and their advisors with some additional training and experience. On the other hand, developing specific habitat characteristics for a prairie chicken would require significant knowledge of the surrounding area and the specific needs of the prairie chicken. Management strategies for more complex resource needs and training for agricultural professionals to develop more general resource needs would be an efficient role for government staff.

Agricultural professionals who move into the natural resource management field will initially have a very wide range of skills and abilities related to natural resource management. These skill bases will coalesce as conservation activities and practices that are most efficient at meeting

EcoCommercegoalsareunderstood. Sincepropermanagementofboththese resources will forever depend on an on-the ground presence, agricultural advisors are well-positioned to provide natural resource assessment and conservation planning advice along with production advice. Currently, agricultural professionals are involved in the conservation delivery system by providing assistance for nutrient, pest, and other management needs to farmers via the USDA Technical Service Provider program. This assistance greatly expands the capacity of the NRCS to deliver assistance to farmers. But by adding farm resource assessments and conservation planning service to their portfolios, farmers and their advisors can take a proactive role in the overall environmental issues.

A Home Inspector Analogy

A farm resource assessment that uses indices and score sheets to rate the quality of soil, water, habitat, energy, and other types of resources can be the starting point for management decisions and can be used as a platform for farmers to reach their objectives as well as government goals. To illustrate the role an agricultural professional may play as a resource assessor, a comparison can be made to a home inspector. The home inspector identifies the quality of the foundation, roof, walls, and major components of the home and provides the initial guidance on issues that need attention. Any repairs are then handled by the homeowner and hired contractors. The home inspector is paid to be the skilled eyes, ears, and feet to assess the home to a particular level of detail.

Since agriculture advisors are already using skilled eyes, ears, and feet, incorporating resource management skills provides additional value with a reasonable level of marginal input. Understanding the status of our states' and nation's farms as it pertains to the natural resources could be considered the backbone of any effort to improve or maintain those resources. There is a tremendous difference in the administrative and assistance burden on local or federal government staff when a comparison is made between that of a farmer entering a government conservation office with a resource assessment to that of a farmer without one. There is also a significant difference in the ability to effectively target state and federal conservation funds when a comparison is made between farms that have or have not completed a resource assessment. There is also a greater sense of ownership by the farmer when the resource assessment and conservation plan are developed by him and his trusted advisor, and therefore, a higher probability that sensible conservation activities will be implemented, regardless of whether they are government-funded or not. The value from just those three aspects should support policies to provide training, certification, and monetary and technical assistance to agricultural advisors who are willing to participate at the ground level of production and natural resource assessment and planning.

Today's agricultural advisors find themselves in a unique position to address the myriad demands placed on agriculture. The issues are related to animal welfare concerns, country-of-origin labeling, and production management criteria and tracking for the use of genetics, water, chemicals, manure, and other inputs that would be considered minutia to the public a decade ago. While these data sets are important and are becoming more prevalent within agricultural production systems, this massive amount of data will not be used as the valuation units. With the access to and understanding of these data sets, agricultural advisors will be the professional group that condenses and assimilates this data into an EcoCommerce format that can be digested by farmers, processors, retailers, and consumers.

EcoCommerce Delivery System

An advantage that the EcoCommerce portfolio has in relation to other ecoservice markets is its use in an index-based resource assessment process. This portfolio can act as a single methodology for farmers to assess resource concerns and benefits, as a foundation for a resource-management plan, and as an assurance document that can then be applied toward various stakeholders' needs and values.

Resource Assessors and Planners

As noted in the Millennium Ecosystem Assessment, the participatory approach effectively incorporates new knowledge into the assessment process that is not currently available to the scientific community. Local resource managers engaged in the assessment process are informed and educated on the status of their resources, and they gain insight into what actions may be needed to generate ecoservices and improve their natural resource base. A potential drawback to this approach is that it may be time-consuming and expensive.

To capture these vital assets of a participatory approach and to mitigate the costs associated with conducting them, an existing on-the-ground agricultural professional workforce would be ideal. Agricultural production advisors, such as those certified by the American Society of Agronomy (ASA) provide farmers with crop-production advice. The ASA has a long history of developing and administering professional certification programs in agriculture. ASA currently has more than 13,000 certified crop advisors throughout the United States and Canada. ASA's certification programs adhere to generally accepted certification standards for examination, credential review of education, experience and references, and the code of ethics. Hence, the certification programs have set standards for practice in both the private and public sectors (ASA 2010).

Most advisors work in the private sector providing agronomic advice and inputs to farmers. Over time, they develop a trusted business relationship with farmers that allows them to influence the farmers' buying decisions and what practices they will adopt to best implement their farm business plans. The focus is on optimizing production while maintaining or enhancing the environmental conditions. In more recent years, the advisors have become more involved with conservation practices and are being recognized by USDA-NRCS as Technical Service Providers (TSP) in nutrient management, pest management, and tillage practices.

To illustrate the relative ease of developing a resource management plan, Table 15.3 consists of the farm's resource assessment that is compared to EcoCommerce management standards (developed by stakeholders). Each farm component is assessed for specific resources, and those management strategies that do not meet the standards are highlighted or indicated in some manner as a strikethrough mark.

To convert this to a universal resource management plan (Table 15.4), the producer would have to provide the management unit, the goal, the action, estimate costs, timeframe, and where they plan on obtaining assistance. By using the common language of management indices, land managers can share their resource management goals to all stakeholders. Since each entity can see the potential partners involved, a higher level of coordination can occur.

Table 15.3		EcoCommerce Assessment								
		Ecoservice Parameters								
		FLi	SCi	fSQi	WQi	CQRi	BTUi	HSi	pIHSi	phHSi
Management Unit	Acres	98	65	77	75	80	80	75	80	80
Farm	500							75	82	80
Farmstead										
Feedlot	5	~~96~~								
Forest	50			75		88		82		
#5001	50			~~75~~		88		82		
Fields										
#1001	100		75		87	92	82			
#1002	100		72		75	88	88			
#1003	100		67		~~72~~	81	~~72~~			
#1004	150		~~62~~		78	~~77~~	~~75~~			
Total	450		68		78	84	~~79~~			
Pasture										
Range										

Table 15.4	EcoCommerce Universal Resource Management Plan							
Management Unit	Goal	Action	~Cost	Schedule	Assistance			
					Federal	State	Private	Operator
Feedlot	Increase the FLi from 96 to 98	Add storage	45k	May-11	x	x	x	
Field 1003	Increase WQi from 72 to 75	Plant buffer	.5k	Sep-10				x
Field 1004	Increase SCi from 62 to 70	Reduce tillage	.8k	Jun-11		x	x	x
	Increase CQRi from 77 to 85	Reduce tillage	.8k	Jun-11		x	x	x
	Increase BTUi from 75 to 85	Reduce tillage	.8k	Jun-11		x	x	x

Of course, this plan needs further details for it to be implemented successfully, but it provides a significant amount of information to the agriculture and resource management professional on the scale and scope of the implementation plan and a significant amount of insight into how that resource management plan can be integrated with commodity production plans. This contrasts with the NRCS conservation planning protocol and process, whose format, while thorough, is not universally applicable and that poses significant communication challenges. Often, it is only the NRCS professional who truly understands the plan's components to the degree that is necessary for successful implementation.

Again, the key attributes that allow this process to function are trusted relationships, knowledge of specific farms, and an understanding of the agricultural community and business. With this existing nationwide resource-management capacity of agricultural professionals, it is quite feasible and cost-effective to develop a training program to incorporate a natural resource assessment and conservation planning capacity into the service portfolio. This capacity would be able to bring back a resource-driven process whose resource management plans can be reintegrated with land management plans.

Professional Organizations

This professional workforce also exists within organization and networks and many are employed by farmer cooperatives. The members of the National Council of Farmers Cooperatives are regional and national farmer cooperatives that are, in turn, comprised of nearly 3,000 local farmer cooperatives across the country. The majority of America's 2 million farmers and ranchers belong to one or more farmer cooperatives. NCFC members also include 26 state and regional councils of cooperatives. Farmer cooperatives handle, process, and market almost every type of agricultural commodity, furnish farm supplies, and provide credit and related financial services, including export financing. Earnings from these activities are returned to farmer members on a patronage basis, helping improve their income from the marketplace. Farmer cooperatives also provide more than 250,000 jobs, with a total payroll in excess of $8 billion, and contribute significantly to the economic well-being of rural America. The potential capacity of professional organizations and members is adequate to assess the natural resources on American farms as the organizational structure and employment is similar to the organizational structure and employment numbers of the conservation delivery system (NCFC 2010).

Parallel Private-Public Sectors

The ASA states it has 13,000 CCAs, and the NRCS has 13,000 employees. The NRCS states that there are 3,000 local soil and water conservation districts serving farmers, and the NCFC states that there are 3,000 local farmer cooperatives. These parallels are more than coincidental if these delivery structures are considered the results of both a centrally planned conservation economy and a market-based production economy. Both delivery structures began about 75 years ago to address the production resources and the natural resources of a farm operation. They remained separate because the impacts of agricultural production on the natural resources remained an "externality" of the market system. As the economy begins to formalize these ecoservice values and costs, the activities and values associated with them will be absorbed by the professionals that have the ability to conduct these activities with the least marginal costs. It appears that the production resource management delivery system has far greater capacity, motivation, and customer relationships than any other economic structure in place, including the existing government-led conservation delivery system. As a result, the resource assessment, planning, implementation, and assurance components (the bulk of the current conservation delivery system) will be carried out by agricultural professionals. The EcoCommerce delivery system will be supplemented by government programs, but not managed by the government as it is currently. It will be guided by value and price of ecoservices, much like other market systems.

EcoCommerce Training

One of the primary needs of the production agricultural workforce is to receive training on adding the skills of natural resource assessment, planning, and assurance. Under the centrally planned conservation economy, this occupation has been handled by a variety of organizations including NRCS, soil and water conservation districts, universities and their extension systems, and the private sector. Funds for these trainings have been derived from various government programs and from professionals attending courses.

By many accounts, deciding what type of trainings that the government agencies should hold has been a challenging task. Since there are no economic signals for farmers and other resource managers to follow as they pertain to ecoservices, no one really knows what the actual training needs are. It is a similar situation with farmers and best management practices (BMPs); since no single agency can tell a farmer which BMPs he must install, decisions on which BMPs to install are lacking. Organizing training courses under this framework is hit-and-miss. If EcoCommerce could begin to provide economic signals to farmers, farmers would, in turn, provide economic signals to their advisors who, in turn, would demand certain training sessions to accommodate their farmer clients. A value would be placed on specific trainings and the private sector would engage in these activities as individuals are looking for jobs.

Index Development Sector

Perhaps a unique sector will be Index Development and Marketing. Since ecoservices and non-point-source pollution are immeasurable in the traditional sense, the development of representative indices will be necessary. Many of the ecoservice indices will be developed under the guidance of government organizations such as the NRCS Office of Ecosystem Services and Markets. But in a market-based or hybrid economy, entrepreneurs have the freedom to seek out new forms of value. Beyond the core indices, new indices will be created to meet the demand of stakeholders that want particular resource management outcomes. If a particular bird species is desired, an organization that wants those types of birds can place a value on an index that describes the location, habitat characteristics, and management of those resources to support that bird population. As these markets mature, specific indices will be created to aid in commerce. Occupations in this sector may be housed in non-profits, academia, government, or the private sector and will become involved in the development of new indices for several reasons:

- The language controls the dialogue.

- The indices express the resource of concern.

- The indices direct the value.

- The management standards are based on the indices.

- The geographical intelligence is generated by the indices.

Occupational Shift

A hybridized EcoCommerce economy presumably would contain both controlled-economy agents and market participants, and the ratio of those two groups would be in direct proportion to the funds that are allocated to each facet of the economy. As EcoCommerce emerges, grows, and matures, the makeup of its participants will generally shift from agents to market participants, as government support is generally needed in the early stage of an ecoservice market and not needed as much if the market is successful. The unique aspect of an EcoCommerce structure, in comparison to today's ecoservice markets, is its objective to integrate itself within the economy at large. By nature, EcoCommerce resides in a larger context than a New York City Regional Watershed ecoservice market from a geographical sense, and it resides in a larger context than a Chicago Climate Exchange from a resource parameter perspective in that EcoCommerce is involved with more issues than carbon equivalents.

Reevaluate Government Roles

Due to these factors, the roles of federal, state, and local governments will be reevaluated in the sense that new capacities will be brought into the conservation economy. Some of the tasks that were included in the all-encompassing role of the government in the centrally planned conservation economy will be addressed by others. Government agencies will have the opportunity to focus efforts on the tasks that they are most proficient at. Non-government organizations that often must leverage government technical and financial assistance may find that they can more effectively leverage these resources from other stakeholders. These other stakeholders would include non-profits, agribusinesses, agro-industries, Walmart and other retailers, bio-refineries, bio-processors, and farmers. The level of influence each of these brings to the table will either reinforce or dilute the influence of other stakeholders, including the government agencies.

If these new and potentially influential EcoCommerce stakeholders accept that farmers and other land managers can provide the ecoservices that their markets desire, they will either align themselves to provide support to the farmer in generating ecoservices, or coordinate the purchase of ecoservices to meet their objectives. By formalizing ecoservices within the economy, EcoCommerce, left to its own capacity, will align the activities of numerous government and private-sector stakeholders. This alignment will produce many of the objectives of today's government conservation delivery system that currently appear unattainable. Such objectives include streamlining the accountability process, determining the value of ecoservices, allotting an adequate amount of funds for desired outcomes, and building cooperation among government agencies with a history of a rather inefficient interaction of competition despite having cooperative intentions. *Beyond the USDA* (Gosselin 2010), a paper by the Institute for Agriculture and Trade Policy, states: "Currently, there is no integrated approach among government departments and agencies to address food-related issues. Thus, the efforts of one entity may undermine the activities of another. With so many government bodies influencing so many facets of our food system, how can we move toward federal food policies that are smart, non-contradictory, and truly serve the public interest?"

The paper answers that question: "The USDA, EPA and Department of Human Health and Services should convene an interdepartmental task force on food policy to bring together the diverse departments and agencies that have bearing on food production and consumption in America. A better understanding of federal oversight of the food system is a prerequisite to a more clear and coordinated approach to food."

Many onlookers and participants in the government process would generally agree with both the question and answer, as each has correct components. But the fundamental problem with the food production business, as is pertains to resource management, is that the federal government can neither adequately manage the economies of configurations nor generate and process the landscape intelligence that is needed to efficiently allocate financial and technical resources and make improvements. Ultimately, landowners and personnel within government, industries, and non-profits will make decisions based on their self-interests and the interests of their organization to advance their causes. Unfortunately, government entities are designed or have evolved to a point that integrating and coordinating themselves as suggested by the IATP paper is not in their self-interests. This is not a cynical perspective, but one that respects the position that government agencies and their professional staff are in. When resource management outcomes are not the valued component in the system, something else *will* become the valued component. The focus either becomes the process, practices, positions, or procedures of generating outcomes.

The reevaluation of government roles will be based on many variables:

• Significant personnel changes that are occurring in USDA NRCS and the similar trends reflected throughout federal, state, and local agencies with a new generation of employees emerging

• Rapid advancements in agriculture with computerized and spatial technology

• Pressures to develop and implement outcome-based policy

• The larger context of resource management participants

As these changes progress, government support will be provided most efficiently by the agencies and personnel who have compatible skills. A brief list of those capacities would include:

• The Farm Service Agency providing spatial records of ecoservices and landscape intelligence

• The NRCS focusing on resource management assessment at various scales greater than the field and farm (similar to its Conservation Effects Assessment Project)

• The NRCS administering financial and technical assistance programs related primarily to structural practices and reducing financial support for cultural practices

• USDA Office of Ecosystem Services and Markets providing oversight for approved management indices and other ecoservice measurements

• Agricultural professionals providing resource assessments, planning, and assurance services

• Agribusinesses and cooperatives providing ecoservice brokerage and related services

• Land managers providing ecoservices in an integrated production plan

Opportunities of the EcoCommerce Commons

The integration of production and natural resource outcomes and the subsequent occupational adjustment and shift will also create opportunities for the stakeholders. Since the farmer becomes the ecoservice supplier of the world, stakeholder organizations, including the government, begin to get a sense of the shared responsibility they have in promoting ecoservices. This becomes even keener as it becomes apparent that sharing this responsibility will reduce costs and address self-interests. Under the centrally controlled conservation delivery system, the burden to succeed was primarily placed on the USDA and local conservation districts, and the burden to implement was primarily on private landowners. This narrowly shared approach was sufficient when the primary goal was to reduce erosion for the purpose of maintaining the soil's productivity to increase the economic well-being of the farmer, the community, and the nation.

As the nation's resource management demands increased and both positive and negative externalities of the farming business were identified, many more government agencies, non-profits, and private-sector entities naturally became involved. With the financial burden still largely placed on the USDA and the farmers, other organizations contribute by providing additional funds and technical assistance to leverage and guide federal dollars. But even today, many state governments, non-profit organizations, and the private sector operate under the premise that the USDA has the primary responsibility to direct and conduct conservation activities on our nation's private farms. This is even to the extent that farmers themselves may view the USDA as the primary party responsible for implementing conservation practices on their land. The winnowing process of conservation programs does not allow the farmer to feel in control of the conservation destiny or ownership of the outcomes. But as bio-refineries emerge from the landscape and new participants, such as Walmart, become part of the "conservation delivery system," it is becoming apparent that the USDA is not the center of resource management - the farmers are.

The USDA does attempt to share in this effort with programs such as the USDA Conservation Innovations Grant and the Cooperative Conservation Program that promote partnerships among private, public, and non-profit organizations. These are successful in bringing people and organizations together and often result in agreements on how conservation outcomes can be achieved. The states often duplicate this model and provide myriad programs such as clean water partnerships. But note that, when the financial contributions of these organized partnerships cease, so, too, do the majority of the common activities. This does not mean that organizational and personal relationships that are beneficial to the cooperation of conservation efforts will not continue, but the self-interests of the organizations and the personnel are quickly informed by the invisible hand that not enough value remains and this lack of value quickly guides those participants to the next activities that provide an income stream. To achieve an enduring shared responsibility, a shared financial stream that is relatively consistent must be formed. Guiding or forcing conservation agencies and organizations to jump from one administration's objectives and Congressional allotments does not provide the required consistency.

In a market economy, the transaction or the exchange of goods and services is the step that defines value and unifies efforts. Entrepreneurs who desire compensation must provide value to the process that aids in the transaction. The profit that is related to the transaction can be increased by lowering both production and transaction costs. The opportunities in EcoCommerce are numerous and symbiotic.

The Advantage of Stacking EcoCommerce Opportunities

Due to the nature of land management activities, several ecoservices may be generated by a single type of activity. Planting a grass or tree buffer strip alongside a stream can create ecosystem functions related to soil quality, water quality, carbon sequestration, and general and species-specific habitat. This buffer strip, in turn, may provide ecoservice values associated with Walmart's Sustainability Index, Game Bird Habitat Unlimited, Valley River TMDL, and Valley Creek WWTP. From this perspective, EcoCommerce opportunities can be stacked for both supply and demand components. From the supply perspective, a single activity can produce multiple ecoservices. The actions and costs required to sequester a ton of carbon may be the same actions and costs to produce an acre-foot of clean water that also produces 10 successful upland bird nestings. An entrepreneur working for the supplier would naturally consider selling the ton of carbon, the acre-foot of water, and the habitat quality to three different entities whose objective is to produce those specific ecoservices. As stated previously, this may be considered double- or triple-dipping by the buyers. It is at this point that the EcoCommerce economy departs from many of the ecoservice markets and allows value to be placed on each symbiotic benefit rather than discounting these natural outcomes of a functioning ecosystem. Since EcoCommerce is an outcome-based process, rather than a practice-based process, it is the value of the outcomes, not the cost of the practice, that carries the transaction. It may appear that the supplier will benefit from the ability to stack outcomes, but in a transparent market, buyers will also be aware of these values. It is no different than a processing plant that generates a primary product and several byproducts. Generally the primary product is the most lucrative, but, depending on market conditions, byproducts may be the more valuable or most profitable outcome. The result of this is generally good for both suppliers and buyers, as both entities are usually knowledgeable about the market conditions and the prices that must be applied to both products and byproducts.

In the buffer example, costs can be shared by several entities providing the opportunity for a greater return to the farmer while costing less for the buyers individually. How these relations and opportunities resolve themselves is embedded in the actions of the EcoCommerce participants and the guidance of the invisible hand.

EcoCommerce Transactions

Nothing turns the gears of a market other than a transaction. With ecoservice, a supply and a demand have always existed at some level, yet without transactions, economic participants cannot have firsthand experience of their economic value and costs. To use the Kimball's integrated commodity and ecoservice production intentions as a starting point, several transaction types can occur. The following pages provide examples of the transaction types that were used by Kimball and the stakeholders. In Chapter 6, six types of transactions were listed than can be used independently or in combination to make the transactions possible:

1. Bilateral agreements

2. Public payment arrangements

3. Tax Credits

4. Clearinghouse

5. Sole-source

6. Market-style trading

Etank Ethanol: Bilateral Agreement, Clearinghouse

Kimball's production and marketing plan includes producing 5,600 bushels of corn for Etank Ethanol within a cropping system that had to meet ecoservice index scores. Kimball forward contracts (bilateral agreements) his 5,600 bushels of corn along with the stipulation that the bushels meet the processor's (EcoCommerce) standards. Meeting these management levels also provides Kimball with the opportunity to make a transaction for 1905 mBTU credits that will be purchased by Etank Ethanol or placed in an internal credit market (clearinghouse) of Etank Ethanol to provide a means for farmer members to purchase these credits.

State EPA-Valley Creek Watershed District- WWTP: Bilateral, Tax Credits

Kimball's operation meets the state's EPA TMDL (water quality) requirement. His WQi score of 78 is the method used to prove to the state that he has met "reasonable assurances." Since the state also uses this method to provide "reasonable assurance" to the federal EPA, he has to certify that his operation meets or exceeds that requirement. While no monetary benefits are exchanged in this bilateral agreement, Kimball becomes eligible for tax credits from the Valley Creek Watershed District.

Kimball is also eligible to engage in the water quality market with credits purchased by the Valley Creek WWTP. The transaction with the WWTP will be in the form of a bilateral agreement with a practice such as a wetland or storage pond with measurable water quantity and water quality parameters.

Electric GenCo – USDA BCAP: Bilateral, Market-Style, Public Payment

Kimball is providing Electric GenCo with 150 tons of corn stover biomass with the requirement that the cropping system meet or exceed certain index scores. He has a bilateral agreement through a forward contract to provide this biomass to Electric GenCo. This also allows him to market carbon credits either through direct purchase from Electric GenCo or through the CCX, a market-style trading system. Since Electric GenCo is on the USDA Farm Service Agency's approved list for biomass conversion facilities and since he meets the BCAP management requirements, he is eligible to receive public payments from the USDA for the delivery of sustainably produced biomass.

Butter Land Company: Bilateral

Kimball has a bilateral agreement with Butter Land Company to deliver a certain amount of milk that is produced under a farming system that meets soil, water, carbon, feedlot and both general and pollinator habitat index requirements. The value of that bilateral agreement is market access for Kimball.

United States Department of Agriculture: Public Payment, Bilateral

Under the EcoCommerce structure (in this fictional scenario), Kimball has a Conservation Reserve Program contract that was generated by a market-based bidding process and completed with a bilateral agreement. His Conservation Stewardship Program III contract is a monetary incentive using a public payment process. He meets his Conservation Compliance objectives via a regulatory compliance process that gives him access to Farm Bill benefits. He meets the USDA Risk Management Agency requirement via a liability protection value and is reimbursed via a public payment process.

EcoCommerce Marketplace

The types of transactions that will occur in EcoCommerce are as numerous and varied as those that occur in the economy at large. While the overall picture of EcoCommerce may be as complex as the overall economy, those who participate in EcoCommerce will only need to interact with the aspect of EcoCommerce that is related to their self-interests. The extent of the EcoCommerce Marketplace may be visualized by illustrating the transaction components and pathways. Two of the EcoCommerce scenarios are applied to a flow chart (Figure 15.1) to illustrate the specific management units that generate the ecoservices (provisional and regulating) and how those values flow to the ecoservice stakeholders. The example on the left side of the figure illustrates multiple ecoservices whose graduated values are applied within a single entity, Etank Ethanol. Kimball basket-bundled the ecoservices required to gain market access to Etank Ethanol. The flow chart represents that Kimball has gained market access and has sold 5,600 bushels of corn. Since Kimball's production strategy of those 5,600 bushels nets 1,905 million BTUs, he is able to gain a resource credit via the Etank Ethanol internal market for BTUs.

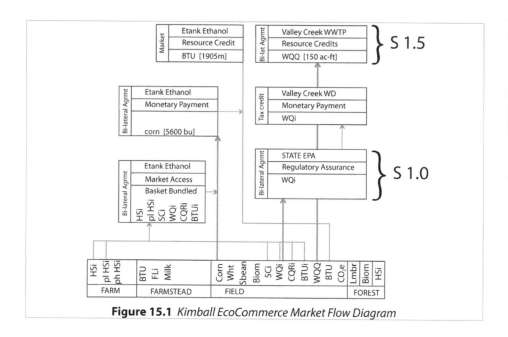

Figure 15.1 *Kimball EcoCommerce Market Flow Diagram*

The example on the right illustrates a single ecoservice parameter (water quality) whose value is applied to three entities: the State EPA, Valley Creek Watershed District, and Valley Creek Wastewater Treatment Plant. Kimball receives assurance from the state EPA that his management strategy meets the water-quality requirements (TMDL) for Valley Creek. Due to this certifiable assurance, he receives a tax credit from the Valley Creek Watershed District. In addition to meeting these standards, Kimball also generated water quality and quantity credits (WQQ) that he is selling to Valley Creek WWTP. The brackets S 1.0 and S 1.5 represent the "sustainability" tiers described in Chapter 12 and in Figure 12.2.

Kimball's EcoCommerce complete market layout is further described in Table 15.5, which lists the 13 major stakeholders that purchase provisional and regulating ecoservices from Kimball's farm operation, including the four entities listed in Figure 15.1. The buyers, how they value the ecoservices, and what means they use to execute the transactions are listed on the left side of the figure. The right side lists the ecoservice types that Kimball produces under each category with the unshaded ecoservices boxes representing the ecoservice that that particular stakeholder is

Table 15.5 — Kimball's EcoCommerce Components and Relationships

Market Components			Ecoservice Type																
			Provisional						Regulating - Management Level (bundled)								Regulating - Credit		
Buyer	Market Valuations	Transaction type(s)	Corn	Milk	Wheat	Soybeans	Lumber	Biomass	SCi	WQi	HSi	CQRi	BTUi	FLi	pIHSi	phtHSi	BTU	CO₂e	WQQ
Etank Ethanol	Market Access	Bi-lateral Agrmt	**Corn**	*Milk*	*Wheat*	*Soybeans*	*Lumber*	*Biomass*	**SCi**	**WQi**	**HSi**	**CQRi**	**BTUi**		**pIHSi**	*phtHSi*			
	Monetary Payment	Bi-lateral Agrmt																	
	Credit Trading	Clearinghouse/Internal Market															BTU	CO₂e	WQQ
State EPA	Regulatory Assurance	Bi-lateral Agrmt							*SCi*	*WQi*	*HSi*	*CQRi*	*BTUi*	*FLi*	*pIHSi*				
Valley Crk WD	Monetary Payment	Tax Credit							*SCi*	*WQi*	*HSi*	*CQRi*	*BTUi*	*FLi*	*pIHSi*				
VC WWTP	Credit Trading	Bi-lateral Agrmt															*BTU*	*CO₂e*	WQQ
Electric GenCo	Market Access	Bi-lateral Agrmt							**SCi**	**WQi**	**HSi**	**CQRi**	**BTUi**	**FLi**	**pIHSi**				
	Monetary Payment	Bi-lateral Agrmt	*Corn*	*Milk*	*Wheat*	*Soybeans*	**Lumber**	**Biomass**											
	Credit Trading	Clearinghouse/Internal Market															*BTU*	*CO₂e*	*WQQ*
USDA BCAP	Monetary Payment	Bi-lateral Agrmt	*Corn*	*Milk*	*Wheat*	*Soybeans*	*Lumber*	**Biomass**											
Butter Land Co	Market Access	Bi-lateral Agrmt							**SCi**	**WQi**	**HSi**	**CQRi**	**BTUi**	**FLi**	**pIHSi**				
	Monetary Payment	Bi-lateral Agrmt	*Corn*	**Milk**	*Wheat*	*Soybeans*	*Lumber*	*Biomass*											
Round Wood Co	Monetary Payment	Bi-lateral Agrmt	*Corn*	*Milk*	*Wheat*	*Soybeans*	**Lumber**	*Biomass*											
Open Market	Monetary Payment	Open Market	**Corn**	*Milk*	**Wheat**	**Soybeans**	**Lumber**	*Biomass*											
USDA CRP	Monetary Payment	Market/Bi-lateral Agrmt							**SCi**	**WQi**	**HSi**	**CQRi**	**BTUi**	**FLi**	**pIHSi**				
USDA RMA	Liability Protection	Public Payment							*SCi*	*WQi*	*HSi*	*CQRi*	*BTUi*	*FLi*	*pIHSi*				
USDA CC	Regulatory Assurance	Bi-lateral Agrmt							**SCi**	**WQi**	**HSi**	**CQRi**	**BTUi**	**FLi**	**pIHSi**				
USDA CSP	Monetary Payment	Public Payment							**SCi**	**WQi**	**HSi**	**CQRi**	**BTUi**	**FLi**	**pIHSi**				

purchasing under the valuation type. The regulating ecoservices in each basket bundle are shown in unshaded boxes.

To read the table, start from the left side to determine the buyer of the ecoservice. As you move right, it lists the market valuation and transaction type. To determine the ecoservice(s) purchased by the stakeholder, continue to move right until one of the three groups of ecoservice categories is encountered. The unshaded boxes represent the ecoservice purchased. Table 15.5 represents the flow of both provisional and regulating ecoservices that are initiated by a stakeholder through a market signal. The market signal is translated via a valuation type and channeled through the necessary transaction process. The provisional ecoservices that flow from the land are accounted for via traditional measurement units such as bushels and pounds. The regulating ecoservices flow from the exact same land unit and management practices that produced the provisional ecoservices. The difference, of course, is that measuring ecoservice quantities requires different measurement techniques. While this difference is significant, it does not warrant a process that isolates ecoservices and their market development from the production aspects of the farm operation. Due to the seemingly insurmountable challenges that ecoservice markets have faced to date, it would seem advantageous to develop and implement the ecoservice markets within the context, personnel, support, and process of the well-developed agro-economic system.

CONCLUSION

Constructing EcoCommerce felt more like a discovery than an invention - or perhaps somewhat of a puzzle as well, since many of the pieces needed have existed and evolved over several decades. Since the economic value of the ecosystems and their life-giving ecoservices has existed long before economic systems were used, EcoCommerce became a matter of describing a method to reveal the values that ecosystems bestow on the economy rather than, of course, creating them.

Due to this absolute and enduring value, I feel confident that an EcoCommerce structure will become integrated within economic systems. As EcoCommerce emerges and begins to provide a glimpse of the ecoservice value and its relationship to existing economic values, it may be a humbling experience for economic participants—humbled by both an awareness of our dependency on ecosystems and an awareness that we will need to begin carrying the burden of economies past. It will also bring recognition that the bio-economy is truly a subsidiary of the ecology. This recognition will also allow for an expansion of the economy. Providing ecoservices and increasing the natural-capital capacity is an investment in the bio-economy infrastructure. This investment will create immediate wealth and renewable wealth.

In January 2010, the Council for Agricultural Science and Technology published an issue paper, "Agricultural Productivity Strategies for the Future: Addressing U.S. and Global Challenges." It stated that numerous factors are converging to make "the perfect storm" in global food and agriculture. These factors included population growth, energy supplies, stagnating yield curves, lack of research expenditures, and diminishing ecosystem services, including existence of 146 hypoxic (low oxygen) zones in the world's oceans (CAST 2010). On issues related to EcoCommerce, the paper specifically listed soil erosion, water quality and quantity, fertilizer resources, and biodiversity as the emerging constraints in United States agriculture.

CAST, an organization of 30 agricultural scientific member societies, sees the solution from the eyes of Dr. Norman Borlaug and his calling for a "Second Green Revolution." The authors of the paper state that the "next green revolution" will include scientific findings related to improved photosynthetic pathways, nitrogen fixation, asexual reproduction, nutrient and water-use efficiencies, efficient conversion of bio-fuels, pest resistance, plant energy-efficiency increases, increased health benefits of food, and seeking innovations.

To date, the market and government policies have supported these types of efforts to advance agriculture production to various degrees, and I expect this support will continue. As a farmer, I also use these types of modern technologies as market forces and government policies create the environment for adopting new production strategies. But from the perspective of EcoCommerce and its recognition of natural capital, I view these scientific advancements as improvements to the productivity of the farm operation, not as an improvement to the capacity of the natural capital of the farm and off-farm resources. The second green revolution must embrace natural capital values and the values associated with ecoservices to the extent that it improves the capacity of both on-farm and off-farm resources. To date, there are no microeconomic forces that provide guidance toward a green revolution that considers ecosystem capacity. Neither does it seem feasible that macroeconomic policies can be developed and implemented to the extent and efficiency that would generate ecoservices within the next green revolution. Therefore, the context of the next green revolution must reside within the scientific community, market economy, government policies, and an EcoCommerce-type framework.

Fortunately there is much to build on. Often, in the passing of societal leaders such as Dr. Borlaug in September 2009, many more leaders are awaken. The next green revolution will need many participants, rather than the scientific breakthroughs of one individual. The 30 scientific societies of CAST are rich in innovation and ambition. The same depth and commitment can be found in ecological, economical, social, government, and agricultural communities. Finding the path toward the next green revolution is in our self-interests as well.

The next steps toward EcoCommerce also have a path to follow. Developing and instituting a new resource management language will be based on the insights and research of Ott in the 1970s and the efforts to refine landscape management indices by state and federal governments in the last three decades. This information capital can rapidly increase. Even the bundle of resource indices available today is far beyond a crude portfolio.

Perhaps more impressive is the human capital available to EcoCommerce. Agricultural professionals have adopted spatial and database technologies that provide site-specific information in useable formats. Their on-the-ground presence is critical for any ecoservice market to function and meet its objectives. Having thousands of these professionals, in conjunction with the government resource professionals, is the deal-maker for EcoCommerce. Combining their capacity with an index-based language, on-farm resource assessments that can readily lead to resource management plans and landscape intelligence are cost-effective.

Landscape intelligence, the missing critical link in the supply and demand equation of ecoservice markets, can be generated and valued. Perhaps the most contentious issue, policies that strive to acquire landscape intelligence must be crafted with significant values in mind. Demanding that producers provide landscape data to be eligible for Farm Bill benefits may be a high political hurdle to clear. Like all commodities, an effectual demand must be generated to motivate entrepreneurs.

An effectual demand, or in a mature market, an aggregate demand, can be generated by those willing to pay. In the last several years, businesses, industries, corporations, and non-profits that are willing to pay have expanded greatly. While once it was just the government in that position, consumers and private business sectors have shown support for ecoservices. With the retail giant Walmart and others following suit or participating in their "Sustainability Index" effort, the tipping point for EcoCommerce may be near. At that point, land managers become the ecoservice suppliers to the nation and world, rather than confined to being the conservation customer of federal and state governments.

That tipping point is what many potential EcoCommerce participants have been waiting for. As I have spent the last three years explaining the potential of a broad-based ecoservice market, I have been repeatedly, asked (and rightly so), "But what is the value of providing ecoservices?" I was fortunate enough to have worked on projects that did value the exploration of a broad-based ecoservice market, so a portion of my self-interests were being met. But the market-based economic value for which they were looking had not emerged. Of course, even with my optimistic conclusion, many readers will not be convinced that such a system could ever be implemented. Amazingly though, as long as someone or some entity deems it to be in their self-interests, however narrow or broad, EcoCommerce can emerge and commence. And that appears to be the case, as a recent caller inquired about my ability to develop a "sustainability plan" for agricultural producers so that they may meet their customers' demands for a product that meets a certain retailer's "sustainability level." The desire to place economic value on a defined level of sustainability is the impetus for EcoCommerce, the same beginning for all emerging markets.

WORKS CITED

APSIM. "APSIM Documentation." www.apsim.info/apsim/Publish/Docs/
Documentation.xml (accessed February 8, 2010).

ASA 2010. "American Society of Agronomy." https://www.
certifiedcropadviser.org/ (accessed February 9, 2010).

Abdalla, Charles. "Land use Policy: Lessons from water quality markets."
Choices, 4th Quarter 2008. http://www.choicesmagazine.org/
magazine/pdf/article_52.pdf.

Abdalla, Charles. "Water quality credit trading and agriculture: recognizing
the challenges and policy issues ahead." *Choices*, Summer
2007. http://www.choicesmagazine.org/2007-2/grabbag/2007-
2-06.htm (accessed February 8, 2010).

Aerts, J.C.J.H. "STREAM (Spatial tools for river basins and environment
and analysis of management options)" *Physics and Chemistry of
the Earth, Part B: Hydrology, Oceans and Atmosphere* 24, no. 6
(1999): 591-595.

Amacher, M. *Soil vital signs: A new soil quality index for assessing forest
soil health res. pap. RMRS-RP-65WWW.* Fort Collins: USDA Forest
Service Rocky Mountain Research Station, 2007.

Anew NZ. "Exxon Valdez oil spill." http://www.anewnz.org.nz/page.
asp?id=3228879138356TLQ (accessed February 7, 2010).

Bell, Simon, and Stephen Morse. *Measuring sustainability: learning by
doing.* 2003. Reprint, London: Earthscan Publications Ltd.,
2006.

Bell, Simon, and Stephen Morse. *Sustainability indicators: Measuring
the immeasurable.* Revised and Updated ed. London: Earthscan
Publications Ltd., 2008.

Bhatia, A. 2005. "Data rich, information poor? Focus on right metrics."
The Data Administration Newsletter. http://www.tdan.com/view-
articles/5115 (accessed February 8, 2010).

Blue Source 2009. "Blue source - A leading climate change portfolio."
Blue Source - A Leading Climate Change Portfolio. http://www.
ghgworks.com/5c-pr09-10-29.html (accessed February 8, 2010).

Boyd, James, and Spencer Banzhaf. "What are ecosystem services?"
        RFF Documents. www.rff.org/documents/RFF-DP-06-02.pdf
        (accessed February 11, 2010).

Burk, A.R. *New trends in ecology research*. ed. Huntington: Nova Science
        Publishers, 2005.

Butt, T.A. "Farm and forest carbon sequestration: can producers employ it
        to make some money?" *Choices*, 3rd Quarter 2004.

CAST. 2010. "Agricultural productivity strategies for the future: addressing
        U.S. and global challenges." *Council for Agricultural Science and
        Technology*. Issue Paper 45 (2010). http://www.cast-science.org
        (accessed February 9, 2010).

Campbell, Neil. *Biology (1996 4th edition) student hardcover text*. 4th ed.
        San Fransisco: Benjamin Cummings, 1996.

Case, Karl E., and Ray C. Fair. *Principles of macroeconomics (Custom
        Edition) by Karl E. Case and Ray C. Fair*. Upper Saddle River:
        Pearson Education, 2004.

Caughlan, L. and D. Hoag. "Feeding elk in greater yellowstone: A case
        study in ex-ante group decision support." iemss.org. www.iemss.
        org/iemss2002/proceedings/pdf/volume%20tre/211_hoag.pdf
        (accessed February 8, 2010).

Christensen, Norman, *et. al.* "The report of the ecological society of
        america committee on the scientific basis for ecosystem
        management." *Ecological Applications* 6, no. 3 (1996): 665-91.

Claassen, Roger, and Cynthia Nickerson. "2008 Farm Bill side-by-side:
        title ii: conservation." USDA Economic Research Service -
        Home Page. http://www.ers.usda.gov/FarmBill/2008/Titles/
        titleIIConservation.htm#market01 (accessed February 8, 2010).

Claassen, Roger. "Cost-effective conservation programs: The role of
        economics." *Journal of Soil and Water Conservation*, Mar. - Apr.
        2009.

Clark, John G. "Economic development vs. sustainable societies:
        reflections on the players in a crucial contest." *Annual Review of
        Ecology and Systematics* 26 (1995): 225-48. http://arjournals.
        annualreviews.org/toc/ecolsys.1/26/1 (accessed February 11,
        2010).

Collins, S. 2009. "Developing markets for ecosystem services." USDA
        OESM Presentation by Sally Collins. www.stateforesters.org/files/
        Collins-2009-NASF.pdf (accessed February 8, 2010).

Conover, M.R. "Perceptions of american agricultural producers about
        wildlife on their farms and ranches." *Wildlife Society Bulletin*,
        Fall 2008.

Cork, Steven. "Ecosystems." http://www.ecosystemservicesproject.org /
     html/publications/index.htm (accessed February 7, 2010).
Costanza, Robert. "The value of the world's ecosystem services and
     natural capital." *Nature* 387 (1997): 253-260.
Cox, Craig. "Beyond T: Guiding sustainable soil management." *Journal of
     Soil and Water Conservation* 63, no. 5 (2008): 162A-167A.
Cox, Craig. "Conservation intelligence." *Journal of Soil and Water
     Conservation* 60, no. 3 (2005): 50A-54A.
Cruse, R.M., and C.G. Herndl. "Balancing corn stover harvest for biofuels
     with soil and water conservation." *Journal of Soil and Water
     Conservation* 64, no. 4 (2009): 286-291.
Cude, C. "Oregon water quality index: A tool for evaluating water quality
     management effectiveness." *Journal of the American Water
     Resources Association* 37, no. 1 (2001): 125-137.
Cukierman, A. 2009. "Forecasting macroeconomic developments -
     Research-based policy analysis and commentary from leading
     economists." http://www.voxeu.org/index.php?q=node/4237
     (accessed February 8, 2010).
Daily, Gretchen. *Nature's services: Societal dependence on natural
     ecosystems*. 1 ed. Washington, DC: Island Press, 1997.
Dasgupta, Partha. "Environmental and resource economics: some recent
     developments." http://www.beijer.kva.se/PDF/15490807_
     Disc186.pdf (accessed February 10, 2010).
Dasgupta, Partha. "The place of nature in economic development."
     IDEAS: Economics and Finance Research. http://ideas.repec.
     org/p/ess/wpaper/id2233.html (accessed February 6, 2010).
Dixon, John, and Kirk Hamilton. "Expanding the measure of wealth."
     Finance and Development, December 1996.
Duraiappah, A. 2006. "Markets for ecosystem services: A potential
     tool for multilateral environmental agreements." International
     Institute for Sustainable Development (IISD). http://www.iisd.org
     /publications/pub.aspx?id=844 (accessed February 8, 2010).
Duriancik, Lisa *et al.* "The first five years of the Conservation Effects
     Assessment Project." *Journal of Soil and Water Conservation* 63,
     no. 6 (2008): 185A-197A.
EPA 1994. "What is nonpoint source (NPS) pollution? US EPA." U.S.
     Environmental Protection Agency. http://www.epa.gov/owow/
     nps/qa.html (accessed February 8, 2010).
EPA 2003. "Final water quality trading policy | Water Quality Trading |
     US EPA." U.S. Environmental Protection Agency. http://www.epa.
     gov/owow/watershed/trading/finalpolicy2003.html (accessed
     February 8, 2010).

EPA 2009. "Air quality index." www.airnow.gov/index.
cfm?action=aqibasics .aqi (accessed February 8, 2010).

EPA 2010. "Section 319 Success Stories - ARIZONA | Polluted Runoff
(Nonpoint Source Pollution) | US EPA." U.S. Environmental
Protection Agency. http://www.epa.gov/owow/NPS/Section319I/
AZ.html (accessed February 8, 2010).

Easterling, W.E 1992. "Preparing the erosion productivity impact
calculator (EPIC) model to simulate crop response to climate
change and the direct effects of CO2. Special Issue: Methodology
for assessing regional agricultural consequences of climate
change." *Agricultural and Forest Meteorology* 59, no. 1-2 (1992):
17-34.

FWS Report. "List of habitat suitability index (HSI) models." Environmental
Laboratory. http://el.erdc.usace.army.mil/emrrp/emris/
emrishelp3/list_of_habitat_suitability_index_hsi_models_pac.
htm (accessed February 8, 2010).

Federal Reserve Bank, 2007. "FRB: Speech, Bernanke--Financial
regulation and the invisible hand--April 11, 2007." Board
of Governors of the Federal Reserve System. http://www.
federalreserve.gov /newsevents/speech/bernanke20070411a.
htm (accessed February 7, 2010).

Friedman, Milton. *Market mechanisms and central economic planning
(The G. Warren Nutter lectures in political economy).* New York:
American Enterprise Institute For Public Policy Research, 1981.

Fulhage, Charles, 1993. "G1881 Generating methane gas from manure
| University of Missouri Extension." University of Missouri
Extension Home. http://extension.missouri.edu/publications/
DisplayPub. aspx?P=G1881 (accessed February 9, 2010).

Gaines, Richard. "NOAA chief steps up push for 'catch shares'
- GloucesterTimes.com, Gloucester, MA." http://www.
gloucestertimes.com/punews/local_story_160223434.html
(accessed February 8, 2010).

Gieseke, T. 2008. "Conservation planning training for private sector
agronomy service and local conservation agencies". http://www.
sare.org/MySare/ProjectReport.aspx?do=viewRept&pn=ENC05-
086&y=2008&t=1 (accessed February 8, 2010).

Gieseke, T. 2007. "Conservation security program drives resource
management." www.mnproject.org/csp/CSP_Report_web_
April_19,_2007.pdf (accessed February 8, 2010).

Gieseke, T. 2008. "Integrating natural resource management into
agronomic centers." The Minnesota Project. www.mnproject.org/
pdf/CIG%20Handbook_web.pdf (accessed February 9, 2010).

Gieseke, T. 2009. "Environmental assistance grants: Ag professionals: A conservation bridge to farmers." Minnesota Pollution Control Agency. http://www.pca.state.mn.us/oea/grants/awarded.cfm (accessed February 8, 2010).

Gieseke, T. 2009. "Domestic Bovine On-Farm Environmental Assessment Final Report" Minnesota Department of Agriculture.

Gosselin, M. 2010. "Beyond the USDA." IATP www.iatp.org/iatp/ publications.cfm?accountID=258&refID=107172 (accessed February 9, 2010).

Govindarajan, Vijay 2004. "Strategy, execution, and Innovation | Fast company." http://www.fastcompany.com/resources/leadership/ vgct/081604.html (accessed February 8, 2010).

Gwartney, James, Dwight Lee, and Richard L. Stroup. *Common sense economics: What everyone should know about wealth and prosperity*. New York: St. Martin's Press, 2005.

Hardin, Garrett. "The Tragedy of the Commons by Garrett Hardin - The Garrett Hardin Society - Articles." The Garrett Hardin Society. http://www.garretthardinsociety.org/articles/art_tragedy_of_ the_commons.html (accessed February 8, 2010).

Harper, Douglas. "Online etymology dictionary." Online Etymology Dictionary. http://www.etymonline.com/index. php?term=economy (accessed February 7, 2010).

Harris, Michael, and Iain Fraser. "Natural resource accounting in theory and practice: a critical assessment." *The Australian Journal of Agriculture and Resource Economics* 46 (2002): 139-192.

Hawken, Paul. *The ecology of commerce*. New York: Harper Collins, 1993.

Helms, Douglas. "Hugh Hammond Bennett and the creation of the Soil Erosion Service." *Journal of Soil and Water Conservation* 64, no. 2 (2009): 68A-74A.

Horan, Richard, and Marc Ribaudo. "Policy objectives and economic incentives for controlling agricultural sources of nonpoint pollution." *Journal of the American Water Resources Association* 35, no. 6 (1999): 1023-1035. http://adsabs.harvard.edu/ abs/1999JAWRA..35.1023H (accessed February 8, 2010).

IMF 2000. "Transition Economies: An IMF perspective on progress and Prospects -- An IMF issues brief." IMF -- International Monetary Fund Home Page. http://www.imf.org/external/np/exr/ ib/2000/110300.htm#I (accessed February 8, 2010).

KDEP. "Division of water." Non-Point source pollution. www.water.ky.gov/ sw/nps/ (accessed February 8, 2010).

King, Dennis. "Will nutrient credit trading ever work? An assessment
      of supply and demand problems and institutional obstacles."
      Environmental Law Reporter, May 2003. www.elr.org (accessed
      October 8, 2009).

King, Grant, and Kevin Parris. *OECD meeting recommendations and
      summary*. Wellington, NZ: Ministry of Agriculture and Forestry,
      2002.

Knight, Bruce 2004. "CSP: A revolution in conservation." Natural
      Resources Conservation Service. http://www.nrcs.usda.gov/
      NEWS/speeches04/knightnltm.html (accessed February 8,
      2010).

Landell-Mills, Natasha 2002. "International institute for environment
      and development." iied. www.iied.org/pubs/pdfs/9066IIED.pdf
      (accessed February 11, 2010).

Lant, C., and S. Kraft. "Using ecological-economic modeling to evaluate
      policies affecting agricultural watersheds." *Ecological Economics*
      55, no. 4 (2005): 467-484. *In* Ruhl, J.B., Christopher L. Lant,
      and Steven E. Kraft . *The law and policy of ecosystem services*.
      Washington, DC: Island Press, 2007

Leopold, Aldo. "Conservation economics" *Journal of Forestry* 32, no. 5
      (1934): 537-544.

Levin, Simon. "Learning to live in a global commons: socioeconomic
      challenges for a sustainable environment ." *Ecological Research*
      21, no. 3 (2006): 328-333.

Levitt, Steven. Freakonomics: The rogue economist explores the hidden
      side of everything. New York: Harper, 2009

Liang, Yi 2006. "ARS | Publication request: Using Cqestr to predict effects
      of management practices on carbon sequestration." ARS : Home.
      http://www.ars.usda.gov/research/publications/publications.
      htm?seq_no_115=211918 (accessed February 8, 2010).

Lone, O. *Natural resource accounting: the Norwegian experience*. Paris:
      OECD Environmental Committee, 1988.

Longva, Petter. *A system of natural resource accounts (Rapporter fra
      Statistisk sentralbyra)*. Oslo: Statistisk Sentralbyra, 1981.

Lorenz, D. 1995. "How much energy does it take to make a gallon of
      ethanol." Ethanol.Org. www.ethanol.org/pdf/contentmgmt/ILSR_
      energy_balance.pdf (accessed February 8, 2009).

MEA Millennium Ecosystem Assessment. *Ecosystems and human well-
      being: A framework for assessment (Millennium Ecosystem
      Assessment Series)*. 1 ed. Washington, DC: Island Press, 2003.

MEA Millennium Ecosystem Assessment. *Ecosystems and human well-being: Synthesis (Millennium Ecosystem Assessment Series). 1 ed, Washington, DC: Island Press, 2005.

MGIO 2010. "Crop productivity index ratings in Minnesota." MnGeo: Minnesota Geospatial Information Office. http://www.mngeo. state.mn.us/chouse/soil_cpi.html (accessed February 8, 2010).

MPCA 2009. "2009 watershed achievements report." Minnesota Pollution Control Agency. www.pca.state.mn.us/publications/wq-cwp8-10.pdf (accessed February 8, 2010).

Maguire, R.O. 2005. "Phosphorus indices to predict risk for phosphorus losses." Southern Extension and Research Activity. www.sera17. ext.vt.edu/Documents/P_Index_for_%20Risk_Assessment.pdf (accessed February 8, 2010).

Maille, P. "Performance-based payments for water quality: Experiences from a field experiment." *Journal of Soil and Water Conservation* 64, no. 3 (2009): 85A - 93A.

Manale, Andrew. "Steering conservation's course using adaptive management." *Journal of Soil and Water Conservation* 63, no. 6 (2008): 183A-184A.

Morris, Daniel 2009. "Ecosystem service stacking: Can money grow on trees (and more)? Common Tragedies. http://commontragedies. wordpress.com/2009/08/03/ecosystem-service-stacking-can-money-grow-on-trees-and-more/ (accessed January 14, 2010).

NASCA 2007. "NASCA resource library." NascaNet. nascanet.org/Index/ search.php?Search=Conservation+Delivery+System (accessed February 8, 2010).

NCFC 2010. "NCFC Members." National Council of Farmer Cooperatives. www.ncfc.org/about-ncfc.html (accessed February 9, 2010).

NCR National Research Council. *Valuing ecosystem Services: Toward better environmental decision-making.* Washington, D.C.: National Academies Press, 2005.

NOAA 2010. "About LIDAR Data." NOAA Coastal Services Center. http:// www.csc.noaa.gov/products/sccoasts/html/tutlid.htm (accessed February 10, 2010).

NRCS 1997. "Minnesota wildlife evaluation system." Minnesota NRCS. www.mn.nrcs.usda.gov/technical/ecs/TechNotes/Biology/ Technote4A.pdf (accessed February 8, 2010).

NRCS 2001. "Cropland rotation intensity rating and diversity index | Montana NRCS." Montana NRCS. http://www.mt.nrcs.usda.gov/ technical/ecs/agronomy/technotes/agtechnoteMT78/index.html (accessed February 8, 2010).

NRCS 2001. "USDA NRCS." American customer satisfaction index.
        http://www.nrcs.usda.gov/FEATURE/survey/ASCINRCSRp.doc
        (accessed February 9, 2010).

NREL 2006. "Century model version 5." Natural Resource Ecology
        Laboratory (NREL) at Colorado State University. http://www.nrel.
        colostate.edu/projects/century5 (accessed February 8, 2010).

NWS 2008. "JavaScript wind chill computer." National Weather Service
        Southern Region homepage. http://www.srh.noaa.gov/ssd/html/
        windchil.htm (accessed February 8, 2010).

Nguyen, N. 2006. "AgEcon2." agecon2.tamu.edu. agecon2.tamu.edu/
        people/faculty/woodward-richard/350/NNGuide.pdf (accessed
        February 8, 2010).

Nickerson, C.. "Cash or credit? Tax credits and conservation outcomes."
        Journal of Soil and Water Conservation 64, no. 1 (2009): 22A-
        26A.

North, Douglass. "Institutions and economic theory." *American Economist*
        36 (1992). http://www.questia.com/googleScholar (accessed
        February 8, 2010).

Odum, Eugene P. *Fundamentals of Ecology*. Philadelphia: W. B. Saunders,
        1971.

OECD 1999. "OECD Proceedings. Environmental indicators for
        agriculture, Volume 2: issues and design "The York
        Workshop". OECD Proceedings. Environmental indicators for
        agriculture, Volume 2: issues and design "The York Workshop".
        |http://www.cababstractsplus.org/abstracts/Abstract.
        aspx?AcNo=19991811351 (accessed February 8, 2010).

Ortiz, Jean. "USDA sued over data rights." *AgWeek (Fargo)*, September 28,
        2009.

Ostrom, Elinor. "A general framework for analyzing sustainability of
        social-ecological systems." *Science*, July 24, 2009. http://
        www.sciencemag.org/cgi/content/abstract/325/5939/419
        (accessed October 16, 2009).

Ott, Wayne R. *Environmental indices: Theory and practice*. Ann Arbor: Ann
        Arbor Science Publishers, 1979.

PBS . "PBS - Bill Moyers Reports: Earth on Edge - Agricultural
        Ecosystems." PBS. http://www.pbs.org/earthonedge/
        ecosystems/agricultural1.html (accessed February 8, 2010).

Paustian, Keith. "Counting carbon on the farm: Reaping the benefits of
        carbon offset programs." *Journal of Soil and Water Conservation*
        64, no. 1 (2009): 36A-40A.

Pearce, D.. *Blueprint for a green economy (The Blueprint Series)*. London:
        Earthscan Publications Ltd., 1989.

Perrot-Maitre, Daniele. *The Vittel payments for ecosystem services: a "perfect" PES case?* London UK: International Institute for Environment and Development, 2006.

Peskin, H.M. 2000. *Environmental accounting: The theoretical foundations of ENRAP.* Manilla: Conference on Resource Accounting and Policy, 2000.

Polasky, Stephen. "What's nature done for you lately: Measuring the value of ecosystem services." *Choices*, Spring 2008. http://www.choicesmagazine.org/magazine/pdf/article_20.pdf (accessed February 8, 2010).

Quade, Henry. "Limnology." Lecture, Graduate Course Minnesota State University, Mankato, Mankato, November 11, 1992.

RFF 2006. "Practical measurement of ecosystem services ." Resources for the Future - RFF.org . http://www.rff.org/Events/Pages/Practical-Measurement-of-Ecosystem-Services.aspx (accessed February 8, 2010).

RFF 2009. "New directions for managing our ecosystems ." Resources for the Future - RFF.org http://www.rff.org/Events/Pages/New_Directions_for_Managing_Our_Ecosystems_.aspx (accessed February 8, 2010).

Read, Leonard. "Read, I, Pencil | Library of Economics and Liberty." Library of Economics and Liberty. http://www.econlib.org/library/Essays/rdPncl1.html (accessed February 7, 2010).

Repetta, Robert. *Report on natural resource accounting : Information paper on the use of natural resource accounting for countries .* Canberra: Australian Environment Council, 1988.

Ribaudo, Marc, LeRoy Hansen, Daniel Hellerstein, and Catherine Greene. "The use of markets to increase private investment in environmental stewardship." USDA Economic Research Service - Home Page 2008. http://www.ers.usda.gov/Publications/ERR64/ (accessed February 8, 2010).

Ribaudo, Marc, and Fred Kuchler. "Market failures: When the invisible hand gets shaky." *Amber Waves*, November 1, 2008.

Robb, Karen. "Management options for nonpoint source pollution greenhouse." 1998 commserv.ucdavis. commserv.ucdavis.edu/CESanDiego/nursebmp.pdf (accessed February 8, 2010).

Robbins, Lionel. "The Concise Encyclopedia of Economics | Library of Economics and Liberty." Library of Economics and Liberty. http://www.econlib.org/library/Enc/bios/Robbins.html (accessed February 7, 2010).

Ruhl, J.B., Christopher L. Lant, and Steven E. Kraft . *The law and policy of ecosystem services.* Washington, DC: Island Press, 2007.

SWCS. *Managing agricultural landscapes for environmental quality:
      strengthening the science base.* Ankeny, Iowa: Soil And Water
      Conservation Society, 2007.

Saaty, Thomas. "Relative measurement and its generalization in decision
      making." *RACSAM* 102, no. 2 (2008): 251-318. http://www.rac.
      es/ficheros/doc/00576.PDF (accessed February 8, 2010).

Sampson, R. Neil. *For love of the land: A history of the national
      association of conservation districts.* League City, Texas: Natl
      Assn Conservation Dist, 1985.

Schmidt, D. 2008. "MinnFarm Index." UMN Manure . www.manure.umn.
      edu/applied/assets/minnfarm_users_guide_2_1_120308.pdf
      (accessed February 8, 2010).

Selman, Mindy 2009. "Water quality trading programs: An international
      overview | World Resources Institute." World Resources Institute
      | Global Warming, Climate Change, Ecosystems, Sustainable
      Markets, Good Governance & the Environment. http://www.wri.
      org/publication/water-quality-trading-programs-international-
      overview (accessed February 8, 2010).

Senge, Peter, Sara Schley, Joe Laur, and Bryan Smith. *The necessary
      revolution: How individuals and organizations are working
      together to create a sustainable world.* New York: Doubleday,
      2008.

Smith, Adam. *An inquiry into the nature and causes of the wealth of
      nations* circa 1775 [*Britannica Great Books vol 39*]. Chicago,
      Encyclopedia Britannica Great Books Vol 39, 1952.

Sowell, Thomas. *Basic economics: A common sense guide to the
      economy.* Cambridge: Basic Books, 2007.

Sternberg, Ernest. "Preparing for the hybrid economy: the new world of
      public-private partnerships." *Business Horizons*, November 1,
      1993.

Stewart, Bob. "National indicators of changes in soil quality." Lecture,
      William E. Larson and Raymond R. Allmaras Emerging Issues in
      Soil and Water from University of Minnesota, St. Paul, April 16,
      2008.

Stoneham, G. *Creating markets for environmental goods and services: A
      mechanism design approach.* Canberra: Land & Water Australia,
      2008.

TCR 2009. "FAQs - The climate registry." The Climate Registry. http://
      www.theclimateregistry.org/about/faqs/#q1 (accessed February
      8, 2010).

Thoma, David, and Satish Gupta. "Airborne laser scanning for riverbank erosion assessment ." *Remote Sensing of Environment* 95, no. 4 (2005): 493-501

UNSD, 2010. United Nations Statistics Division." United Nations. unstats. un.org/unsd/sna1993/introduction.asp (accessed February 10, 2010).

USDA 2005. "Water quality eligibility tool." USDA. ftp://ftp-fc.sc.egov. usda.gov/AL/tech/csp06/csp06_wq_eligibility_tool_instructions. pdf (accessed February 8, 2010).

USDA 2006. "USDA 2007 Farm Bill theme papers." USDA . www.usda. gov/documents/FarmBill07consenv.doc (accessed February 8, 2010).

USDA 2008. "Soil and water eligibility tool." USDA NRCS. www.nm.nrcs. usda.gov/programs/csp/fy08/swet-instructions.pdf (accessed February 8, 2010).

USDA 2009, Office of Communications. "Release No. 0383.09." USDA Newsroom. www.usda.gov/wps/portal/!ut/p/_s.7_0_A/7_0_10B ?contentidonly=true&contentid=2009/08/0383.xml (accessed February 10, 2010).

USDA 2009. "WIN-PST." NRCS Engineering Standard Drawings Catalog. http://www.wsi.nrcs.usda.gov/products/W2Q/pest/readme. html#intro (accessed February 8, 2010).

USDA ARS 2008. "Revised universal soil loss equation v2." Official NRCS RUSLE2 Program. fargo.nserl.purdue.edu/rusle2_dataweb/ RUSLE2_Index.htm (accessed February 8, 2010).

USDA FS 2008. "Ecosystem services and the farm bill." US Forest Service - Caring for the land and serving people.. http://www.fs.fed.us/ ecosystemservices/Farm_Bill/index.shtml (accessed February 8, 2010).

USDA FSA 2006. "Environmental benefits index." Conservation Reserve Program Fact Sheet. www.fsa.usda.gov/Internet/FSA_File/ crp33ebi06.pdf (accessed February 8, 2010).

USDA GLTI 2001. "Guide to pasture scoring." Grazing Lands Technology Institute. ftp://ftp-fc.sc.egov.usda.gov/GLTI/technical/ publications/pasture-score-guide.pdf (accessed February 8, 2010).

USDA MRBI 2009. "MRBI factsheet." USDA NRCS Programs. www.nrcs. usda.gov/PROGRAMS/pdf_files/mrbi_factsheet.pdf (accessed February 8, 2010).

USDA NRCS 2004. "Phosphorus index | NRCS." Natural resources conservation service . http://www.nrcs.usda.gov/technical/ecs/ nutrient/pindex.html (accessed February 8, 2010).

USDA NRCS 2004. "Strategic plan | NRCS." Natural Resources
     Conservation Service . http://www.nrcs.usda.gov/ABOUT/
     strategicplan/ (accessed February 8, 2010).
USDA NRCS 2005. "Human capital strategic plan | NRCS." Natural
     Resources Conservation Service . http://www.nrcs.usda.gov/
     ABOUT/humancapital/index.html (accessed February 8, 2010).
USDA NRCS 2005. "Soil tillage intensity rating." USDA NRCS. ftp://ftp-fc.
     sc.egov.usda.gov/WI/Pubs/stir.pdf (accessed February 8, 2010).
USDA NRCS 2009. "Background | conservation effects assessment
     project | technical resources | NRCS." Natural Resources
     Conservation Service . http://www.nrcs.usda.gov/technical/NRI/
     ceap/about.html (accessed February 8, 2010).
USDA NRCS 2009. "USDA-NRCS technical services provider registry."
     USDA-NRCS Technical Services Provider Registry. http://techreg.
     usda.gov/ (accessed February 8, 2010).
USDA NRI 2009. "National resources inventory | NRCS." Natural
     Resources Conservation Service . http://www.nrcs.usda.gov/
     technical/NRI/ (accessed February 8, 2010).
USDA OBPA 2009. "Office of budget and program analysis." www.obpa.
     usda.gov/budsum/FY10budsum.pdf (accessed February 8,
     2010).
USDA OESM 2008. "Conservation land management." Ecosystem
     Services. www.fs.fed.us/ecosystemservices/pdf/farmbill/ESB_
     Charter.pdf (accessed February 8, 2010).
USSC 2010. U.S. Senate Committee on Environment and Public Works
     http://epw.senate.gov/public/index.cfm?FuseAction=Minority.
     Blogs&ContentRecord_id=28fa840a-802a-23ad-4bfe-
     e571c55c5de3 (accessed April 26, 2010).
Vilsack 2010. Testimony of Thomas J. Vilsack, Secretary of Agricultural
     before House Agricultural Committee. April 21, 2010. http://
     agriculture.house.gov/testimony/111/h042110/Vilsack42110.
     pdf (accessed April 26, 2010)
Vitousek, Peter and Paul Ehrlich. "Human appropriation of the products
     of photosynthesis." *BioScience* 36, no. 6 (1986).
WAC 2010. "WAC | About Us." Watershed Agricultural Council. http://
     www.nycwatershed.org/index_wachistory.html (accessed
     February 8, 2010).
Wackernagel, Mathis, and William Rees. *Our ecological footprint:
     Reducing human impact on the earth (New Catalyst Bioregional
     Series)*. Gabriola Island, BC: New Society Publishers, 1995.

Wagar, Tim. "River friendly farmer." River Friendly Farmer. www.extension. umn.edu/specializations/environment/HD1002.html (accessed February 8, 2010).

Walmart 2009. "Walmartstores.com: Sustainability index." Walmartstores.com. http://walmartstores.com/ Sustainability/9292.aspx (accessed February 8, 2010).

Weinberg, M., and R. Claassen. "Rewarding farm practice versus environmental performance." *Economic Brief 5*. Washington DC: USDA Economic Research Service, 2006.

Whitten, S., and J. Bennett. *Managing wetlands for private and social good: Theory, policy and cases from australia (New Horizons in Environmental Economics)*. illustrated edition ed. London: Edward Elgar Publishing, 2005.

Williams, Jeffery. "What is the carbon market: Is there a final answer?" *Journal of Soil and Water Conservation* 64, no. 1 (2009): 27A - 35A.

Willliams, David. "Colorado firms skewer U.S. Chamber of Commerce for fighting climate change legislation." *The Colorado Independent (Denver)*, October 22, 2009.

WEF, 2010. "Redesigning Business Value: A roadmap for sustainable consumption". http://www.weforum.org/en/initiatives/ DrivingSustainableConsumption/index.htm (accessed April 15, 2010)

Wright, Janice. *Natural resource accounting : an overview from a New Zealand perspective with special reference to the Norwegian experience*. Canterbury: Centre for Resource Management, Lincoln University & University of Canterbury, 1990.

York, Dana. "Plenary II Session." Address, SWCS Annual Convention from Soil and Water Conservation Society, Keystone, Colorado, July 23, 2006.

AUTHOR BIO

During the last 20 years, Tim Gieseke has strived to understand the ecological and economical balance needed within agriculture. On completing his MS in Environmental Sciences in the early 1990's, he spent nearly a decade learning the technical and engineering skills of landscape management. During this time he also returned to the farm he grew up on in south central Minnesota and began his farming career that he is still engaged in. He and his wife and their three boys represent the fourth and fifth generations that have lived on the farm.

These experiences led him to participate in farm policy at the federal level and environmental and agricultural policy at the state and local levels. As it became more apparent that the demands on agriculture were increasing and the existing conservation model weakening, he startedAg Resource Strategies, LLC and then created The EcoCommerce Company to implement this business and policy model that provided him the flexibility to deliver on those demands. In his exploration to find the means to unify agro-economy and agro-ecological objectives, he discovered EcoCommerce.

INDEX

F

M